Money Meltdown & Climate Change

Defeating crime, corruption, poverty and starvation
in a single nation world, administered through an entrenched
policy of collective and participative secular governance
of the people, by the people and for the people.

Money Meltdown
&
Climate Change

The Penalties of Infinite Economic Growth

Bob Robertson

Order this book online at www.trafford.com
or email orders@trafford.com

Most Trafford titles are also available at major online book retailers.

Printed in the United States of America.

ISBN: 978-1-4269-2974-8 (sc)

Trafford rev. 05/31/2011

www.trafford.com

North America & International
toll-free: 1 888 232 4444 (USA & Canada)
phone: 250 383 6864 • fax: 812 355 4082

To thewonderful memory of my late wife Yvonne,
who was my most treasured friend and companion for fifty years.

Preface

I originally intended this book to become a helpful lifestyle guide for my children and grandchildren.

When I became a father, I began wondering why children throughout the world, including myself, have always been denied education about some of the most important aspect of survival in life.

I had long suspected there might be a conspiracy of denying children education about money, and how it works, for some dark and unknown reason. I have since become convinced the reason has been a deliberate and cruel way of ensuring a constant supply of young, poorly educated and malleable human resources, conditioned to become totally dependent upon the reward of money for their labours throughout their entire miserable working class lives.

I then considered matters relating to patriotism, and the respect we are required to have for national, political and religious leaders. Those requirements become seeded into the impressionable minds of children from an early age, while simultaneously discouraging debate about the alleged importance of such things.

These and other forms of intensive subliminal mental conditioning have been extremely successful for millennia, to the point that the majority of people have obediently accepted their intended positions of subservience to the power of the ruling elite. So much so, that parents automatically encourage their children to walk the same narrow and dimly lit road of ignorance about financial matter; about entrapment within country borders; about the greed and corruption of politics and about highly questionable and flawed religious doctrines.

Since the industrial revolution, however, subtle changes have been taking place in the composition of the ruling elite. The reins of world leadership have been moved quietly from within the traditional grasp of nation rulers, politicians and religious leaders, into the manicured hands of the wealthy capitalist elite. The multinationals and money are now the indisputable rulers of the world.

While contemplating how to give guidance to my children a new and more menacing problem came into sight.

The global warming and climate change phenomenon moved from being a subject of casual discussion into something far more intense and worrying. I perceived it as becoming something that would eventually relegate all other worldly disasters into less important irritations. My 'guide book' suddenly became something of potential importance to a much wider readership than my children and grandchildren.

As the manuscript grew and global problems became more clearly defined under predicted climate change conditions, I discussed my remedial hypothesis with friends and acquaintances. Some offered constructive criticism and input while others believed my proposed solutions might be considered too radical and controversial.

Wishing to include their valued observations within the pages of my book, I decided to 'write in' an accompanying casual interactive observer, incorporating some of those comments and questions. These interactive exchanges are shown in bold italics to provide a conversational style of writing, which I believe adds a little life to an otherwise subjective text. It is a style that is difficult to apply in a disciplined manner and literary purists might express disapproval, or consider it to be an unfortunate choice.

The subjective nature of the text is unavoidable because, apart from informative comments from specialised professionals, I express my personal opinions relating to the societal problems under consideration. I also express my concerns about the consequences of the global warming and climate change phenomenon, which must not be regarded as being unrelated to other global lifestyle problems. We must give serious consideration to those consequences, certainly for our own sakes but more importantly for the sake of future generations who will inherit whatever legacy we leave behind.

Much has been written about the state of today's world order and armies of experts have written millions of words explaining the problems, some telling us they will get much worse while others assure us recovery has already started. However, I could found no credible proposals for solutions to the mountain of problems, nor how we should prepare ourselves to create conditions by which we, and future generations, might best survive the consequences of years of environmental abuse and gross mismanagement of the global economy and monetary system.

Whatever those solutions might be, they should form the core of a legacy for future generations to inherit and should include guidance for the creation of a new world order that guarantees participative governance by the people, for the people and of the people.

I provide solutions, and present a template for the creation of a uniquely different and more preferable new world order in which to accommodate them.

The book underscores the many obstacles created by our ancestors and made worse by successive generations, including ourselves, that have prevented us achieving the obvious and glorious alternative life styles we should have had. The alternative has been sacrificed at the altar of greed and corruption.

We have all been lied to and deceived by the ruling classes since time immemorial. We have become enslaved to cultural prejudices and denied access to the truth about so much that affects our lives.

I hope this book will encourage the people of the world to consider the alternatives that are within our reach and leave a legacy of hope and opportunity for future generations. We dare not fail them.

In this regard I commend the words of Frederick the Great (1712-1786) for your consideration:

"The greatest and noblest pleasure which men can have in this world is to discover new truths; and the next is to shake off old prejudices."

out of control abuse and gross mismanagement of the global economic and monetary system.

Whatever these solutions might be, they should form the basis of a legacy for future generations to inherit, and should include a plan for the creation of a new world order of governance of the people, for the people and by the people, [illegible] [illegible] solutions, and [illegible] a [illegible] for [illegible] [illegible] unique, cultures and [illegible] [illegible] world [illegible] access to a [illegible] life.

The book articulates the many obstacles encountered by our ancestors and made worse by successive generations, including ourselves, that have prevented us achieving the objectives and goals of a [illegible] [illegible] [illegible] had. The [illegible] has been sacrificed at the altar of greed and corruption.

We have all been led to [illegible] [illegible] [illegible] time immemorial. We have become enslaved to cultural programs and denied access to the truth about ourselves and others [illegible].

This book has been [illegible] to encourage the people of the world to [illegible] the alternative [illegible] with [illegible] a legacy of hope and [illegible] for future generations. We [illegible] fail them.

In the [illegible] [illegible] [illegible] [illegible] [illegible] [illegible] [illegible] [illegible] [illegible] enlightenment:

"The greatest and noblest pleasure which we can have in this world is to discover new truths; and the next is to shake off old prejudices."

Contents **Page**

Preface vii

Chapter 1 - The need for change 1

Chapter 2 - The Culture of Conflict 8

Chapter 3 - Climate Change - Is humanity really at risk? 19

Chapter 4 - Money - the stuff of dreams and nightmares 39

Chapter 5 - Politics & Politicians - The League of Scoundrels .. 62

Chapter 6 - A History of Religion 130

Chapter 7 - Sovereign State Countries 194

World Governance organogram 230

Conversion of countries 231

Chapter 8 - Solving the Problems 239

Summary 243

Chapter 9 - The Plan for Change 245

Chapter 10 - Handling the need for change 280

Chapter 11 - The Solution Proposals 282

Annexure 297

About the author 301

Contents **Page**

Preface .... [illegible]

Chapter 1 - The need for change .... [illegible]

Chapter 2 - The Culture of Control .... [illegible]

Chapter 3 - Climate Change – Is humanity [illegible] .... [illegible]

Chapter 4 - Money – the stuff of dreams and nightmares 39

Chapter 5 - Politics & Politicians – The League of Scoundrels .. 62

Chapter 6 - A History of Rebellion .... [illegible]

Chapter 7 - Sovereign State Gov[illegible] .... [illegible]

World Governance organogram .... [illegible]

Conversion of countries .... [illegible]

Chapter 8 - Solving the Problems .... [illegible]

Summary .... [illegible]

Chapter 9 - The Plan for Change .... [illegible]

Chapter 10 - The [illegible] .... [illegible]

Chapter 11 - The Solution Proposal .... [illegible]

[illegible] .... [illegible]

About the author .... [illegible]

Chapter 1

The need for change

Life is full of changes and we wouldn't be who and where we are today if nothing had changed over millennia.

In my own lifetime I have seen many changes, some good some not so good. Life has conditioned me to expect change and to recognise conditions that will make change either welcome or necessary.

Conditions in 1980 alerted me to the need for change. The need grew stronger over the ensuing years. By 2008. I could not understand why the powers that be were doing nothing about them.

If you say 2008, I imagine you are referring to conditions relating to the sub prime mortgage collapse in the USA

Absolutely, and it rocked the USA's financial market causing shock waves to reverberate around the world with some devastating effects.

You will recall first world economies took the initial impact, which triggered off a series of major corporation and bank collapses in a number of developed nations.

The destructive power surged around the globe taking no prisoners and leaving no national economy unaffected.

It was proclaimed to be the worst financial crisis since the Wall Street crash of 1929. It was later upgraded to the worst in recorded history.

The Bank of England, for example, dropped its lending rate to the lowest level in 300 years.

Ah! Yes, that was quite a disaster and we are all still feeling the effects but, they will not last forever. Economies will recover and we shall soon get back to normal again

I am not too sure about that. If economies get back to 'normal' as you say, I am sure the problem will linger to hit us again.

People around the world have become the victims of an economic meltdown. The inherent flaws I detected in the global monetary system years ago are bringing about its rapid demise. This is particularly worrying because the dependability of money can no longer be relied upon by anyone, rich and poor alike.

As money continues depreciating in real value, many of the rich will see their carefully accumulated assets sucked into the black hole of negative equity.

The poor, the homeless and the world's starving millions, who have been desperately reliant upon grants and aid to ease their plight, will suffer when grants dry up because of money losing its value and availability.

I agree this is very worrying but world leaders and the banking industry are beginning to turn things around. Economies will start picking up again.

I am not convinced. Let us review what happened.

Some governments chose to give their reserve banks worthless paper securities to print fiat money as bailout funding for sinking banks and large corporations, in the forlorn hope of stimulating economic recovery and to prevent massive unemployment.

Bailouts will fail and aggravate an already desperate situation because the flawed monetary system is in a state of collapse which has been getting worse for decades.

Back in 1935, American economist Irving Fisher (1867-1947) summed up the worthless nature of money at that time when he said:

> *"Thus, our national circulating medium is now at the mercy of loan transactions of banks, which lend, not money, but promises to supply money they do not possess."*

Almost forty years later, Fredrich August von Hayek (1899-1992), Nobel Laureate of Economic Sciences 1974 said:

> *"With the exception only of the period of the gold standard, practically all governments of history have used their exclusive power to issue money to defraud and plunder the people."*

From these and similar observations, the unsecured value of the world's monetary system became a ticking time bomb, which has inevitably exploded.

Investment security will become increasingly volatile and banks will become increasing reluctant to lend money to each other and to people applying for loans, particularly as interest rates drop.

Low interest rates on deposits will affect people living on fixed incomes and those reliant upon interest earned on savings.

Larry Parks, Executive Director, Foundation for the Advancement of Monetary Education summed it up when he said:

> *"With the monetary system we have now, the careful saving of a lifetime can be wiped out in an eye blink."*

People who have been surviving by the grace of bank credit may experience a small margin of relief on their monthly repayments, but much of the apparent saving will be lost in real terms due to escalating cost of living expenses.

The question arises:

"How was money permitted to become a weapon of mass economic destruction?"

Answer:

"Because man's inherent vice of greed has grown stronger by the pursuit of infinite economic growth in the hope of accumulating the wealth and power it is expected to yield."

South Africa contains textbook examples of how wealth has enabled power and corruption to thrive in both the private and public sectors.

Crime and corruption have become two of the country's most successful growth industries.

The pursuit of infinite economic growth is an extremely dangerous philosophy.

Infinite means never ending. The only way to achieve never ending economic growth would be to keep printing never ending supplies of worthless fiat money to meet the never ending rewards that never ending growth demands.

If the world remains on that course it will lead to inevitable self-destruction.

The more fiat money that is printed, the lower its disposable income value becomes. Prices of goods and services are force upward, matched by demands for increased salaries by human resources.

The inevitable losers will be the ordinary people who have no influence over the acquisition of stability.

Winning will be reserved for the economic oligarchy of multinationals and bankers who profit through the control of the world's monetary system.

The shattered lives of so many losers will lead to experiences of the horrors of debt-related domestic violence, alcoholism, drug abuse, prostitution and other forms of crime.

Sadly in South Africa, where non-whites are in the majority, they are the ones becoming increasingly affected.

The country's policy of Black Economic Empowerment (BEE), which was intended to uplift the previously disadvantaged black majority, has been accused by many of having enabled, and possibly encouraged, the creation of black elitist minorities.

Whereas great wealth and positions of equally great power for some have become synonymous with BEE (Black Elite Enrichment?) policy, the swelling ranks of disadvantaged poor and un-empowered blacks underscores the fact that South Africa has become one of the most financially imbalanced and socially unequal nations in the world.

South Africa is not alone though.

As global recession bites deeper into economies around the world, examples of corruption and obscene financial rewards for managerial failure have been surfacing everywhere.

The deep seated inherent flaws of the world's monetary system are also becoming apparent.

Money no longer has the dependable value that people need in their lives, and it is only a matter of time before economies start collapsing completely.

But it won't end there. More problems are yet to come, the effects of which are expected to be even more catastrophic.

I refer to global warming, climate change and the potentially horrendous consequences they are expected to have for our future generations.

I believe there are solutions. I also believe we can change course to achieve them, but we must first bring stability into our lives.

Stability will enable us to make informed and rational decisions rather than being driven by panic and desperation into making wrong ones in haste.

We need to unburden ourselves from the financial pressures that prevent us making carefully considered decisions.

Economists, influenced by their age old gospels of conventional economics, will tell us too much stability stifles economic growth. That's good news because, as we are witnessing right now, the pursuit of infinite economic growth destroys the stability we need in our lives.

The way forward to finding solutions appears to be straightforward.

We must bring equitable and sustainable financial stability into our lives, by creating a stable and controlled form of global economy that is not dependent upon growth, infinite or otherwise. The trick, of course, is learning how to do it.

It will not be easy. Oligarchic interests will do everything possible to prevent it happening. They will never surrender their enormous wealth and power simply to enable their human resources – that's you and me and everyone else – to have financial stability in their lives.

Also, there are other obstacles threatening attainment of stability in our lives.

Even before the economic meltdown began, humanity has been living in an environment of escalating global conflict.

There are four prime distilleries of conflict that have bedevilled humanity for centuries:

- 1) money which, as we are witnessing now, has brought with it a whole basket of new and worrying social issues;
- heightened intransigence and intolerance on issues relating to:
- 2) politics and
- 3) religion;
- 4) ongoing xenophobic and warring conflicts erupting within and between various countries.

In one way or another, money, politics, religion and national sovereignty have always been the common denominators found in all forms of global, community and domestic problems around the world.

We will only achieve desirable change if those trigger devices of conflict are removed. To do so we must learn everything possible about them and about how, when and by whom they were created.

With this in mind, the following six chapters dealing with those common denominators go back in time, searching for their origins, purposes and the adaptations over centuries that some have undergone to accommodate changing conditions.

The final four chapters explain how the process of change should evolve and the rewards for getting it right.

The process of change will take time and it will be extremely challenging. Millions of our present generation may not live long enough to experience the final beneficial results. Billions of others will, particularly our future generations, which makes it all so important and essential to be thorough.

The approaching global warming and climate change phenomenon must not be underestimated. It cannot be circumvented to avoid, nor can it be removed from our lives, despite all the technological wizardry at our disposal. It is unstoppable and will become an ever increasing penalty weight to be carried throughout the whole process of change, and for a very long time thereafter.

Scientific consensus suggests climate change will damage the environment and destroy much of what we dependent upon for survival. It will be life threatening to all life forms on Earth, not just ourselves, and it is predicted to endure for perhaps a thousand years.

My solution proposals take these factors into account, with recommendations for early defensive and reparation tasks that should, and can, be initiated now rather than later.

Mankind will gradually become compelled to adapt to the consequences of climate change, and to accept the need to adopt some radically new and untested lifestyle changes in the process.

Climate change has not yet reached the stage at which the need for adaptation will become an obvious and inescapable fact of life. That moment is not very far away though, perhaps only ten or fifteen years.

In fact, Britain's Prince Charles has said the world only has *"less than 100 months to act"* to save the planet from irreversible damage due to climate change.

He warned that a failure to act by 2017 will have catastrophic effects for the planet and, more particularly, for all life forms dependent upon a healthy and vibrant environment.

To make that moment of realisation for proactive action much easier to accept and adapt to, we should be planning for changes in the world's monetary systems now.

The present and ongoing global economic crisis, the credit crunch, job losses and money meltdown, provide us with immediate and compelling reasons, and opportunities, to begin the planning process as quickly as possible.

Those planning foundations will require some careful and probably unconventional thinking.

As the late Professor Albert Einstein said:

"There are problems in today's world that cannot be solved by the level of thinking that created them."

I kept his words in mind throughout the entire process of writing my book. We all have to think big and differently and outside of the box.

The benefits of acting now must not be sacrificed at the altar of complacency. If we fail to act now future generations will never forgive us – assuming there will be future generations.

Chapter 2

The Culture of Conflict

There have always been incidents of human conflict of one type or another throughout history, generally occasioned by political, religious, financial or territorial differences of opinion.

In more recent times there have been shocking incidences of children murdering others at school, intimidating their teachers, peddling drugs and participating in overt sexual activities. This growing culture of violence at a young and impressionable age is very worrying.

We are witnessing the emergence of a violent future generation greatly disadvantaged by the disgraceful legacy of recession, failed education systems and unemployment inherited from their elders.

What type of future leaders will result from this ugly cultural metamorphosis?

A generation embroiled in conflict and violence will be disinclined to unite and adapt to a culture of survival while struggling under climate change conditions.

You make an interesting and disturbing observation but, what if the prophesies of global warming and climate change never comes to pass? There are many experts who tell us the "Al Gore" clan got it all wrong and made alarmist and unsubstantiated statements of pending doom and disaster.

You make a fair point but the majority view warns us to prepare for the worst.

For example, Tim Wirth, president of the United Nations Foundation, is reported as saying:

"It is time now to hear from the world's policymakers."

"The so-called and long-overstated 'debate' about global warming is now over".

Nevertheless, if the predictions of disaster are eventually found to be mistaken, I believe a worsening and widespread culture of conflict will continue to ravage our species, probably with more damaging consequences than those of global warming and climate change.

Whereas the global monetary meltdown alone is going to have harmful effects upon us all, we are presently confronted by many problems. I am focussing more specifically upon two that I believe are particularly serious and worrying right now: climate change and the culture of conflict.

Global warming is a potentially serious problem over which we really have little or no control at all, and if scientific predictions are proven correct, we could be looking at the risk of an enormous loss of human life and the possible extinction for many lesser life forms.

The cultural metamorphosis to which I referred could have similar life threatening consequences for humanity but, it is within our power and ability to prevent it happening.

If we fail to do so, global warming becomes something of a secondary problem.

If I have understood you correctly, you seem to be implying that the cultural change you perceive, or the demise of some of the older cultural norms, has become a problem of greater urgency for humanity to resolve than the predicted horrors of global warming and climate change.

In effect yes. I believe the climate change phenomenon will, if it reaches scientifically predicted proportions, affect the survival of all life forms, not just mankind. We must acknowledge that mankind's survival is absolutely dependent upon the continued survival of all other animals, mammals, birds and insects. If they perish we are bound to follow.

We must also understand that all life form species are dependent upon a continuity of supply of an enormous variety of foodstuff, which is also under threat of destruction from the destabilisation of climatic conditions.

Mankind is the only life form that possesses the cognitive intelligence, the technology, the physical capability, the communication facilities and organisational skills, to possibly minimise the long term devastating effects of climate change.

It will become increasingly evident that such an enormous campaign of sustainable protection and continuous recovery, will only be attainable if the entire human race unites under a common sense of urgency, of determination and co-operative intention to make it happen.

If the present culture of conflict becomes worse, such a campaign is unlikely to ever come to pass.

We need to create a universal culture of understanding that survival of the majority overrules the selfish demands of the few.

That prerogative is sadly not a universal commitment throughout the world today.

If the culture of conflict permeates the very fabric of global society it could mutate into an uncontrollable form of anarchy, which would probably relegate a universal survival campaign to a "mission impossible" status.

With that dreadful prospect in mind I am compelled to suggest that a review of mankind's cultural inclinations has become urgent.

My goodness, you are certainly painting a dreadfully gloomy picture of the human race. The world has always had its share of militants, rebels, gangsters, ruffians and murderers. I have no doubt they will always be part of social structures. But I'm sure it's nothing to get overly concerned about. There has always been a lot more good than bad in the world and I have no reason to expect that to change in the foreseeable future.

I agree that people should certainly be taking climate change a lot more seriously, but I have no doubt that if the predictions become irrefutably confirmed, everyone will knuckle down to do something about it.

Well, as much as I respect your point of view, I believe widely reported facts and the opinions of experts would appear to disagree with your expectations.

The youth of today comprises a growing number suffering from drug abuse and alcoholism. Others are in drug trafficking. Schoolgirl pregnancies are on the increase, as are paedophilia and child prostitution.

An increasing number of husbands, faced with seemingly insurmountable financial problems, murder their wives and children before committing suicide.

These and other disturbing trends are synonymous with what I perceive as the growing cultural of conflict and societal violence.

So many people are struggling to find solutions to financial and marital problems weighing upon their troubled minds.

I believe the problems are the consequence of a failed monetary system, aggravated by self-inflicted pressures brought about by people living beyond their means on credit terms who have become buried under a mountain of debt.

They become further overwhelmed by the relentless increases in food, fuel, transportation and energy costs.

Increasing numbers of people are losing their jobs, their incomes, their savings, their homes and possessions, their lines of credit and are finding it unbearably difficult to survive one day after another.

It is hardly surprising, therefore, to learn the UK has been experiencing an expanding £2 billion a year growth industry. It's called Customer Theft, a.k.a. shoplifting.

Almost predictably, drug addicts are among the most prolific and persistent shoplifters.

The average British addict needs £200 a day to feed the habit and whatever they steal has to be sold as quickly as possible to secure a fix.

Many work through 'fences,' sometimes working to a prepared list of items. The fences pay approximately 30% of the resale value so addicts have to steal £600 to £800 worth of goods for every fix needed.

Many of the fences sell stolen goods over the Internet through sites such as eBay. The practice has become known as e-fencing.

If it is a growth industry in a country like the UK, which prides itself on having good social security facilities designed to assist the jobless, the poor, the under nourished and destitute members of society, how much faster might it grow in countries that lack these social support benefits, and where policing services are stretched to the limits of human and financial resources?

The traditional ways of combating crime have been through community education and attempts to increase the size and efficacy of policing. Both tend to become diluted by the common constraints of finance and skilled human resources.

Money has an irritating habit of being scarce when finance for social services is needed, yet plentiful when it comes to financing projects targeting the demands of multinationals for economic growth.

Not surprisingly, infinite economic growth is actually running out of fuel. Money is losing its value and the global monetary system is collapsing rapidly. Infusions of fiat money will not revive it.

Well, I certainly agree with you that times are undoubtedly tough but we haven't hit rock bottom yet. Countries have experienced periods of recession before, and we are aware of the Wall Street crash of 1929.

But history shows that things do get turned around and the world does survive. As bad as it appears to be right now I have every confidence we shall overcome, pick ourselves up and return to normality. It might take a while but we shall make it.

Obviously I would very much like to agree with you but conditions today are far different and much worse than those of 1929.

To begin with, there is far more cash in circulation per capita globally and a greater number of people wanting access to it.

The need for credit facilities has become far more widespread throughout the world than ever before. People have become accustomed to living far beyond their means and, although banks are aware of this, too many have been providing under-secured credit facilities. Some have gone far beyond a prudent fraction of their own cash and deposit reserves.

For example, as stated by the Federal Reserve Bank of New York:

"Because of the 'fractional' reserve system, banks, as a whole, can expand our money supply several times, by making loans and investments."

However, when banks grant loans that exceed the fractional security of cash deposits on their books, they create money out of nothing by charging interest on the funny money they advance as loans.

The consequences were pointed out by the Federal Reserve Bank of Philadelphia:

"Without the confidence factor, many believe a paper money system is liable to collapse eventually."

The confidence factor in the global money system has been rapidly declining for years so it's eventual and inevitable collapse should not surprise us.

Governments regularly tell their publics that sound economic fundamentals are firmly in place and that growth is assured and, in political parlance, "there will be a better life for all."

Meanwhile, infrastructure remains un-maintained; roads become increasingly potholed; health and education services decline; energy sources continue to fail; food and other cost of living expenses increase relentlessly and the atmosphere and water resources become increasingly polluted.

These failures fertilize the growing conflict of violence.

As the world moves ever deeper into recession we have to ask:

"How did the financial and political decision-makers get it so terribly wrong?"

I believe it was because they couldn't bring themselves to get outside of their conventional boxes and think differently.

Today's financial problems cannot be solved by applying the failed economic philosophies that caused them.

Our political leaders will be unable to lift us out of recession because they will be too busy protecting their own selfish interests.

Hopes of recovery will be constrained by the multinational oligarchic corporations who choreograph global politics. They call the shots. Inevitably we shall have to save ourselves and we have strength in numbers to do so. Collectively we are more than six billion people and the law of averages favours us greatly.

After all, what would we be fighting for. What are the fundamentals that most people want out of life?

1. Full and sustainable employment opportunities at all levels;
2. Free schooling from kindergarten to high school;
3. Free tertiary education for successful and meritorious entrants;
4. Free medical and hospitalisation services worldwide;
5. Quality residential housing for everyone;
6. A healthy and well maintained environment;
7. A stable unit of currency;
8. A dependable and stable global monetary system;
9. A Basic Income Grant for those who are unemployable;
10. A stable pricing structure for goods and services;
11. The abolishment of all forms of existing taxation and duties;
12. The removal of inflation and the means by which it has been traditionally created;

13. An abundance of free and low-cost passenger transportation services;
14. The creation of a low-to-no premium insurance service for every conceivable risk;
15. Sustained quality accommodation, frail care and financial income for retirement;
16. Low-to-no cost funeral expenses.

With the possible exception of point 6, none of the above will ever be attainable under existing world order and leadership conditions. I am inclined to believe, however, that even point 6 is beyond the achievable capability of world leaders.

Collectively, we have allowed ourselves to become the 'work fodder' and consumers of the world, serving the needs of the multinational and elitist minorities. We have provided them the wealth and power that enables them to control the global economy and our lives.

It's payback time.

Well, I am not going to contradict you on that particular point because I am inclined to believe you. However, from the little I know and understand about national and global economics, I challenge the ability to achieve all those fundamentals you have listed, without taxation or monetary input from a financial source of some description. They all have to be paid for, so from whence will the money come?

That is exactly how we have all been conditioned to think. Nothing is possible without money. I shall reveal later how the survival dependency upon traditional money must, and can, be removed from our lives completely.

Meanwhile, a clue is in points 7-12 above. We need an entirely new and equitable unit of exchange with a guaranteed stable and sustainable collateral security. That security is Earth's abundant resources which, as I shall explain later, can be taken under the people's collective control and management.

Over the centuries, members of the elitist body corporate have masterfully and diligently stolen Earth's resources, the land, the waterways and oceans and the very air we breathe. They have even taken from us the will to rebel and to resist. They can be credited with an enormously brilliant achievement – at our expense.

What do you mean by 'stolen' relating to resources and land etc?

I mean they have taken land by force, or coercion or through the exercise of some self-proclaimed right or entitlement harking back to the early days of royalty and imperialism.

Consider this:

Who, at any time in our history, was the planet's Realty Agent with the power and authority to permit tracts of land and sea to be allocated for selective human ownership?

Who was the planet's Resources Distribution Authority who permitted select human beings to have exclusive rights to extract or otherwise acquire and process the planet's entire stock of resource assets?

Such authoritative entities have never existed because there is no resident owner of the planet and its huge stock of resources to appoint them.

Seizure of land and assets was all done in the glorious name of conquest and the conquerors claimed exclusive ownership of the spoils.

The culture of possession reigned supreme in those ancient times and the peasant-stock communities learned quickly how to submit and to become obedient battle fodder to make it all possible.

We don't regard ourselves as peasants today but, because our psyches have been expertly conditioned over the years, we remain inclined to submit to authority obediently.

Reverting to the wish list of fundamentals, I can give you advance notice of some of the long-awaited spin off benefits we could enjoy under my proposed new world order relating to points 7 and 8 i.e. a stable unit of exchange and a new stable global monetary system. These points would see the end of cash as we know it.

We would be able to create a new and unique cashless society, bringing with it an immediate end to all traditional cash-related criminal activities such as drug trafficking, money laundering, cash robberies of every description, fraud, corruption and the fencing of stolen goods. They would all simply, and thankfully, dissolve into history.

A regulated cashless societal lifestyle enhanced by guaranteed employment, free and low cost services, stable prices and zero inflation, will remove the tension, frustration and anger prevalent in so many family homes today, much of which is associated with financial problems.

My proposed new and greatly improved global monetary system would render it impossible to run into debt or to have poverty thrust upon us.

Global poverty, hunger and starvation would be completely eradicated, subject always to possible food security problems caused by the vagaries of climate change conditions.

This all sounds wonderful. Too wonderful to be true I would say, and I am looking forward to learning how you believe this Utopian lifestyle can be achieved.

One big question keeps coming to mind. If you are saying all this is possible, why has it never been attempted before?

I could reply by saying nobody thought of doing it before, but that would not be entirely correct.

You mentioned Utopia, which is a word used by Sir Thomas Moore back in 1516 when he wrote his book of the same name, about an imaginary island inhabited by an idyllic society.

His decision to use an island was, I believe, symptomatic of what had happened to the world over millennia. People had become conditioned to accept being divided into separately bordered nations as perfectly normal.

Moore did not propose a global Utopia because he too was conditioned by the conventional philosophy of creating his own separate nation within a world of foreign nations.

This same philosophy was the norm for all leaders throughout history.

They conquered other nations in order to bring wealth and prosperity back for themselves, while often expanding their territorial domains.

The creation of the British Empire was an excellent example of that phenomenon.

The British conquered a huge percentage of the Earth's land mass. So much so that it was said the sun never set upon the Empire. It extended so far around the world that the sun was always shining on part of it.

The intention of Empire remained exactly the same as territorial conquests had been throughout history, to bring wealth and prosperity to the conquerors, or in this example, to the British royal family and friends of the court.

Typically, the British public at large were very minor beneficiaries, becoming little more than poorly paid workers of the large human resources community that kept the imperial harvesting machinery turning.

Britain shamefully continued to have more than an acceptable amount of poverty, illiteracy and hunger within its own borders.

But that elitist culture has endured since time immemorial.

It could be argued, perhaps, that my proposal would be a similar form of conquest by taking from the rich to give to the poor, which would not be so. Nothing would be taken into ownership by or for anyone in the accepted sense.

As will be seen later, my proposal enables the planet's entire population of life forms, particularly mankind, to share equitably in the benefits derived from the world's complete and bountiful inventory of natural resource assets. This would be achieved through a harvesting and beneficiation process designed along unique socially responsible lines.

As previously mentioned, man is the only animal possessing the essential skills to tackle such a huge and challenging administrative task. Leadership to do so would be nominated and elected from within the entire human race. There would be no elitist multinational corporations formed to have exclusive commercial rights to carry out harvesting and processing functions.

This is beginning to sound like another version of an alternative elitist group of people ruling the world. How do you propose avoiding such an undesirable world domination state of affairs occurring?

No individual or elitist group of any size will rule the new world order of my vision. Indeed, no group of people, not even the total global community will rule the world in the historically accepted sense.

Humanity will be subject only to the rule of common law and the entire human race will be able to participate in the law making process, and in the creation of a supreme global constitution.

The global community will have the collective right to nominate and elect its chosen legislators, who will be charged with administering the rule of law without fear or favour.

In the present world order, people's lives are ruled by minorities in various countries. Those different and sometimes conflicting forms of rule would come to an end under my proposed Global Administration process.

Throughout my eight years of research, I reviewed a number of prophecies and philosophies which attempt to explain mankind's place and purpose in life. The only words resembling my own thoughts are those of Moses in the Old Testament, Genesis 1:27-30.

Using the fundamentals of my proposal for change as an interpretation of his words, he and I appear to be on the same wavelength. We both believe mankind has a responsibility to protect and preserve the interests and well-being of every creature on earth.
Whereas Moses proclaims it to be by divine order, I believe it is the only intelligent option we have for our own sustained survival.

Sadly throughout the ages, there have always been those who devote their considerable energies and power to control the survival process themselves, and to determine who shall be the favoured beneficiaries. We find them within the domains of money, politics, religion and particularly in sovereign territories. Together with their lieutenants and aides, their councillors and administrators, and many hard working faithfulls all over the world, they work behind the protection of a veritable firewall of security.
That firewall must be breached if every man, woman and child is to be provided with a safe, happy and peaceful place in the sun.

In chapters dedicated to each of those domains, I show how they evolved and how the power to the firewall must and can be switched off.
Meanwhile, let us consider the climate change phenomenon.

Chapter 3

Climate Change

Is humanity really at risk?

According to all available and dependable expert opinion the short answer to this question appears to be 'yes,' very much so.

Mankind's long assumed assurance of continued normal evolutionary progression on planet Earth, appears now to have become far from guaranteed.

In reality, of course, it never has been.

So, are you telling us the planet is doomed? Prophesies of doom have been abounding for years but we are all still here.

Quite so, and I have found no evidence to suggest our planet is doomed or in any form of danger. Far from it in fact.

Throughout her 4.5 billion or so years of existence, Mother Earth has been bombarded by an assortment of space debris. Some resident life forms have been affected in the process but, to the best of scientific knowledge, there have been no dramatic changes to our planet. She will continue her uncharted course through the endless vacuum of space until she eventually dies.

Indeed, her journey towards eventual decay, hopefully billions of years from now, is far more guaranteed than mankind's survival into the next millennium.

Excuse the pun, but how on earth can it be predicted that our survival as a species is at risk of being snuffed out within such a brief moment of Earth's billions of remaining years? That sounds quite alarmist to me.

Well, there has always been a risk of being "snuffed out" as you so colloquially put it, by the same phenomenon that brought about the devastating end to the dinosaurs that had been roaming the earth for many millions of years.

We are told it happened when a chunk of rock in outer space, about ten kilometres in width, plunged to Earth some 64 million years ago.

The possible risk of a similar occurrence has not been completely dismissed by modern science and there are a number of recorded close encounters with such a destiny in the past. We can reasonably expect there will be others in the future.

As worrying as that form of possible devastation clearly is, it is not the type of risk that should concern us too much at the moment.

I'm inclined to agree. We have far too many other things to worry about at the moment, many of which seem to be getting worse on a daily basis.

Indeed, and mankind should be more concerned about the possible devastation his species is bringing upon itself, and upon other life forms which, according to Moses, mankind has been commanded to protect and preserve.

For a number of years there has been broadly based speculation that man's meteoric advances in science and technology, and particularly his industrial revolution will, if left unchecked, kill the planet and everything on it.

While there might be reason to believe an element of truth exists in this prophesy of doom hypothesis, insofar as it relates to vegetation and lesser life forms, there are no authoritative reasons to fear we are on course to destroy the entire planet itself.

She has been around for a very long time and some believe she has a form of life and intelligence far beyond man's understanding. Some think she has become far too wise to allow microbes such as ourselves to become anything more than a slight irritation.

She has endured the extremes of ice age conditions, the blistering heat caused by massive eruptions from within the bowels of her internal thermonuclear chamber, huge continental shift movements, tsunamis of great magnitude and some unimaginable growing pains.

No, despite his self-assumed superior intelligence and technological skills, man possesses neither the ability nor the energy source to destroy her.

He certainly has the ability to destroy himself by contaminating the delicately balanced life support systems Mother Earth has so freely provided, and is headed in that direction. Sadly he could undoubtedly take a lot of other life forms with him in the process.

It has become increasingly important, particularly now, for us all to get a much better perspective and understanding of our very elderly home planet, that we might make more informed distinctions between the levels of power embodied within it, compared to the small levels of power and energy we have managed to acquire throughout our extremely short existence.

Mother Earth is an entity of our universe, of the entire cosmos and of the black hole from whence she is said to have originated in the form of pure energy.

We are hitching a ride for as long as we don't make nuisances of ourselves, which we have begun doing.

I can't argue too much with that in principle, but I have no doubt millions of people are going to be upset by being referred to as microbial hitchhikers. Many will regard it as degrading and outrageous. Some may call it blasphemous, especially the black hole theory of origination. However, the overriding necessity to prevent, or at least to prepare for climate change conditions might dampen cries of dissent.

I hope so, because that overriding necessity is very important. It gets right to the heart of man's dilemma, which might become particularly worrying for those with strong religious beliefs and convictions.

Whereas global warming and climate change are no longer debatable issues, the consequences for life as we know it are still being assessed. Debatable issues now will focus upon the severity of climatic conditions, how they might differ in various parts of the world and what collective actions must be taken to survive under them.

Informed sources predict unprecedented declines in sustainable life support essentials, such as nutritional food and potable water, enormous shrinkage of some coast lines, perhaps millions of lives being lost and the risk of deceases that might be created from irrecoverable bodies.

We shall soon be asking how the dilemma can be averted; what must be done to stop it; and what world leaders are doing to save us.

Millions will turn to prayer, possibly seeking guidance to be given to world leaders rather than divine intervention to end the dilemma itself.

If prayer fails, as I fully expect, and world leaders remain as far away from solutions as they presently appear to be, the world will urgently need a viable Plan 'B' and a succession of alternatives to fall back on.

Today's problems are the penalties of pursuing infinite economic growth. Climate change aside, our lives have become increasingly disrupted by those who are addicted to the relentless quest for infinite economic growth, and who have redesigned world order structures in pursuit of that goal.

They refer to this new world order as 'globalisation,' with promises of broad based economic benefits accruing to the whole human race. Predictably, globalisation is not working and we are seeing no economic benefits.

Globalisation is a word with no singular definitive meaning whatsoever. It can be, and invariably is, preceded by any number of activity captions such as Cultural; Economic; Political; Commercial etc.

Economic globalisation is certainly not working and there is a growing scrap-yard of redundant, retrenched and job seeking people to prove it. They are the victims of the transnational and multinational conglomerates who believe economic globalisation will guarantee the continuation of infinite economic growth.

Pursuit of this unreachable goal has contributed to the unstoppable global warming and climate change phenomenon. Increased unemployment and a devastating worsening of global recession is now a certainty. Inevitably the 'haves' will shrink in size while the 'have nots' will increase alarmingly.

We have allowed this to happen and must now act to ensure this destructive lifestyle is replaced by one of social responsibility.

A nice thought, and communism attempted to achieve that goal, unsuccessfully I might add, over many years. The pressures of supply and demand always get in the way. Sadly, we shall never achieve a global community of 'haves.' There will always be have-nots. My concern is how you intend addressing that problem while ensuring the have-nots can be saved from utter poverty and starvation.

My proposal addresses that worrying issue while putting forward a uniquely different, and no doubt controversial alternative to globalisation.

The additional climate change problem has to be addressed deliberately, emphatically and in ways that will require us all to jettison much of the social, cultural, political and religious conventionalism that has contributed, in one way or another, to the many problems confronting us now.

Climate change has certainly added a new and dangerously complex dimension to our present lifestyle problems and I will show how we can accommodate it by reshaping our lifestyles.

From what has been taking place amongst nations participating at the Kyoto Protocol meetings and subsequent venues, global political consensus relating to change will not be achieved. We are already some twenty years late in navigating the obstacle course of political and commercial private agendas.

With our monetary system in a state of collapse and climate change bearing down upon us, our chances of survival in a financial vacuum and a failed economic globalisation crisis are zero.

I agree the state of the global economy is looking very shaky at the moment, but the world has experienced periods of recession in the past and always managed to overcome them. As worrying as things clearly are at the moment I have no doubt they will pick up eventually – they always do. I am also sure we shall have the financial resources and the will to prevent irreparable climate change damage occurring.

I accept there have been previous recessions, but each has left a larger scar on global societies than its predecessor. Each has heightened the probability of another in the future. Recessions have tended to increase global unrest and poverty, both of which are certainly prolific at the moment. The fact that we have had previous recessions should have warned us our financial systems are gravely flawed.

Climate change is going to make this present period of recession very different to all others, and economists predict it will take a very long time to recover. I do not believe we shall ever recover.

Although natural resources abound in great abundance for survival purposes, we shall never have the necessary guaranteed financial resources to gain access to them and to get them working for us.

To understand the magnitude of the problems we have created, we need to look critically at our failures as an intelligent species on this planet.

We have failed to maintain unity of identity and purpose as a species;
We have failed to maintain a clean and healthy environment;
We have failed to enable equitable distribution of resources globally;
We have failed to monitor and maintain essential food security;
We have failed to protect and manage wild life territories;
We have failed to realise we do not exist in exclusive isolation from everything around us.

We have lost sight of the fact we are an integral part of everything on the planet and failed to fulfil the functions and responsibilities that would have ensured the well-being and preservation of us all.

Having considered our failures let us remind ourselves what our planet actually is.

As mentioned earlier, Mother Earth is scientifically acknowledged to be a product of what has become known as the "Big Bang" phenomenon. Together with billions of other bundles of pure energy created at the time, she is moving at great speed away from the point of creation in no preordained direction whatsoever.

She has transformed from her original state into what she is now and continues to change in ways that few of us have the ability to perceive or to comprehend.

An extremely high percentage of her mass is still energy with the power to move continents and to form new land masses and remove others.

All life exists upon the extremely thin and fragile layer of crust that covers her body which, on a scaled down model of the planet would be no thicker than a sheet of paper.

From this thin layer, all living things gather whatever scraps they can find to live, to grow and to procreate.

With the notable exception of mankind, most life forms take and give something of value back in return.

Like an intelligent and destructive virus, man takes and pollutes the environment in return.

Is man reading from a different page to all others on the planet or have his destructive inclinations been deliberately programmed into his DNA for a particular reason?

We have a reasonable, albeit incomplete record of our planet's present life form tenants. We have also been able to trace back to others that existed many millions of years ago.

If we regard the very oldest of what we know and that which exists today as being a substantial part of a complete life cycle on Earth, some interesting thoughts come to mind.

Have we, the human element of the whole, been designed to bring this particular cycle to an end?

If so, will another cycle of unimaginable description arise like a mutant Phoenix from the ashes?

Is it unreasonable to imagine that over a time period of 4.5 billion years other cycles might have existed before ours began? Cycles that our technology is presently unable and unlikely to trace? If so, did any of them contain life forms intellectually comparable to ourselves? If so what caused those possible earlier cycles to end without a trace?

As you say, interesting questions to which we shall never know the answers, and I'm not entirely sure I really want to know anyway. But, where are you going with this. Is it pertinent to the problems we are now facing?

Perhaps not but, as you say we might never know.

I sometimes wonder if people think about the incredibly short period of time that humanity has been in existence, compared with other life forms that have family roots going back many millions of years.

For example, creepy crawly spiders have been spinning webs for more than 400 million years.

Then there are other species, long since extinct, that roamed around Earth many millions of years earlier.

Is it not possible that a species similar to ourselves, with comparative or even more advanced intelligence, existed all over the world a billion years ago?

If so, did their technology and lifestyles bring about a global warming and climate change phenomenon similar to, or worse than, that which we have brought about in our own short life time?

Could the evidence of that era have long been converted to lava, by the heaving and turning of the planet's paper thin surface like a bubbling Bolognese sauce, leaving no geological traces?

In other words, are we the first intelligent life form of our type to bring about such potentially life threatening devastation, or are we repeating a time in history about which we have no knowledge?

Just a thought, from one who likes thinking outside the box!

Returning to the question of whether humanity might really be at risk from climate change. It is scientifically acknowledged that humanity certainly is at risk, and unless bold and decisive steps are taken by the entire human race now, to bring pressure to bear upon world leaders and decision makers to confront the problems, the consequences might be devastating.

When I began researching information in 1998, relating to the subjects that would form its originally intended focus, the words "global warming and climate change" were rarely, if ever, seen in publications of broad readership interest.

They have now become words uttered by many but, perhaps not entirely understood by all, so we should review how the issue has been addressed thus far.

In February 2007, forty-five nations joined France in calling for a new environmental body to slow global warming and to 'protect the planet.' It was to be a body that could potentially have policing powers to punish violators.

The United States, China and India were noticeable and predictable absentees from the meeting.

The day before, a scientific report stated that global warming is 'very likely' caused by mankind and that climate change will continue for centuries even if heat-trapping gases are reduced. These were words that underscore exactly what I have predicted, with only one difference. Rather than mankind having 'very likely' caused our problem, I maintain he very definitely did.

Former US vice-president Al Gore, whose Oscar-nominated documentary "An Inconvenient Truth[1]," was of the same opinion. As dramatically informative as it undoubtedly was, I got the distinct impression its main thrust was to promote Al Gore's public spirited persona to the American nation as being 'the right stuff' to save the world.

There appears to be a popular belief amongst many U.S. citizens that saving the world is a mission reserved exclusively for them.

"We are at a tipping point," Gore told the conference by videophone. *"We must act, and act swiftly ... Such action requires international cooperation."*

That message has been endorsed by scientists and some international leaders who said the science was so well documented that action was clearly the next step.

As encouraging as such statements of urgency quite clearly were, the issue has become relegated to a lesser level of priority by heads of state confronted by domestic problems of their own. Problems like recession, money meltdown, unemployment and rising crime rates for example. It's the conventional and traditional nature of political expediency.

Some of the burning questions (and probable answers) confronting the citizens of the world right now are:

- will we hear credible and believable words of commitment from all the world's leaders?...No;
- will they all be in agreement regarding the essential steps to be taken?...No;
- will the incredibly heavy burden of cost be overcome?...No;
- how many humanitarian relief programmes will be affected?...Perhaps all;
- what retaliation might we anticipate from fundamentalist groups? ...Much;
- how much time do we actually have left to make a difference?...Very little.

There will, of course, be many other questions but these are particularly relevant in my opinion.

Interestingly, the London-based International Institute of Strategic Studies, in its annual *Strategic Survey* in 2007, identified climate change as a major issue of international security, predicting it would become more evident as the effects become more apparent.

Experience suggests that most localised societal problems arise from issues relating to money, politics, religion and territorial sovereignty. Those engaged in these historically deep rooted and vigorously protected acts of wealth generation and population control, can be expected to deny compromise, to oppose change, and to stall progress in the quest for climate change solutions.

Will the frightening magnitude of climate change be seen by world leaders as sufficiently important to demand a truly collaborative and focussed search for a solution, or will domestic problems continue to take precedence? I am inclined to expect the latter.

That's an extremely pessimistic approach which does no justice to the concerns expressed by those with whom you have debated issues, and who have supported the principles of the need for change.

You really must have some faith in human nature and believe that our elected national leaders do understand, and can be persuaded to unite together for a real and lasting global solution.

I confess to ownership of a pessimistic psyche concerning politics and politicians.

As such I expect the actions of most world leaders and so-called policy makers to be characterised by deliberate intentions to ensure the traditional and entrenched political prerogatives of trade offs, corruption and quid pro quo arrangements. This has been so blatantly displayed during various Protocol conferences relating to carbon trading processes, which I discuss later.

I have little doubt the ordinary people of the world will become compelled to take the global warming and climate change phenomenon very seriously indeed. I am sure they will eventually become united in a quest to help guide their children, and their grandchildren to survive the expected consequences.

When world leaders predictably fail to provide supportive guidance, the people's huge superior numbers must come together, under controlled conditions of their own making, to plan and implement a process of action that will optimise survival of Earth's abundant resources and ensure a future, for as long as that might be, for as many of Earth's life form generations as possible.

How can such a monumental task be accomplished?

What are the priorities and where does one start?

These are but a couple of the many questions I have already asked myself and I now know exactly what has to be done and how best to do it.

All well and good, but you have to sell it to the rest of the world first and get them to buy into your proposals for what you allege is a workable solution. This is one of those moments when optimism has to come into play, particularly for a pessimist such as you.

Anyway, when are you going to reveal your solution?

My solution will be revealed in due course but I must first give a clear understanding of how I perceive the nature of the problems before revealing how I believe the solution must be crafted to overcome them.

To begin with, there are no documented precedents upon which we can draw to guide us in our preparation to meet global warming and climate change. Conventional occurrences such as hurricanes, tornadoes, earthquakes, raging fires and flooding have become common events and experiences for us to deal with. We mop up, repair, rebuild and get on with our lives.

Unconventional occurrences will be something quite different.

The tsunami that occurred off the coast of Sumatra in December 2004, affecting coastlines as far away as Sri Lanka, India and even South Africa, took the world completely by surprise, and was certainly not a conventional happening in the accepted sense.

Authorities were neither prepared for the event nor for its disastrous consequences. There were no conventional routines in place to immediately deal with it.

The devastating earthquake and tsunami that hit Japan in 2011, causing damage to the Fukushima Nuclear atomic power plant was another unexpected and dangerous experience.

Imagine the effects of a weekly tsunami of similar or greater intensities occurring in different parts of the world, under conditions where the world's coastal high tide levels had earlier become 'conventionally' six metres higher than they presently are.

With regard to rising tide levels, scientists have been studying two huge ice masses of the world: Greenland and West Antarctica, which account for 99 percent of the freshwater ice on our planet which is relentlessly melting.

It has been estimated that if the 5.4 million square miles Antarctic ice sheet melted completely, sea levels around the world would rise 61 metres (200 feet).

Some predict a 6 metre rise in sea levels before the end of this century and hundreds of millions of people around the world are expected to perished and millions more will become displaced and homeless.

To where will the survivors flee in desperation?

A permanent six metre rise in sea levels would probably wipe out half the world's major international shipping ports, rendering many of the remaining accessible ports largely redundant, because cargo fleets would have fewer, if any, serviceable trade ports at which to call and to bunker. Ocean-going vessels can only refuel at fully equipped commercial ports, the majority of which will have been rendered inoperative with no available bunker refuelling facilities.

A twelve metre or more rise would definitely bring an end to the world's maritime shipping and deep sea fishing industries. It would also close down the pumping, transportation and refining of crude oil worldwide

At what additional cost might replacement ports and infrastructure perhaps have been constructed and for whose account? How many traditional humanitarian causes will have been abandoned due to diminishing financial, material and shipping resources?

What effect would this have upon the real value or worth of conventional money and what would be the cumulative effect as climatic conditions worsened and endured for a thousand years?

Frightening, isn't it?

Yes it is, but from what I understand, the six metre rise in sea levels is only expected to happen in about 2100, so there will still be time to prepare ourselves.

That might be true but the jury is still out on the actual rate of yearly increase.

It might be moderate over the first 30-40 years, accelerating annually over the remaining years. A moderate increase might conceivably add one metre to high tide levels twenty years from now, which could still have serious degrading effects upon coastlines and habitation in many parts of the world.

When you say there will be time to 'prepare ourselves,' I have to ask: prepare for what? How and when should we start preparing and who will give direction?

We can prepare to see the words 'traditional' and 'conventional' morph into ever changing meanings in the years ahead.

What is traditional and conventional today might have no lasting reference in the near future, other than what used to be.

Maybe so, but religious and cultural heritages will endure. They won't change. People will still find strength and support from them in troubled times.

Well, only time will tell. Over the years I have developed reservations concerning the true relevance of various cultures to humanity's well-being. In my opinion cultures should be living things, evolving with the changing lifestyles of those who follow them.

The fundamentals may stay constant but some of the associated customs and ritual practices should be constantly reviewed by the custodians of culture.

Some cultures appear to remain locked into the eras of their origins centuries ago, having little or no relevance to modern lifestyles and perceptions.

I perceive culture as being the perpetuation of believing in a collection of long established bad habits.

Perhaps we should start thinking about creating a new secular global culture of good habits. Those that focus upon the interdependence of all life forms and upon the essentials for ensuring a collective survival. A culture of survival that future generations can build upon.

We should all be asking ourselves what needs to be done to prepare for climate change conditions. What aspects of national and global governance need to be reviewed and changed? Is the total global community capable of becoming united and committed to prepare a legacy of survival for the world's children of tomorrow?

There are so many questions to be answered before we can make considered decisions about planning for the future. There are also many existing problems we have to solve first. The most important of these is money and the whole monetary system. Until we get that sorted out very quickly, we shall never be able to work on a recovery plan for the future.

Money presently rules our lives. It determines the success or failure of every venture embarked upon. A venture is more likely to succeed when input costs are stable and income targets are attainable. Success is far from being assured under present volatile financial conditions and the expectations for the future are not optimistic.

Does this mean you are not absolutely certain that your solution will work under prevailing conditions?

I am certain it will work, if the executors are empowered to revise the monetary system to accommodate the objectives of the solution. One of those objectives would be to ensure income stability for the employed people throughout the transitional period, while eradicating unemployment and poverty for the disadvantaged masses.

I have interrogated my proposal very critically over a number of years. I am satisfied it forms a solid and credible foundation upon which to build a truly just and equitable lifestyle formula for every man, woman and child on the planet.

I searched for flaws or weaknesses that might obstruct that objective and made appropriate adjustments where necessary.

For example, how could I eradicate poverty completely, simply by replacing conventional money with a paperless unit of exchange? I also needed to keep a door open for the entrepreneurial spirit and for man's incentive to improve his lifestyle and financial security. Those and other questions have been addressed and accommodated. Indeed, the rewards for personal achievements would become more broadly based and of far greater personal value than ever before.

Being cognizant of the fact that one can never please all the people all of the time, I turned my attention to seeing who might become losers, or disadvantaged, if my proposal is adopted.

In the final analysis the principal losers would include those who had amassed personal wealth and power through the deliberate and dedicated pursuit of organised crime, and those who did so in the pursuit of illegal and nefarious activities such as corruption and exploitation of human beings. Also, those who have abused their positions of trust, and all other personal gain pursuits conducted in ways contrary to fair and honourable behaviour.

I get the impression you might be taking on the planet's entire criminal population? You are going to have your hands full and it could become bad for your health.

Indeed I would fully expect to rock a few criminal boats, in far more assured and efficacious ways than has been achieved through a number of conventional crime and corruption combat methods.

Since an important element of my proposal dispenses completely with all forms of conventional and traditional cash, replacing it with a system of accountable non-negotiable electronic credits, every form of traditional cash-dependent crime will simply dissolve. From the sneaky pick-pocket of wallets and purses, up to the hi-tech money launderer and every activity in between. They will all join the ranks of the unemployed.

I also expect to see a welcome end to grievous bodily harm and death synonymous with cash-related criminal acts.

Although entrepreneurial wizards within the criminal underworld, will undoubtedly apply their minds and skills to acts of crime that will reward them with my proposed new type of money (called Credits), they will very quickly learn they are on a mission to nowhere. They will definitely become losers.

Others who might also regard themselves as having been wronged, or unfairly disadvantaged, might be those who have acquired positions of power and rule over their territorial subjects, and perhaps over the subjects of other territories, through hierarchal, special appointment or election processes and in some cases by militarily enforced and dictatorial means.

However, not all will experience a complete loss in material terms or public status. Indeed I am sure that some amongst them would be invited to accept nomination for important positions within the proposed new Global Administration body, the establishment of which would coincide with the termination of those existing dominions.

I am satisfied my proposal embodies all the essential ingredients to benefit every member of the human race, even some of the crooks who would be offered rehabilitation training and rewards in an extensively enlarged range of global community service skills.

A few of the non-negotiable prerogatives of my plan are the complete removal of poverty, illiteracy and starvation. Also the provision of the finest education and health care facilities that technology can provide, guaranteed employment opportunities for life, culminating in dignified and carefree retirement.

So, you want to ensure a beautiful sunset period throughout the remaining years of your life?

That would certainly be nice, wouldn't it?

Unfortunately, I shall not be a beneficiary of those enviable benefits. Time is definitely against me in that regard. If my proposals received total global acceptance tomorrow, with the process beginning the following day, it would probably take twenty or thirty years before a new Global Administration governance structure could be celebrated. I do not anticipate becoming a centenarian!

How much time do you think we have?

If you mean how much time do we have before preparing for the effects of climate change, I would say we are already running out of time. We should be in the preparation stage already.

We know the phenomenon has already begun and we are just beginning to experience the leading edge of its long term cutting effects.

We have been assured it cannot be stopped and it will not pause to allow us to make whatever preparations we think appropriate to readjust our lifestyles.

The process will continue relentlessly, at its own pace, bringing with it a complement of conditions the like of which we have never before experienced, and against which we have no tested protection plan.

Expert opinion suggests things will get much worse before the entire population becomes sufficiently challenged to attempt survival strategies.

We have to address the problem proactively rather than finding ourselves struggling to deal with a variety of unprecedented problems reactively.

What sort of unprecedented problems do you have in mind?

These will be discussed later based upon available scientific reports, which will become more voluminous and informative in the coming months and years.

As an example, the Arctic Circle region was described by scientists as resembling a Ticking Time Bomb[2] when they initially discovered an estimated 400 billion tonnes of highly volatile methane gas, escaping from previously trapped reservoirs below the protective permafrost.

Ice and permafrost have been protecting us from this highly explosive and dangerous gas for millions of years, but global warming is steadily melting our protective coat of frozen armour away.

According to geologist John Atcheson, melting permafrost and methane gas release has occurred on the planet twice before.

The most recent was about 55 million years ago in what geologists call the Palaeocene-Eocene Thermal Maximum, when methane 'burps' caused rapid warming and massive extinctions disrupting the climate for more than 100 000 years.

A 'burp' is similar to the human experience, requiring no descriptive explanation whatsoever!

In geological language, when the mean constant atmospheric temperature increases by a few degrees, it causes these gases to volatilise and 'burp' upwards into the atmosphere, causing it to become even warmer thus releasing more gas, and so on.

The most damaging of these catastrophes is said to have occurred 251 million years ago, at the end of the Permian period, when a series of methane burps came close to wiping out all life on Earth, long before we arrived on the scene.

Over the ensuing half-a-million years a few species struggled to gain a foothold in the hostile environment.

The really frightening fact about 'burping' is that once the process of atmospheric warming gets started, and the temperature continues to rise, there's no turning back. It's likely to play out all the way. Liver salts won't stop it!

With the permafrost ground steadily unfreezing and melting away, 1.5 trillion tons of carbon dioxide are also being released and near-perfectly preserved Mammoths have become exposed.

While the dangers of carbon dioxide (CO_2) being released into the atmosphere have been widely spoken about, scientist inform us the greenhouse warming effect from methane gas is 23 times stronger.

Tests are regularly carried out and I was horrified to learn of revised estimates suggesting as much as 100 000 billion tonnes of methane is waiting to burp skywards.

This appears to be far in excess of the amount by which we could reduce our present release of CO_2 into the already polluted atmosphere.

Although I have seen no informed reports on the subject, I am aware that biologists have discovered bacteria, fungi, viruses, algae and yeast hibernating under as much as four kilometres of ice all over the world. I am bound to wonder how many different prehistoric viruses might be receiving a new lease of life after millions of years in hibernation in the deep-freeze permafrost regions.

As worrying as this obviously is, I'm sure that all available data will be flowing steadily to those who will be able to thoroughly assess it and produce well informed proposals to enable precautionary plans to be drawn up.

You are undoubtedly right about the flow of data, but one is compelled to question whether there is sufficient, if any, commercial and political will to take early proactive steps to protect us from the increasing number of damaging effects we are told to expect from climate change?

There is a continuing trend to concentrate solely upon commercial trade-offs to reduce carbon emissions only, which scientists warn us are unlikely to have any guaranteed preventative effects against global warming.

I'm trying to predict possible occurrences under unpredictable conditions, where knowledge of hindsight will eventually have little or no meaning or relevance.

Presumably there are hundreds, if not thousands, of scientists and academics all over the world, struggling to come to terms with the questions arising from the climate change problem drawing ever closer.

Hopefully many solution proposals will be tabled for consideration. Mine is but one.

We might be presented with scientific assessments, presented to us as politically inspired solutions, in the predictable quest for kudos, but I guarantee we shall never see a politically created solution with unanimous endorsement from world leaders.

In the unlikely event of it happening I guarantee the paramount components of money, politics, religion and sovereign territories will be retained. The struggle for survival will be lost for ever.

Yes, and you will say 'I told you so,' adding a warning to people to prepare to meet their doom.

But seriously, as I have said before, world leaders have far more information at their finger tips than you, than me and the rest of the global population. They have access to the finest brains in the world and to the most informed advisors. I still remain confident we can rely upon the right decisions being made by world leaders.

It would be highly irresponsible of me to argue with some of the points you raise. The finest brains are indeed there, no doubt pulsating with informed advice and guidance for consideration by our world leaders. However, they presently remain singularly focused upon reducing carbon emissions and the quest for alternative energy sources.

We should be asking them if their carbon emission reduction strategy is dependably founded upon informed scientific recommendations. Also, are the majority of experts now convinced that reduced carbon emissions will avert or slow down global warming and climate change?

We should also ask them which scientific hypothesis they have accepted – the one that says global warming has actually stopped or the one proclaiming an escalating tendency?

If it has actually stopped, for how long will it remain so, and can we now be assured that polar ice regions will stop melting and return to the desirable cyclical periods of re-freezing?

Until world leaders inform the people what they intend doing and why, speculation will abound and confidence of survival will wane quite quickly. The persistent societal problems will continue to worsen and economies will decline relentlessly.

If a politically motivated solution is adopted and the conventional financial and monetary systems prevail, disposable incomes will continue to depreciate at a steady rate globally, and the spiralling cost of living syndrome will continue its upward climb, as will unemployment and poverty. We can also expect the culture of conflict to worsen.

Let me summarise the question of climate change and its future effects upon all life on our planet.

The opinion of many of our scientists and other professionals leans towards a forecast of unprecedented disaster if the rise in temperature cannot be persuaded to stabilise. We have progressed beyond the 'wait and see before we act too quickly' syndrome and reached the 'let's get started now, before it's too damned late' stage. This means proposals for solutions must flow thick and fast and be assessed by minds that are free from the agendas of political and multinational imperatives.

They must also be free from the conventional and burdensome considerations of cost, which my proposal achieves.

Chapter 4

Money - the stuff of dreams and nightmares

The Survival Constraints of Money

In all its various forms, money has become the fuel, the weapon and the reward of power.

Before any survival proposals can be debated, we must first reach consensus on how to convert the present flawed world monetary system into a stable instrument of exchange that will equitably benefit the entire human race rather than privileged minorities only.

Money should never have been allowed to nourish an already advantaged elitist minority while depriving the desperately disadvantaged majority of sufficient for their sustained survival.

That's all very bold and noble but please be gentle, because money is the one thing to which most of us can relate, regardless of how much of the stuff we may or may not have. It's what we work for to bring some level of security and stability into our lives. Without it there is virtually no incentive to get out of bed every morning.

Believe me I do understand but money has become a monstrous necessity in our lives. We have been deliberately conditioned to regard it as a strong and dependable unit of exchange which, in all its various designs, appearances and international denominations, enables economies to grow and to provide the stability in our lives to which you alluded.

However, as Reginald McKenna (1863-1943) said, when he was British Chancellor of Exchequer:

"Those who create and issue money and credit, direct the policies of government and hold in the hollow of their hands the destiny of the people."

Across the Atlantic, in August 1957 H.L. Birum Sr. wrote in the American Mercury magazine:

"The Federal Reserve Bank is nothing but a banking fraud and an unlawful crime against civilization. Why? Because they create the money made out of nothing, and our Uncle Sam Government issues their Federal Reserve Notes and stamps our Government approval with no obligation whatever from these Federal Reserve Banks, individual banks or national banks, etc."

And this fraud has continued for many years.

Money was created for a number of reasons, not least of all to replace the centuries old system of bartering. It also became a more convenient way for rulers to value their material possessions and to collect taxes from their subjects. With variations, the tax principle has endured over the years.

We all think we know and understand what money is and we certainly know how it touches human lives, particularly those who have it in abundance, and painfully for those who possess little or none at all. Interestingly, money has not been officially defined by banks or governments, so if you think you know what money is let them know!.

Regrettably, money is no longer the dependable instrument for measuring the real values of what you referred to as 'security and stability' in our lives.

That ended when the gold standard, which had previously given global currencies a common measurement of value, was abandoned and world currencies became commodities traded on global markets.

Because people spend much of their lives competing for money in the market, it is not surprising that those who have no tradable assets or resources will become greatly disadvantaged in the process.

What do you mean by 'compete for money?' Surely that sort of thing only takes place on stock markets and in various forms of gambling.

Absolutely, but I am talking about things happening at a more general and basic level.

For example, when a man attends an interview for a job he is trading his skills and experience for money. He is competing with other job seekers for money through employment.

When we move into the realms of the unemployed masses, particularly those who have no skills or experience whatsoever as collateral, we find millions of unfortunate people who may remain eternally reliant upon grants, and the compassion of others, probably for the rest of their lives. Unfortunately, as happens in so many instances, some become forced in desperation to steal their daily bread or join the ranks of organised crime.

Sadly, millions of disadvantaged people become abused, persecuted, violated and exploited by people who trade upon the misery of others.

Although the lack of money is a sad and worrying problem for so many people, the principle of money as an instrument of exchange has not always been a completely bad thing in principle.

We know that money collected in taxes buys the public facilities and services essential in a well-managed community environment.

Those who receive money from employment are able to use their income to buy their homes, clothing, food and other necessities in their lives.

As you implied earlier we all need money to sustain our livelihoods and our dignities. For most of us our only legitimate access to it is through the job market and we are all competing with each other for money from the same universal pot.

We have become slaves to the wretched stuff. It rules our lives and has become the prime essential possession that we absolutely must have above all others.

Oh! Come on now, there are many other things that are far more important in our lives and more rewarding than money.

Things like good health, our beliefs and faith, family, friends and many other things. Things that make us feel good and things that we can do for the good of others.

Money isn't everything, you know.

As true as that might appear to be, we cannot achieve any of those things without the presence of money in our lives.

When our health fails we need money for expert medical attention.

Millions of starving and impoverished children do not get a meal a day, simply by praying "give us this day our daily bread."

A happily married couple can only house, clothe, feed, educate and generally care for their children and themselves by the grace of money.

People tend to make some very emotional statements about the greater importance of many things in life compared to money, albeit with the clear understanding that money doesn't have to be trashed in the process.

I know all the things to which you alluded are important to us but they will not always be within our grasp if money moves beyond our reach. When money deserts the family unit, discord and violence all too often fill the void.

The cruel and brutal fact of life is that without money in our pockets or hand-outs from the charities that rely upon donations from others, we cannot exist. Many simply fade away and die.

Children have never been taught anything at school about money because, over the years, the ruling elite have conspired deliberately to prevent their human resources understanding the mechanics and nuances of the monetary system. They prefer to let them work to earn money, without showing them how to make money work for them. To do so would have been very counter-productive.

People have been encouraged as adults to invest money in banks and insurance companies that were then enabled to make such deposits work harder and more profitably for themselves than for their investors.

Money as we presently know it must be taken out of our lives and replaced by something more accessible to every member of the human race. We should never have to compete against each other simply to gain access to enough money to keep ourselves and families alive.

I will introduce you to that unit of exchange later on and explain how it would work.

I'm looking forward to hearing about that and particularly how people will no longer have to compete to get some of it. However, if you do away with money, what will happen to incentive, the thing that makes us want to earn as much

money as possible to improve ourselves and the lives of our families?

As I mentioned earlier, incentive and the entrepreneurial spirit are wonderful things when used honourably and must always be encouraged. The replacement monetary system I propose is very supportive of incentive, particularly when it benefits society at large.

Meanwhile, let's look at the monetary system we presently have and compare it with something I believe to be vastly superior. We can first review some of the very harmful effects that conventional money can have upon family and community values.

The majority of families today cannot survive on the disposable income of a single breadwinner. Many of today's married couples are compelled to be joint breadwinners. The safety, security and welfare of their children during working hours are invariably delegated to third parties, usually at a cost.

The use of credit facilities has become a normal way of life and huge numbers of people are deeply in debt, confessing they cannot survive on disposable income alone and are dependent upon credit facilities, which is precisely what the money system intends should happen.

The household debt to income ratio for South African families is approximately 75%-80%, which is dangerously high.

According to South Africa's National Credit Regulator, 45.3% of the 18.07 million consumers with outstanding credit are struggling to meet repayment obligations. Those who are three or more months in arrears rose by just over half a million to 10.16 million at the end of December 2009.

In the UK, PricewaterhouseCoopers claimed in November 2007, the average personal debt of British citizens was £33 000.00 (R465 300.00) arising from mortgages, credit cards and personal loans. An increase of 94% since 2000. Total consumer borrowing at the time stood at £1.3 trillion (R20.15 trillion).

UK Credit card providers were confronted with lost profits of almost £4 billion (R60 billion) through loan defaults.

We are told some 60% of economic growth derives from high spending consumers. If they are denied credit or become retrenched, consumer spending drops off and economic growth take a dive.

This tells us the pursuit of economic growth, particularly the infinite variety, is highly irresponsible and dangerous. It's a stability crusher.

It requires the employed human resources of the world to spend more of their disposable income than they can afford, to keep economies growing. They are tempted to spend more by borrowing to do so. Live now, pay tomorrow and spend the rest of their lives regretting it!

These are just a small sample of problems relating to conventional money.

My vision of a global renaissance revolves around a World Governance Standard supported by a strong, equitable and stable monetary system. Stability would be assured by the absence of demands for economic growth, which would be completely unnecessary and impossible to pursue.

Stability would go far to free us from the present culture of conflict and violence as well as other disruptive issues prevalent in political, religious and sovereign territory structures.

The conversion of money into a common worldwide unprintable electronic unit of exchange will not be far removed from certain popular features of the present system.

I'm particularly interested in the new unprintable form of money you talk of. You also referred to it as a worldwide unit of exchange. What does that actually mean. Also, if it's not printed or minted what will we have in our pockets, a bunch of credit cards?

Not quite credit cards as we now know them but something very similar but much more expansive.

Money is universally accepted as being a unit of exchange to acquire goods and services from suppliers. It has no intrinsic value or other beneficial qualities. As Voltaire (François Marie Arouet 1694-1778) wrote:

"Paper money eventually returns to its intrinsic value -- zero."

As to it being unprinted, that is not unusual in terms of the financial transactions that millions of ordinary people apply today.

What do you mean by that?

Since the coming of Internet facilities and on-line banking, an increasing number of people receive their earned incomes as electronic credit transfers to their bank accounts, and have become accustomed to paying their creditors in a similar manner.

However, people are required to carry a certain amount of actual cash on them because not all purchases can be transacted by the use of cheques or credit cards.

Indeed, because of the relatively high cost to provide credit card facilities for customers some small-size traders are obliged to demand cash for purchases.

Notwithstanding these variables and the continuing need for cash for a number of other purposes, the growth of electronic transactions has been quite phenomenal during the past fifty years, and is quickly establishing itself in the minds of upcoming generations to be perfectly normal.

Some of the money transactions affecting our daily lives, such as bank interest on overdrafts and home loans is fiat money created electronically out of nothing by banks and other financial institutions.

When borrowers default on their repayments to banks, which millions all over the world are doing, the banks are left with a huge amount of liability, very little cash in hand and an assets ledger of questionable value. They become technically insolvent.

Through mechanisms put in place by Reserve Banks and governments for such predictable emergencies, taxpayers become the involuntary guarantors of bailout payments to the failed financial institutions. The taxpayers will have been given no choice whatsoever over such decisions. It's all done in terms of the multinational doctrine that the elitist minorities shall prevail and the rest of society – that's you, me and everyone else – shall, without reward, be compelled to ensure they do.

Thankfully, there would be no place or need for banking services in my proposed World Governance Standard.

OK, I get your point but where is it taking us? We need money and lines of credit so how do you propose we overcome the present status quo?

An understandable point and I'll come to that in a moment. Let me just say at present we do need conventional money but we should do everything possible to avoid needing lines of credit.

Allow me to highlight some of the anomalies associated with traditional cash, as well as the increasing tendency towards credit and the use of credit cards, which make it so desirable to adopt a more soundly based, user friendly, equitable and humanely responsible monetary system.

There have always been hazards associated with hard cash and the potential risks to which human beings are exposed simply by having cash in their pockets or at their homes.

We are aware of cash-in-transit heists and of ATMs being blown up by robbers.

Reports abound concerning so many different cash-related crimes and dreadful injuries, and often death, inflicted upon the victims of cash related crimes.

Then there are other more sophisticated money related criminal activities. The crimes of bribery and corruption, embezzlement, fraud, and drug trafficking involving billions, most of which involve actual cash, sometimes moving through electronic banking services as part of the money laundering process.

Others, notably bribery and corruption, might involve the movement of high value material items such as luxury vehicles and homes from grateful beneficiaries.

Although the removal of all forms of conventional money from society would obviously end all traditional cash related crime, how will the lives of ordinary people be affected?

The design of a new, unconventional and universal single monetary system must focus upon many non-negotiable prerogatives. Apart from removing the scourge of cash related crimes, it must provide mankind with the means of pursuing a quality lifestyle, customised to the personal ambitions and capabilities of every individual. Above all, it must remove completely the unbearable sufferings of worldwide poverty and starvation of which we are so sadly aware.

My proposal achieves these prerogatives together with a number of other highly beneficial value-added features and I call my proposed new single monetary unit a Credit. Its title reflects the status by which lifestyles should be lived and the financial state in which people will be enabled to conduct their lives – in credit rather than in debt.

The need for a viable alternative to conventional money is not just a figment of my own imagination, nor is it a belief to which I alone subscribe.

Belgian currency expert Bernard Lietaer:

"The biggest issues that I believe humanity face today," he said, "are sustainability and the inequalities and breakdown in community, which create tensions that result in violence and wars.

"We can address both these issues with the same tool, by consciously creating currency systems that will enhance community and sustainability."

"I propose that we choose to develop money systems that will enable us to attain sustainability and community healing on a local and global scale.

"These objectives are in our grasp within less than one generation's time. Whether we materialize them or not will depend on our capacity to cooperate with each other to consciously reinvent our money."

While he gave no suggestions relating to the composition of new monetary systems, I perceive his understanding of money matters and the inherent flaws in the present money system, as being very profound and informed. Not just because his perceptions so closely mirror my own, but because he is a man who has a far more intimate relationship with global monetary structures and their workings than I am ever likely to have. He participated in the design and implementation of the Euro – the single European currency system – and has personal experience of currency trading and its effects.

So too has billionaire currency speculator George Soros, who is reported as saying:

"Instability is cumulative, so that eventual breakdown of freely floating exchanges is virtually assured."

In a BBC interview, Soros said:
"The International financial system has collapsed and cannot be restored in its current form. It will have to be restructured because it was flawed and collapsed under its own weight."

This underscores the devastating effects that currency trading and volatile exchange rates have had, and continue to have, particularly on the economies of soft currency nations and their consumer publics.

People like Lietaer and Soros and many of their peers, all of whom are very experienced in matters related to banking, the financial markets and currency trading, appear to share a common philosophy that proclaims the present global money system is destined to collapse.

Having reviewed lifestyle hazards associated with our conventional money, I asked myself why our disposable incomes have been allowed to become so increasingly unstable?
Two answers came to mind:
1. As will be shown later, the IMF and World Bank have allowed currency trading to destabilise disposable incomes worldwide;
2. The world's reserve and central banks, which do not trade directly with the public, tend to create money out of nothing and lend it to commercial banks, who lend it to their borrowing clients. They then create more money out of nothing by charging interest on the funny money.

The inevitable consequences of increasing fiat money in circulation are inflation, a weakening of the purchasing power of disposable income and an increasing need to stimulate economic growth, in a futile bid to give value to the worthless fiat money in circulation and to keep the flawed monetary system afloat.

Banks should only lend to borrowers no more than a certain percentage of the value of real money they hold from depositors, thereby ensuring they are always in a solvent position.
The amount of money they lend is traditionally termed as fractional money, the real value of which is equal to the percentage, or fraction, of deposited money they hold.

Because the business of lending money has become such a profitable and attractive business for banks, some lent a higher fraction of their deposited securities to earn greater amounts of interest and to create more money out of nothing. Some have gone as high as 90 percent or more.

According to G. Edward Griffin in his book *"The Creature from Jekyll Island*[4]*"* this appears to produce something of an accountability problem for banks.

Having issued receipts for the 100 percent of deposits and 90 percent for the borrowers, total receipts become 190 percent.

Griffin asserts the banks have created an extra 90 percent of money to be in circulation which is covered by only 52.63 percent of the original value of cash collateral deposits e.g. (100 ÷ 190 × 100 = 52.63%).

This would become one of the prime contributing inflationary effects upon economies and force a sharp reduction in the purchasing power of money in circulation.

The fact that so many banks around the world were hit by the U.S.A.'s sub-prime home loan crisis in 2008, necessitating billions of dollar bailout injections from the Fed, the Bank of England and other Reserve banks, suggests there is probably a huge amount of fiat money in circulation, chasing the defaults on repayments of funny-money lent to those sub-prime home buyers.

This and several other destabilising effects upon disposable incomes, makes yet another compelling case for replacing conventional money with a different, non-manipulative and far more stable unit of exchange, and for dispensing with banking services completely.

Concerns about the banking fraternity have been expressed by eminent people throughout history.

The U.S.A.'s third president Thomas Jefferson said:

"'I believe that banking institutions are more dangerous to our liberties than standing armies. If the American people ever allow private banks to control the issue of their currency, first by inflation, then by deflation, the banks and corporations that will grow up around the banks will deprive the people of all property until their children wake-up homeless on the continent their fathers conquered."

From my research, the person who actually came closest to my perception of the monetary system is Richard C. Cook.

He worked for the Carter White House and NASA, then spent 21 years with the U.S. Treasury Department.

In April 2007, he wrote a hard-hitting report entitled *"An Emergency Program of Monetary Reform for the United States."*

It explains why he believes the U.S. financial system has failed and why only an emergency program of monetary reform can address conditions which are leading to catastrophe.

“"Dollar hegemony" he said, “has flooded the world with U.S. currency, loans, or debt instruments to support our fiscal and trade deficits, pay for our extraordinary level of resource utilization, induce foreign governments to purchase our armaments, ensure the allegiance of their governing elites, and maintain their economies in subservience through World Trade Organization and International Monetary Fund trade and lending policies. ....

One thing is connected to another. A good investigator always asks, "Who benefits?" The most salient feature of our financial system is that the creation of new purchasing power through credit - loans, mortgages, credit cards, etc. - is controlled by private financial institutions and, though regulated, works principally for their profit.

Because we are never taught about alternative economic structures, we take this system for granted. ....”

The section that so accurately mirrors my own thoughts was this:

“But the system is man-made, with functions and effects that can be measured and analysed. The system was created by historical forces, but if we want to, we can identify these forces and change the system. What we have lacked is the understanding of our possible choices, along with the discernment and moral courage to act on our understanding. The direction in which change must be sought is that of greater economic democracy; that is, a higher degree of sharing of the bounty of the earth by more people." *(My underscoring.)*

If the American monetary system collapses the rest of the global system will surely follow. While there is no firm consensus about the timing of this calamitous probability, some say “within the next ten years” – i.e. perhaps by 2015.

But, there is another consideration.

It is axiomatic that money rules the world and the USA is the richest nation in the world. So, we must assume that in economic terms the USA rules the world.

Not quite so according to Paul Craig Roberts, who was Assistant Secretary of the Treasury in the Reagan administration.

He was also Associate Editor of the *Wall Street Journal* editorial page and Contributing Editor of *National Review*.

He is co-author of *The Tyranny of Good Intentions*,

With credentials like that I believe anything he has to say on the subject of money and the power it wields should be taken seriously.

In an article he published in August 2007, captioned *"Uncle Sam, Your Banker Will See You Now"* he revealed how the American 'Goliath' at the time named Bush could be controlled by a 'David' called China with potentially disturbing consequences for the entire world.

Here is a slightly abridged version of his open message to American readers:

"On the morning of 8 August 2007, China let (those) in Washington, and on Wall Street, know that … China's considerable holdings of US dollars and Treasury bonds 'contributes a great deal to maintaining the position of the dollar as a reserve currency.'

Should the US proceed with sanctions intended to cause the Chinese currency to appreciate, 'the Chinese central bank will be forced to sell dollars, which might lead to a mass depreciation of the dollar.'

If Western financial markets are (able) to comprehend the message, US interest rates will rise regardless of any further action by China. At this point, China does not need to sell a single bond. In an instant, China has made it clear that US interest rates depend on China, not on the Federal Reserve.

The precarious position of the US dollar as reserve currency has been thoroughly ignored and denied. The delusion that the US is 'the world's sole superpower,' whose currency is desirable regardless of its excess supply, reflects American hubris, not reality. This hubris is so extreme that only six weeks ago (end June 2007) McKinsey Global Institute published a study that concluded that even a doubling of the US current account deficit to $1.6 trillion would pose no problem.

Strategic thinkers …. will quickly conclude that China's power over the value of the dollar and US interest rates also gives China power over US foreign policy. The US was able to attack Afghanistan and Iraq only because China provided the largest part of the financing for Bush's wars.

If China ceased to buy US Treasuries, Bush's wars would end. The savings rate of US consumers is essentially zero, and several million are afflicted with mortgages that they cannot afford. With Bush's budget in deficit and with no room in the US consumer's budget for a tax increase, Bush's wars can only be financed by foreigners.

No country on earth, except for Israel, supports the Bush regime's desire to attack Iran. It is China's decision whether it calls in the US ambassador, and delivers the message that there will be no attack on Iran or further war, unless the US is prepared to buy back $900 billion in US Treasury bonds and other dollar assets.

The US, of course, has no foreign reserves with which to make the purchase. The impact of such a large sale on US interest rates would wreck the US economy and effectively end Bush's war-making capability. Moreover, other governments would likely follow the Chinese lead, as the main support for the US dollar has been China's willingness to accumulate them. If the largest holder dumped the dollar, other countries would dump dollars, too.

The value and purchasing power of the US dollar would fall. When hard-pressed Americans went to Wal-Mart to make their purchases, the new prices would make them think they had wandered into Nieman Marcus. Americans would not be able to maintain their current living standard. Simultaneously, Americans would be hit either with tax increases in order to close a budget deficit that foreigners will no longer finance or with large cuts in income security programs.

The only other source of budgetary finance would be for the government to print money to pay its bills. In this event, Americans would experience inflation in addition to higher prices from dollar devaluation

This is a grim outlook. We got in this position because our leaders are ignorant fools. So are our economists, many of whom are paid shills for some interest group. So are our corporate leaders whose greed gave China power over the US by off-shoring the US production of goods and services to China. It was the corporate fat cats who turned US Gross Domestic Product into Chinese imports, and it was the 'free trade, free market economists' who egged it on.

How did a people as stupid as Americans get so full of hubris?"

Roberts pulled no punches in his hard hitting condemnation of the Bush administration nor, by inference, of the flawed mechanics of the global monetary system, to which his experience has enabled him to be so very closely attached.

His insinuation that heads of state can be, and invariably are, far removed from reality at ground zero is well taken.

I devote a lot of attention to this and the related effects in chapters addressing politics and sovereign nations.

His mention of the U.S.A.'s Federal Reserve was interesting because it has been my lay opinion that the Fed. has probably played a bigger role in causing the American economy to become so financially vulnerable than is generally accepted Indeed the Fed. can be held largely responsible for the predictable collapse of the entire world monetary system.

A little piece of history about the Fed:

It was conceived by a cartel of bankers in 1910, and born in 1913 by the passing into law of the Federal Reserve Act.

Congress had obviously been convinced the stated objectives of the Fed, righteously proclaimed to include bringing stability to the American money market and protection of the peoples' best interests, were sound enough reasons to pass the Act into law. Because such humanitarian principles are regarded by many to be at variants with those of the banking profession generally, the Fed. is unlikely ever to fulfil its proclaimed objectives.

The book I recommended earlier - *"The Creature from Jekyll Island"* - for those interested in money matters generally and the Fed. in particular, sub-titled 'A second look at the Federal Reserve' is well worth reading.

The Fed., or people associated with it, might have another agenda for us to worry about.

I logged onto Youtube during some research and found a video clip relating to talk of a One World Government.

In it were words attributed to Paul Warburg, Council on Foreign Relations and architect of the Federal Reserve System, quoting a statement he made in an address to the U.S. Senate 17th February 1950:

"We shall have World Government, whether or not we like it. The only question is whether World Government will be achieved by conquest or consent."

Further on in the clip was a statement alleged to have been made by David Rockefeller of the same Council in an address delivered to a meeting of top business people:

"We are grateful to the Washington Post, the New York Times, Time Magazine, and other great publications whose directors have attended our meetings and respected their promises of discretion for almost 40 years.

It would have been impossible for us to develop our plan for the world if we had been subjected to the lights of publicity during those years.

But now the world is more sophisticated and prepared to march towards a world government.

The supra national sovereignty of an intellectual elite and world bankers is surely preferable to the national auto-determination practiced in past centuries."

I have been unable to confirm the validity of Rockefeller's words but, if true, were they a declared intention of bankers and the intellectual elite to rule the world, with the masses following obediently behind?

> ***OK, so you have managed to shatter my long-held view that money is one of the more reliable aspects of our lives and that my bank manager is one of the few people I can trust. I agree money certainly does not go as far as it used to, nor as far as we now want it to go. But it's the only stuff we have.***
>
> ***So, are you now going to explain how your proposed new money system is going to work and – dare I say it – save us all?***

My proposed new money system will not exactly "save us all," but it will certainly make it easier for us to save ourselves.

Before explaining how, I believe it is important to stress that all aspects of new world order changes must be planned by the will and participation of the world's total population, rather than by multinational and minority interests.

I also need to show the criterion my proposed Credit money system had to satisfy before I could propose it as an alternative unit of exchange.

1. **Simplicity** – it must be fully understandable by every literate member of the global community.
2. **Global accessibility** – every eligible person must have access to it worldwide.
3. **Security and stability** – Its availability and stable purchasing value must be linked directly to non-tradable collateral assets. The assets must be guaranteed and sustained, enabling the prerogative of zero inflation to prevail.
4. **Ecologically friendly** – It must protect the global environment, the ecology and the planet's natural resources as well as the elements that enable production of life supporting resources.

Let me expand upon each of the stated criteria to show how the Credit would meet them on a sustainable basis:

1. Simplicity

The Credit will never be available in a material form, thereby overcoming the present expensive process of production and distribution of printed notes and coin, and of protecting the integrity of traditional money from highly skilled forgers and counterfeiters. It also disposes of the additional expense incurred to eventually destroy old, soiled and damaged money.

It also dispenses with the humanitarian need to incorporate special design features enabling, for example, blind people to determine the values of notes and coins they handle.

As previously mentioned, cash in transit heists, ATM robberies and theft of every kind for financial gain would no longer occur, neither would drug and human trafficking, money laundering and all other cash dependent criminal activities.

The Credit will become a unique and equitably distributed unitary share of Earth's entire inventory of resources. Every member of Earth's human population will become lifetime shareholders and the Credits will be accountable resource acquittal dividends.

Credit allocations will be electronically credited to the recipient's Status Card account (discussed later), in similar manner to present ways by which people's bank and/or credit card accounts are electronically credited by their employers and debtors on a monthly basis.

The enormity of the task to complete and sustain a global registration process is not underestimate. There will be opportunities for huge numbers of people with operational and management skills capabilities, and for many others with the competence to be fully trained.

The manner in which the Credit monetary system will operate will lead to the redundancy of all present financial markets, the banking system and peripheral components, as well as all related industries. Similarly, all other traditional cash related services performed within our present private and public sectors would cease to exist.

Many new and comparable disciplines will be created, providing important and essential redeployment opportunities for those with the will and competence to manage a new and truly global monetary system.

2. Global accessibility

Availability of and access to Credits will be on a totally global basis.

For example, when travelling from one's home to any other part of the world, people will simply take their Status Cards with them and use them in exactly the same way as at home for purchasing goods and services.

The purchase price of goods and services throughout the world would be similar, if not identical, everywhere.

Exchange Control would no longer obtain because Credits would be the common form of money worldwide in a single nation environment.

3. Security and stability

These attributes require deeper consideration.

Being the only form of money on the planet, distributed and transferred electronically, and constantly measured against monitored global resource inventory stocks, the security of Credits on a worldwide basis would be automatically guaranteed.

The commencement unitary value of Credits will have been determined by a select committee of eminently qualified people. The results will be formally proclaimed upon a date not less than one year preceding adoption throughout the world.

Throughout the Status Card registration process, global population census numbers will become accurately measurable and the essential monitoring and revision mechanisms will be constantly refined.

A sustainable population number will have to be factored into long term life support capabilities, and I estimate the target total will probably be no more than six billion by the end of the first 200 years of Global Administration governance.

The optimum sustainable population factor will be continually monitored, relative to the availability and utilisation of resources and the effects of climate change.

These factors will be affected by food security; the availability of potable water; planned and mobilised ecological and environmental recovery and growth; the expectation of extended years of life for people surviving the effects of climate change conditions; the increasing number of people moving from poverty into the Basic Income Grant (BIG) status, and for the gainfully employed majority.

The Basic Income Grant is explained further on.

Purchasing values of Credits will be monitored for stability, perhaps initially over twenty stages of five year periods during the first hundred years of the new Global Administration, with possible adjustments thereafter.

This all sounds very complicated to me, particularly that part about an optimum sustainable population factor. What does that mean?

In a nutshell, long term family planning on a massive scale.

I predict you are going to have problems with that one. There are millions of people out there who do not agree with family planning.

Yes, I'm aware of that and the subject will have to be handled responsibly, under conditions of mutual respect and tolerance on both sides of the debate, which should be achievable 100-200 years from now.

We are presently aware that a high percentage of those who lack the resources to support the products of their traditional beliefs, are often those who eventually, and very sadly, decline into poverty dragging their dependents down with them.

For this and many other reasons, I continually stress the importance and absolute necessity for us to look at the practical realities of the bigger picture of sustainable survival for the entire species. I predict future generations will consciously review and assess all aspects of inherited cultural and religious beliefs that pose a potential threat to achieving that goal.

We must remember that over a period of time spanning approximately 2 000 generations up to 1950, the mean average human population of the world had been estimated to be in the region of two billion people. That was the number I personally recall at that time.

From 1950 to 2000, the population was shown to have increased to 6.5 billion, an apparent increase of 225 percent. Seven short years later it jumped to almost 9 billion, which is a further 34.46 percent increase and perhaps a total of 350 percent over 57 years.

It has been revealed that mankind's activities giving rise to our present global warming and climate change predicament, occurred during that extremely short fifty seven year period.

A recent report by the UN Food and Agriculture Organisation (FAO) states that over the past twenty years alone, food output has risen at 1.3 percent a year, while the number of mouths to be fed has increased by 1.35 percent, approximately 13.5 million.

Food security has turned attention towards concerns relating to bio fuels. It presently takes 232 kg of corn to make 50 litres of bio ethanol and a child could live on that amount of corn for a year.

As bleak as you continue to paint your picture of our future world, I still believe we really do have the money and resources now to either prevent it from having such a devastating affect, or to possibly retreat from the threatened coastal regions and rebuild in preparation to meet the challenges head on.

Well, let us examine the realities of your suggestion.

The majority of the world's busy commercial ports and highly populated towns and cities that have grown up around them, evolved over many years. Some took hundreds of years to reach their present size and density.

Attempting to replace all this to alternative locations further inland would take many years to accomplish at unimaginable cost.

Bearing in mind that many hundreds of such rebuilding projects would have to be undertaken simultaneously around the world, from whence would the human resources, billions of tonnes of materials and equipment come and who would be paying the astronomically high costs? I cannot imagine projects of this nature ever being contemplated under prevailing conditions.

Another consideration would be the effects upon the disadvantaged masses throughout the world. We know how much they rely upon relief aid from donor nations. If the existing money system is retained, what will happen to them when maritime trade links collapse and when money and resources become diverted for purposes other than remote humanitarian aid? Conventional money holds no hope whatsoever for their future survival, nor for others.

4. Ecologically friendly

Whereas the proposed new Credit would represent a share of the global resources assets, its disposable income value relevance will not yet be immediately apparent. It will become so further on.

As a prelude thereto, let us consider the relationship between our presently eroding environment and the reparation cost arguments. Under prevailing conditions they are weighted with some justification in favour of those who consider reparation to be economically flawed.

A number of commercially credible submissions, sponsored by major industrialists from the richer nations, were presented to Kyoto Accord signatories underscoring their warnings of severe economic risks associated with some of the proposed remedial actions. They maintain the cost in terms of money and job losses to correct environmental and ecological disasters would be enormously and unacceptably high.

Those were the reasons promoted by multinational corporations and their political allies for not throwing money at a clean-up operation to remove pollution from the environment, despite clean-up recommendations tabled at Kyoto Protocol meetings.

Amongst other things, the Kyoto Convention addressed the problems of CO_2 emissions and the manner by which they should be reduced. From this came the proposals of Carbon Trading which were adopted in 1997 and there is an excellent and very informative overview of the topic in the Dag Hammarskjöld Foundation's "*What Next*[5]" project publication.

The United Nations Framework Convention on Climate Change (UNFCCC) treaty finally came into force on 16 February 2005, having been ratified by 127 countries responsible for 61 per cent of global greenhouse-gas emissions.

The Protocol binds 38 industrialised nations to reducing their emissions by an average of 5.2 per cent below 1990 levels by 2008-2012.

We have been told the cost in terms of money and job losses to correct environmental and ecological disasters would be enormously and unacceptably high.

My proposed World Governance Standard Credit system changes all that. It gives birth to a socially responsible resources management process, working within a money-less social structure, enabling the delivery of goods and services without the traditional considerations of conventional monetary costs and profit generation.

The Credit's prerogative of being ecologically friendly will be achieved.

This is particularly so when addressing the urgent need for reparations of our atmosphere and environment, and perhaps slowing as much as possible the devastating effects that climate change will have upon us all.

Your words are all well and good, full of promise and hope but I don't see the substance. To replace conventional money with a different monetary system is one thing but the economic fundamentals of supply and demand, profit and loss, investment, competition and all the other paraphernalia

common to all monetary systems, must still surely come into play and you will still be left with the haves and the have-nots, the wealthy and the poor.

That might indeed be true if we were debating the introduction of an alternative conventionally minted currency, but we are not.

The Credit will not be something to carry in ones wallet, pocket or purse. Nor will it be something to be traded on commodity exchanges. It will never be affected by the traditional economic fundamentals of supply and demand.

It will no longer be the traditional financial medium of conventional trading activities because trade in the accepted sense will no longer take place. Accordingly, there will be no capital investment and related profit and dividend considerations.

The Credit will be a predetermined unit of disposable income, paid by electronic transfer to the registered Status Card account of every adult member of the human race worldwide for conventional life support purposes.

It will be argued, I am sure, that conventional money will be needed to 'save the world.'

I would certainly not support such an argument. I would counter by saying conventional money is not saving everyone from the agonies of hunger; it is not providing everyone with dependable health care; it is not providing every child in the world with sound education, and it is certainly not ensuring carefree retirement for the world's elderly folk.

It will certainly not save the world from the onslaught of global warming and climate change.

The value of any unit of global currency today is not measured against the life sustaining needs of humanity. It is measured against the market value of commodities, including all other currencies, all of which are subjected to those market influences of supply and demand you mentioned.

Money must be recreated to meet the survival needs of the majority rather than the rewards of wealth and prosperity for the few.

In Chapter 9 – The Plan for Change - you will see how that will be achieved.

Chapter 5

Politics & Politicians

The League of Scoundrels

What is politics actually all about?

Let us find out what people of historical prominence had to say about politics, politicians and government?

George Washington (1732-1799), 1st US President under the Constitution, in his farewell address said:

"Occupants of public offices love power and are prone to abuse it."

American statesman John C. Calhoun (1782-1850)

"Government has within it a tendency to abuse its powers."

John Hospers, Professor Emeritus of Philosophy at the University of Southern California:

"By far the most numerous and most flagrant violations of personal liberty and individual rights are performed by governments. The major crimes throughout history, the ones executed on the largest scale, have been committed not by individuals or bands of individuals but by governments, as a deliberate policy of those governments, that is, by the official representatives of governments, acting in their official capacity."

Ludwig von Mises (1881-1973) Economist and social philosopher:

"The worst evils which mankind has ever had to endure were inflicted by bad governments. The state can be and has often been in the course of history the main source of mischief and disaster."

From these observations one might expect politicians throughout the world to expect to be regarded as being members of what I call "The League of Scoundrels," and from my own experience that is exactly what so many of them are – absolute scoundrels.

If politicians are the dangerous, uncaring and self ingratiating people so many believe them to be, how was politics ever allowed to get started in the world and who do you believe was the world's first "scoundrel" who got the political ball rolling?

That's an interesting question and I think the answer can be found in ancient scriptures. In my opinion the foundations of political and religious philosophies and leadership were laid more or less in tandem with each other and have remained umbilically connected ever since.

The partnership has not always been overtly close and harmonious. Indeed, over the millennia there have been a number of tempestuous partings and reunions by mutual agreement and understanding. The volatile nature of their relationship has always been inevitable and remains so even today.

Both have been generating their wealth and power from the same source – the ordinary people within their domains. The rulers and politicians wanted peoples' bodies, while the religious leaders wanted their minds and souls. Both demanded respect, allegiance and obedience for quite different reasons but, for identical purposes – power.

Over the years both have succeeded but to vastly different degrees of self benefit. The nation rulers and politicians won the bodies of the people within the boundaries of their own dominions, while the religious leaders eventually won the minds and souls of the people in many dominions.

As to the world's first politician, I think we might look back to the pre-flood era and consider the tyrannical and murderous scoundrel Cain. He was an empire builder, self appointed monarch and creator of governance, all of which will have presumably disappeared into oblivion with the coming of the great flood.

Nimrod was possibly the very first post-flood politician, gathering people around him to do as he commanded. The meaning of the verb form nimrodh is "let us revolt" and according to scriptures Nimrod certainly revolted against God's commandments. A political scoundrel personified.

Nevertheless, I have devoted an entire chapter to the subject of religions further on so let me concentrate upon politics.

Right. Keep your eye on the ball.

Absolutely.

Researching politics entails looking into its origins, development, expansion and acquisition of power and influences.

By learning from history we become able to see how the traditional structures and practises of politics might now be demolished and replaced by a truly democratic regime of secular and globally participative governance, serving the collective interests of the entire human race.

To determine how the future establishment of a Global Administration might affect the conventional and traditional science of politics, and the psyche of modern day politicians, it will be necessary for those charged with doing so to have an intimate understanding of all aspects of this complex, rotten and corruption-prone profession.

My own experiences in active politics are very limited indeed, being confined to a three year period of time commencing June 1997, when I joined Roelf Meyer's New Movement Process (NMP) in South Africa, which was intended to become a credible opposition party to Nelson Mandela's ruling African National Congress (ANC).

Three months later the NMP merged with General Bantu Holomisa's NCF movement and the amalgam was renamed the United Democratic Movement (UDM) and remains part of South Africa's political fabric today.

Good grief, are you telling me you were a member of the dreaded "League of Scoundrels" yourself?

Yes, but only for a very short time and with no personal prominence whatsoever.

I became one of the many founding members of the UDM and was appointed chairman of the Gauteng Finance Commission for a while.

For the benefit of non-South African readers, Gauteng is one of the nine provinces created by the ANC when they came to power in 1994, replacing the original four provinces of Transvaal, Orange Free State, Natal and the Cape, with Gauteng, Mpumalanga, Free State, KwaZulu-Natal, Eastern Cape, Western Cape, Northern Cape, North West and Limpopo.

Gauteng is the smallest province in size but the largest in terms of economic activity, incorporating Johannesburg and Pretoria and the lion's share of the country's commercial, industrial and gold mining activities and interests. It also hosts the Johannesburg Stock Exchange (JSE) which later moved from the Johannesburg CBD into the northern suburbs.

In preparation for general elections in 1999, Roelf Meyer effectively handed leadership of the UDM over to Bantu Holomisa and went into private practise.

The UDM scraped through the elections and secured two parliamentary seats.

Although I gained no practical experience whatsoever of post-election opposition strategies, my involvement and participation in the pre-election policy-making processes and electioneering strategies, nevertheless provided me with a practical insight into the manipulative tactics of politics, and the equally manipulative and oft devious nature of the psyche of some politicians, particularly the emergent 'struggle' converts entering conventional politics at that time.

Suffice it to say these insights convinced me I no longer wished to pursue a political career. I wasn't the 'right stuff.'

So, you got out?

Yes, I stepped down in 2000.

From what I observed and learned, my assessment of the South African political system at that time, which is not dissimilar to global practise, can be summarized as follows:

Regardless of differences of opinion regarding the party's policy issues, the policy line will be adhered to unquestioningly.

In effect some career politicians are conditioned to accede to the commandment that prescribes all social issues shall be deemed subordinate to the party line, pending their future assessed values as possible electioneering vote catchers.

Politicians are perceived by many to be singularly and collectively focussed upon maximising their own self interests, their career positions and their eventual retirement status.

The political party can be regarded as the structure, or club, formed by like-minded members, to become the enabling structure through which those personal ambitions are pursued.

The ultimate value of a politician's career objectives will invariably depend upon the level of influence he or she attains within the party hierarchy and the manner in which it is deployed to protect the party's credibility and its leader.

A career politician is virtually guaranteed a retirement status of greater than reasonable comfort and security, whereas the ultra ambitious politician will either retire in opulence or burn his fingers in the attempt to do so.

But what about those pre-retirement years? How can an ambitious politician gain interim beneficiation during his active political life and lay solid foundations for the future, preferably with monetary dividends along the way?

That's easy. He can do what all ordinary people try hard to do throughout their lives, through savings, investments, insurances and retirement annuity plans.

Indeed he could but many politicians regard themselves as members of an elitist group, occupying space at an altitude of importance much higher than ground zero.

Politics can be a serious business for those in pursuit of power and wealth, disguised as a selfless crusade fighting the good fight for their constituents in general and the nation as a whole.

It is a business that has nothing tangible to sell other than unqualified assurances of "a better life for all" and a rewarding existence for those who put their trust in the manicured hands of the political candidate and mandate he or she propounds.

You really are being very cynical.

You are virtually saying that a politician's word should not be trusted because the needs of his constituents are not high on his list of priorities. In fact, you are saying his personal interests are his highest priority. I find that very difficult to believe.

Well, let us not forget the shenanigans of many British MPs who were exposed for having defaulted on their expense allowances, their privileges, their tax returns and a number of other perks.

American political history contains volumes of reports linking Senators, Congressmen and others to acts of corruption.

In South Africa, only twelve short years after the country's quantum leap into national independence, the country's official opposition party, the Democratic Alliance (DA), made public to the media a list of 1 792 names of public servants found guilty of receiving social grants to which they were not entitled.

Wow! That's a lot of 'scoundrels' as you call them.

Quite so!

It was reported that the government's Social Development Minister Zola Skweyiya, had provided the names to the DA in response to a parliamentary question and the DA had decided to publish the names despite the minister's request for confidentiality.

> "The government has developed a tendency to hide from the public important information about the state of our country," DA Social Development spokesperson Mike Waters said in a statement.
>
> "We find it strange and somewhat offensive that the minister would ask the DA to be complicit in this kind of behaviour."

In his reply the minister asked Parliament to apply discretion in the publication of the information.

The DA said it had committed itself to respecting the confidentiality of information deemed to potentially put the nation's security at risk, but information on corruption it said, should never be swept under the carpet.

> "We understand that the individuals named in the minister's reply were caught stealing and agreed to sign admission of guilt statements."
>
> "It is perhaps appropriate therefore, that they have not been charged criminally but, the state's generosity should not extend to protecting their anonymity."
>
> "Taxpayers had a right to know who had been stealing their money," said Waters.

The DA said the named public servants were not being charged interest on repayments of the stolen money. They were also not required to pay a fine and were given extremely lenient repayment plans.

> "In some cases, people can take as long as 31 *[interest-free]* years to repay the amount owed."

The individuals owed a combined total of just under R11 million (+- $1,6 million).

Of the total group of offenders, 241 were employed by the SA Police Service. There were also 425 teachers, nine school principals, 29 education specialists and seven legal support service personnel.

My goodness this is dreadful. Perhaps bringing such things into the public domain will prevent further malfeasance.

A reasonable assumption but unlikely to have the desired results.

South African readers will be familiar with the so-called 'Travelgate' affair relating to travel voucher fraud by political figures, and the ongoing allegations of bribery and corruption relating to the R30 billion "Arms Deal.[6]" (*Note: This link provides access to a very comprehensive record of events*).

In February 2007, Douglas Gibson, D.A. Chief Whip at the time, speaking during debate in the National Assembly on president Thabo Mbeki's state-of-the-nation address, raised the point that four years into the fraudulent 'Travelgate' saga it had yet to be concluded and about 20 MPs were still in Parliament after pleading guilty to charges of defrauding the people.

The next surprise was that as many as 200 MPs had been sued by the liquidators and had paid, or were paying money back. The public did not know who these MPs were nor how or why they incurred these debts.

Two Cabinet ministers had to repay more than R300 000.00 to the liquidators.

Former ANC Chief Whip Mbulelo Goniwe had to repay R70 000.00.

Gibson said it was surprising that members of parliament could "make mistakes" amounting to these amounts of money yet, according to the powers that be, were deemed to have done nothing illegal rendering them liable to criminal prosecution.

On the worrying question of crime, president Mbeki at the time, labouring under a bout of denial, had publicly expressed his opinion on a number of occasions that despite public opinion, crime was in fact under control and actually decreasing.

Members of the public clearly disagreed with him and there were, quite literally, barrow loads of dissenting letters and emails delivered to his office prior to his state-of-the-nation address, which were deemed to have influenced its final draft.

Admitting that crime was of "great concern" he presented a wish list of things that government would be 'considering' to improve matters.

Wish lists are political instruments of public appeasement but implementation is generally conspicuous by its absence.

The DA's Douglas Gibson reinforced this perception when he said:

"The real surprise was that the president, as leader of the ANC, had said nothing about crime in Parliament and had failed to act.

"Surely the ANC considers that those among us who have stolen money from the people are not fit to be parliamentarians?".

I agree with Mr. Gibson. If politicians have admitted their criminal activities they must become automatically liable to prosecution and then, as seems inevitable because of their admission of guilt, they should be sentenced by the court accordingly.

Also, as he had pointed out, a person with a criminal record is precluded from being a member of parliament.

Those are reasonable assumptions which would certainly have force and effect if you or I, or any other ordinary member of society, had committed the offences.

But of course, parliamentary offenders do not regard themselves as ordinary members of society.

They are paid up members of the elitist League of Scoundrels enjoying the benefits of what one might call diplomatic immunity within their own national borders. The great untouchables.

Your reference to a criminal record precluding membership of parliament is extremely pertinent and appears to have no relevance in parliament itself as far as the ruling ANC party was concerned.

In August 2007, the *Sunday Times* newspaper reported that the then Minister of Health Manto Tshabalala-Msimang was suffering from chronic alcoholism, and that doctors and staff at the hospital where she underwent a liver transplant, knew she had been drinking before her operation.

Standard procedure is that alcoholic patients stop drinking for between six and twelve months before surgery and permanently thereafter, the report read.

It was certainly a little disquieting to learn that the person in charge of the nation's health service was an alcoholic, particularly after having informed the nation and the world that beetroot and garlic were combatants against HIV and Aids!

Further journalistic research revealed that while she was serving as superintendent of a hospital in Botswana in 1976, she had been convicted of stealing a watch from a patient under anaesthetic.

She was then expelled from the country and declared a prohibited immigrant!

The report quoted an employee at the Athlone Hospital at Lobatse near Gaborone as saying: "Everyone here thinks it's hilarious that she is today a health minister in South Africa."

How can politics be taken seriously?

From time to time religious leaders chip in with support for their political compatriots in an attempt to convince the world that politicians, even those with the most heinous track records, need to be treated with dignity and humility.

For example, Archbishop Desmond Tutu felt Zimbabwe's president Robert Mugabe needed help when he said:

> "I would hope that there might just be a way of providing face-savers that would enable people to exit without feeling that they had lost a great deal of personal stature," he said. "We need to provide that for the sake of the people."

I cannot imagine this having any relevance of being "for the sake of the people."

How does one measure the personal stature of such an intransigent and despicable dictator?

Tutu, who has been an outspoken critic of human rights violations by Mugabe's government, has highlighted one of the inherent vices of politics, particularly at national leadership levels worldwide, which the hierarchy of religious leadership acknowledges and largely endorses in keeping with the historical bond that has endured between them for centuries.

It is an assurance that heads of state who abuse their power, enrich themselves, impoverish their citizens and brutalise opposition, shall never be punished by their global peers.

They must be afforded an opportunity to step down with grace and dignity and to retire in opulence for the remaining years of their lives.

The League of Scoundrels must, and shall, prevail.

Reverting to South Africa's politics, the new crown princes of political corruption became established in the newly decorated corridors of power and influence, and absolutely nothing would be done to ensure that heads of political wrongdoers would roll.

It is not unusual for the converted to surpass the corrupt performances of those they emulate or replace.

> ***Yes, and some members of the "old guard" Nationalists were also suspected of being masters at feathering their nests through corrupt activities. But of course that was said to be 'par for the course' for all whites during the apartheid regime era.***

I cannot agree with such a sweeping statement as that. Some whites did indeed take advantage of the system but not all.

Most got on with their lives the best they could under a despicable system that was common to all.

It was the whites exclusively who, prior to the first democratic elections in 1994, responded with a resounding "Yes" vote to the referendum initiated by the state president at the time, F.W. de Klerk, calling upon whites to declare whether or not they were in favour of the blacks taking control of the country's governance with Nelson Mandela at the helm.

That affirmative vote gave de Klerk the confidence and resolve to take the quantum leap forward into the unknown and uncharted territory of national unity and democratic governance. I'm sure it will have also given Nelson Mandela enormous assurance that the road ahead would not be marred by dissenting violence and widespread conflict and bloodshed.

As bad and unjust as apartheid obviously was, people tend to forget how the seeds of racial discrimination were sown in South Africa.

South Africa's early history shows that British colonial governance introduced separatist rule in the colony during their period of imperial administration, denying non-whites access to economic participation.

So the fundamentals of racial discrimination were well entrenched by the British Crown before the Nationalists came on the political scene.

When they eventually took political control of the country, they introduced the principle of dedicated and independent homeland regions for the various black tribal peoples to develop their own economies, pumping millions of white taxpayers' money into their misguided venture. It was greatly flawed and few believed it would actually work.

The Afrikaans word describing this type of separate development is 'apartheid', and this is the word with which the rest of the world became familiar when the Nationalists formalised their policy.

They were also intent upon raising the Afrikaner culture to a position of political and social prominence and to create sustainable employment opportunities for the large numbers of poor and disadvantaged members of the Afrikaner community.

They achieved this in no small measure by becoming public sector employers of large numbers of Afrikaner civil servants and in hospitals, schools, railways and harbours, agriculture and forestry, the mining industry, the national defence forces and the police services.

The English-speaking whites largely, but not exclusively, occupied the commercial, business and finance sectors.

As difficult as it undoubtedly was for blacks and other non-whites to live normal lives under abnormal conditions, all whites, regardless of their cultural backgrounds and political inclinations, were subjected to very stringent and restrictive laws relating to all forms of personal contact they might have with non-white members of society, particularly blacks.

Contravention of the law could, and occasionally did, give rise to pre-dawn knocking on doors by law enforcement officials and the removal of suspected "offenders" to be taken into custody and subjected to hours of questioning.

Whereas blacks were unquestionably the most disadvantaged under apartheid rule, whites were not precluded from the draconian conditions of enforcement.

Interestingly, it was estimated at some time during the 1970s that approximately two million white family homes, each employed an average of two black domestic servants, each of whom would have had at least two or three other dependents.

In that sector alone some 8-12 million or more blacks would have derived a degree of financial income support and sustenance from the white domestic sector. A large percentage of domestic staff had their own on site quarters with water, power and toilet facilities. They will have been provided food and paid weekly or monthly wages.

The picture is somewhat different today.

Because many white homeowners can no longer afford to employ living-in domestic workers, a high percentage now have more than one casual employer for whom they might work one or two days a week.
They will not have on site accommodation, they might not be provided with food and will invariably have to pay their own transport costs to get to and from each place of work.

The domestic workers of today enjoy Constitutional rights, freedom of movement, speech and choice, previously denied their disadvantaged predecessors, but are they better off financially? It remains a debatable question.

Reverting to the scourge of corruption in high places, I imagine Mr. Mandela will have been deeply saddened, in his post-presidential life, to see that many of the participants in crime and corruption are ANC politicians in positions of power at national, provincial and local government levels.
They are seen to have taken such a commanding lead in the race to attain personal wealth and prosperity while the numbers of homeless, jobless, illiterate and impoverished blacks at ground zero have steadily grown over the years of ANC governance.

So you think the country's greatest and most respected statesman experienced disappointment in his twilight years?

I would imagine so but I am not privy to what goes on in the old man's mind.
He had a noble vision for the nation in general that would enable social upliftment for previously disadvantaged blacks in particular.
He gathered around him people of assumed like-mindedness and equally assumed leadership qualities and determination, to transform his vision into a reality.

So you think he was let down by his own comrades, is that it?

Not by all of them. But those who failed the challenge and lost sight of the old man's vision also lost sight of the bigger picture it represented.

Predictably South Africa's black ruling class appears now to be pursuing a course of racial discrimination through the process of Affirmative Action and Black Economic Empowerment now they have the political power and the enabling mechanisms to do so.

Wait a minute! Are you saying the South African government is deliberately taking over control of the country's economy from the whites, rather than becoming part of the economic and development process?

Well that is certainly what a large body of people interpret the definition of Black Economic Empowerment (BEE) to imply.

That perception is reinforced in the wording of the definition of BEE as formally adopted by the BEE Commission in 2000, part of which states:

> *"It is aimed at redressing the imbalances of the past by seeking to substantially and equitably transfer and confer the ownership, management and control of South Africa's financial and economic resources to the majority of its citizens."*

The majority of citizens in South Africa are the blacks, to the exclusion of all others, including Indians and coloureds.

Additionally, here are some quotations from the Executive Summary Report of the BEE Commission in 2001.

From the opening introduction:

> *"The domination of business activities by white business and the exclusion of black people and women from the mainstream of economic activity are causes for great concern for the Reconstruction and Development Process.*
>
> *A central objective of the RDP is to de-racialise business ownership and control completely, through focused policies of black economic empowerment."*

I imagine that "de-racialise" means the removal of whites and the transfer of economic power to blacks in the context of that statement.

In an attempt to justify a BEE strategy under the cross heading of 'Meeting the Challenge of Disempowerment' we find:

> *"South Africa's present Government inherited a mismanaged economy, designed to serve the needs of a minority of the population and condemning the black majority to a vicious cycle of extreme poverty, unemployment and underdevelopment."*

What had the situation for the black majority become fourteen or more years after those words were penned?

In terms of poverty and unemployment both have reached very worrisome heights, well above the levels applicable before the ANC took over political control.

I can't see how you can justify that statement having said the Nationalist apartheid policy denied blacks access to the mainstream economy.

I agree blacks would have found it extremely difficult, if not impossible, to become part of management structures of long established white owned business interests. Legislation would have prevented this happening. It did not mean, however, there were no employment opportunities whatsoever for black people. Indeed, a number created profitable businesses for themselves.

Millions of others were employed in the mining, farming, forestry, railways, harbours, airport, and transportation industries; by the police and defence forces.

From talking with black people within my age bracket I learned much about the repressive indignities experienced by blacks living under apartheid conditions. I was also told that family unity was much stronger and supportive in those times than it has become today. Although wages were low, money went much further than it does today. Generally speaking millions of black people were better off financially than they are today.

Since acquiring political power the ANC regularly complain they inherited a grossly mismanaged administration, blaming this for their inability to uplift and improve the lives of their disadvantaged kin.

These excuses have exceeded their 'use before' date by a number of years, particularly since the ANC government has now been fingered as being unable to manage the country's finances.

For example, an overview of the audit outcomes of government departments over a number of years proves that too many ministers and directors general have been unable to provide proper financial management of public money.

Indeed in many cases the overview paints a picture of financial disarray and mismanagement on a grand scale.

"The consequence of this is serious indeed," according to a statement issued by the DA.

Why do you keep making reference to the DA and what they have to say? Are you an avid supporter?

No, not at all. I make mention of the DA's comments because they are the official opposition party in South African politics.

I assume they will research their subjects very carefully and prepare their battle tactics with reliable ammunition, sourced from armouries to which I do not have access.

Working on the premise that a responsible opposition party will never fire blanks, I feel quite comfortable quoting them in matters that are in the public domain.

OK. Fine.

Returning to the DA's observations, out of the 135 annual audits conducted by the Auditor General on the 34 government departments and public entities over the subject period, there were only seven 'clean reports.'

In contrast, 35 were 'qualified', received an 'adverse opinion', or a 'disclaimer'.

A total of 128 reports had an 'emphasis of matter'.

Entities that receive 'qualified reports', 'adverse opinions' or a 'disclaimer' from the AG are deemed to be in a state of financial disarray and mismanagement.

Entities receiving a report with an 'emphasis of matter' were deemed to have failed to comply with their agreed programme of action or with statutory requirements.

This is all very informative, educational and no doubt more than a little worrying for South African readers but, why are you not taking a more global approach to politics?

I have been focusing upon disturbing aspects of South African politics because my book was originally intended for South African readers. Any attempt to focus upon the politics of many countries would make this particular chapter extremely long and tiresome.

South Africa's parliamentary superstructure comprises elements similar to systems elsewhere in the world. Also, the country's Constitution is recognised as being the most well composed document of its type in the world.

Historically, represented by General Smuts, South Africa played a major founding role in the formation of the United Nations in 1945.

Another consideration is also worthy of mention.

Working on the palaeontological declaration that South Africa hosts the location of the cradle of human kind for the entire planet, makes it an excellent place to use as a point of departure in search of solutions to all humanity's problems, including politics.

The entire world's developmental problems have an umbilical attachment to the cradle of mankind here in South Africa.

Aren't you now getting off the political track altogether and moving into history? You are certainly stretching a point.

Just a little perhaps but it's exciting to remember those who trekked out on extraordinary evolutionary and exploratory journeys from the Sterkfontein region of South Africa became the ancestors of the entire global population.

They pioneered the world we have today comprising many countries, many cultures, many languages, many religions and various forms of political governance.

I could hypothesise that the entire world stems from the global region that has since become known as South Africa and that it was those very early South African globetrotters who colonised the world.

On that basis my South African-based proposal for a single nation world has deep historical relevance and credibility, by inviting the entire global community to unite and return to its ancient ancestral family roots.

Interesting hypothesis and I confess it does appear to have a degree of relevance. It would be interesting to learn how other people perceive the concept. The thought of having come from one family setting in the beginning, makes it a lot easier to accept, in principle at least, your proposal that we all become a single world nation again. Very interesting.

Yes, and those early trekkers will have created the many and varied forms of civilisation prevalent today.

Meanwhile, returning to the present time.

When the ANC eventually came to power the country was welcomed back into the open arms of international politics and commerce, due very largely to the much-liked charismatic nature of Nelson Mandela.

Old anti-apartheid hurdles and obstacles were removed from the course and South Africa was all set to get back in the race, to rebuild harmonious international relations and to right the wrongs of the past at home.

Needless to say the previously oppressed and disadvantaged masses went into a joyous mode of great expectations.

But let us not forget that white "Yes" vote during the referendum that contributed to making it peacefully possible.

So the country was off to a good start with the blessing of the white minority?

Well the majority of South Africans certainly thought and hoped so at the time.

While having good relationships around the world was naturally expected to benefit the economy as a whole, the non-white majority was particularly looking forward to economic upliftment at home and the long-awaited recovery of their personal dignities as human beings.

However, when Nelson Mandela eventually retired and made way for his chosen successor Thabo Mbeki, the road to recovery seemed to lose direction.

Mbeki was perceived as the Nero of South Africa, strumming a forlorn tune of African renaissance while his own countrymen suffered the burning agonies of societal collapse.

HIV and Aids, raging unemployment, poverty, declining standards of education, of healthcare and the justice system, were some of the pressing issues marking his reign of denial about HIV and crime.

Sadly, twelve years down the road, expectations of the masses were not fulfilled to any meaningful extent. Poverty, unemployment, crime, corruption in high places, and poor service delivery at community levels became worse than ever.

Mbeki's government acknowledged some failures at national, provincial and local government levels, blaming it all upon their "inheritance" of old apartheid policies.

Imagine a soccer coach apologising to his team's supporters' club for having lost every match over a twelve-year period, blaming it all upon the strategies employed by the coach he replaced.

I think they would probably lynch him!

Or worse.

It has been said by political analysts; specialists in social sciences; newspaper editors and others who study the ebb and flow of public perceptions of political performances, that the ruling party in general and Thabo Mbeki in particular had been out of touch with the masses they had sworn to serve.

Just days after being overtaken by Jacob Zuma in the ANC leadership nomination race in November 2007, Mbeki postponed indefinitely the handover ceremony of the African Peer Review Mechanism (APRM) report, "due to other urgent government matters" he had to attend to.

This might have been expected particularly since some believed the report was very critical of the ANC government's failure in tackling one of the world's highest crime rates.

Interestingly, shortly after Mbeki's insistence that crime was not running out of control, a wall was built around his official residence at a cost to taxpayers of R90 million! Crime would not be much of a threat to anyone living behind such an expensive and sophisticated protective barrier, even though it failed to prevent the theft from his roof of R25 000.00 worth of aluminium wire!

Then came the interesting interview he had on South African Broadcasting Corporation (SABC) television in January 2007, saying it was just a perception that crime was out of control.

> "It's not as if someone will walk here to the [television] studio in Auckland Park and get shot. That doesn't happen and it won't happen. Nobody can prove that the majority of the country's 40-million to 50-million citizens think that crime is spinning out of control," he said.

Ironically two months later a group of men armed with rifles and pistols robbed a Coin Security van collecting money at the very same SABC building in Auckland Park.

But let us not dwell too much upon Mbeki's unfocussed views of the realities of life.

If we consider the bigger picture of the global political structure, where the focus upon social issues has become so blurred, we find the majority of the world's population is suffering the consequences of failed service delivery in one form or another.

Private sector growth in profitable medical health care, private education, private home security and a number of other privately managed social services has been thriving, because the public sector has continually failed to provide many essential services on a well managed and efficacious basis.

Only 14 percent of South Africans can afford to pay for private medical aid cover. The remaining 86 percent are reliant upon the country's inadequate, overworked, under resourced and poorly managed public health service.

So why are we experiencing such a massive erosion of political competency?

Is it something new or has it always been there, only to have become so vividly exposed by media investigative reporting and increased awareness through improved information technology?

Is humanity perhaps evolving and progressing at speeds beyond the administrative and intellectual capabilities of politicians and their service delivery structures?

Or has the value of money simply depreciated at such an alarming rate that the cost of providing efficient and equitable governance can no longer be afforded on the scale needed?

For example, over the past 15-20 years budgetary provisions for large public sector development projects, that used to be quoted in the hundreds of thousands in monetary terms, have moved up through the millions and are now being written in billions and in some cases trillions.

Add to this the almost forgotten fact that South Africa's currency has devalued against hard global currencies by about 700 percent over the past thirty years, and one begins to understand why the poor have become poorer and why their numbers are increasing relentlessly.

Poverty has no right of way in the corridors of political power. According to a report in the respected *Financial Mail*, forty percent of ANC MPs in parliament were directors of companies at the time, many owning them outright in the lucrative construction and mining industries. Manipulative Black Economic Empowerment at work!

Extra-political activities are increasingly perceived as reasons for non-performance at all levels of governance, particularly at local and municipal levels where the effects touch public life more directly.

But the quest for power remains the most disturbing and destructive aspect of politics, particularly at the pinnacle positions of national leadership. History shows us how it can be wielded with such devastating effect upon the unfortunate and defenceless citizens of countries in so many parts of the world. Insidious acts of genocide have been inflicted upon many millions of people over millennia by power crazed political leaders.

Having researched a great deal of information on the subject, records pertaining to the twentieth century cover a period of time to which citizens of the world today can best relate are available at a web site compiled by Piero Scaruffi[7].

In his preamble to the data covering 92.131 million deaths of civilians, Piero mentions the numbers do not include military deaths. Nor do they include civilian deaths caused by wartime activities. For example the many thousands of civilians killed at Hiroshima and Nagasaki by atomic bombs dropped there in bringing about a closure to Japan's horrific, shameful and brutal involvement in World War II.

They do, however, include civilians deliberately targeted and killed by two US presidents during the Vietnamese war.

More than half the total are attributed to Mao Ze-Dong (China, 1958-61 during the "great leap forward" and 1966-69 the "cultural revolution") 49 million.

These are horrendous statistics which not only remind many of us of what actually happened during parts of our own lifetime but also add weight to the compelling reasons why proposals for a Global Administration, structured by a participative involvement process of the global masses, should be seriously considered and assessed.

China's history of having slaughtered 49 million of its own people in pursuit of its communist cultural revolution, tells us its leaders have little respect for human life. Indeed its current record of human rights violations is universally acknowledged. Its textile and garment manufacturing industries, fuelled by what has been described as slave labour, has caused rising unemployment in the home industries of countries that import its products.

South Africa is one such country and its retail outlets have become full of Chinese low cost, low quality, short life expectancy garments of every description, as well as potentially dangerous children's toys.

When Britain handed Hong Kong to China on a plate, Beijing took possession of the one piece of artillery missing from its world commerce domination arsenal, a golden key to gain entry into the global capitalist economic market.

Communism cannot survive in isolation from capitalism and the vibrant Hong Kong stock exchange was going to enable China to flex its economic muscles throughout the world's financial centres. They have been rippling with great effect ever since.

Crime – a growth industry

Crime has become a worrying factor worldwide and South Africa has sadly become a world leader in what has become one of the largest and most successful growth industries in the country. For example, according to a South African Institute of Race Relations Survey more than 230 criminal syndicates have been operating in South Africa since 1994, when the ANC came to power.

Syndicate bosses make money from activities such as drug peddling, prostitution, kidnapping, credit card scams, car theft, dealing in stolen goods and money laundering.

Included among the figures for various serious categories of crime for the 2003/04 financial year, were:

- 19 824 murders (2.26 per hour);
- 52 733 rapes (6 per hour);
- 30,076 attempted murders (3.43 per hour);
- 133 658 robberies with aggravating circumstances (15.25 per hour);
- 13 793 carjackings (1.57 per hour);
- 299 290 burglaries at residential premises (34.14 per hour); and
- 64 629 burglaries at business premises (7.37 per hour).

And those only cover the cases that were reported.

The report says South Africa is one of the top six countries in the world for murder. It is also one of the world's most violent countries.

According to the Institute for Security Studies, South Africa's national average is 43 murders per 100 000 of the population while the world average is eight.

During 2011 the government will spend R86.18 billion on the criminal justice system. This represents an increase of 213 percent since 2001/02. In contrast, it will spend only R13.8 billion educating school children from Grade R to Grade 12.

The South African Police Service (SAPS) is somewhat frustrated in its crime busting tasks, having about seven police officers for every murder committed, which is substantially below the world average of 158.

There are also exacerbating intellectual problems. About 25 percent (30 000) of SAPS members remained functionally illiterate ten years after the integration of law enforcement agencies.

In 2008 Minister of Safety and Security, Charles Nkaqula admitted that 6 888 firearms comprising pistols, rifles, shotguns and revolvers had been lost or stolen from the South African Police Service since 2004, which is an increase of 425 percent! Only 158 of these were recovered while 439 firearms had not been returned from ex-policemen who left the service.

Questions obviously arise concerning how many of these stolen arms have been or, will be used in acts of crime.

With statistics showing a prison occupancy of 411 prisoners for every 100 000 people in the country, South Africa locks up nearly three times more people per capita than the average of a sample of 84 countries. The implication of this is that the workload in SA's criminal justice system is substantially greater than in many other countries.

Staffing levels in South Africa's criminal justice system are a great deal lower than the average for other countries when compared to the level of crime (e.g. murder). South Africa has about 0.14 prosecutors for every murder committed compared to a world average of 2.6 (putting South Africa 94.6 percent below world average).

When it comes to life expectancy generally in South Africa, the numbers are not very encouraging.

According to a Survey report issued by the South African Institute of Race Relations, life expectancy for South African men in 2010 was 53.3 years, and for women 55.2 years. Between 2010 and 2030, the country's population will grow at a decreasing rate each year. Estimates show that from 2030 onwards, South Africa will have a decreasing population.

By 2030 the population will be 53.81 million, which will then decrease to 53.74 million by 2035, and to 53.28 million by 2040, according to data from the Institute of Futures Research at the University of Stellenbosch cited in the Survey.

One of the main reasons for this is the long term impact of HIV/AIDS.

In South Africa, the number of deaths in a year is making up an increasingly higher proportion of the number of births. In 1985, deaths were only 25 percent of births. This was expected by the Actuarial Society of South Africa to increase to 87 percent of births by 2021.

According to Thuthukani Ndebele, a researcher at the Institute, "If this trend continues, there will soon be more deaths than births in South Africa."

But, what about the life expectancy, and protection thereof, for the "League of Scoundrels" and VIPs?

Taxpayers paid R350 million ($50 million) a year for VIP protection for the president and other members of government.

This was six percent more than the R330 million ($47 million) it spent on nationwide crime intelligence which is vital to the prevention of crime in general and the dismantling of highly sophisticated criminal syndicates in particular.

This would suggest the government appears to have a problem with its crime prevention and public safety priorities.

On the contrary, the politicians know exactly where the priorities are. With themselves.

The fact that more money is spent on security for politicians than on national crime intelligence indicates government's security priorities for the country's citizens and tourists are of lesser importance.

By example, there are twice as many posts allocated to the SAPS unit that provides protection to a handful of VIPs in the country, than there are to the unit that protects the country's women and children from abuse.

A violent crime against a child is reported every six minutes in South Africa yet there are only 1 439 approved posts across the entire country for the Family Violence, Child Protection and Sexual Offences (FCS) Units attached to the SAPS.

Shamefully, highly specialised units like these are closed down and the skilled and experienced officers integrated into the short-staffed structures of police stations around the country, thus diluting the efficacy of the specialised skills they have.

In contrast to the dismantlement of a much needed and respected community service and the apparent failure to efficaciously train FCS officers, there are 2 800 posts allocated to the VIP protection unit whose sole function is to provide protection to the president, deputy president, former presidents and other VIPs.

That sounds quite obscene to me.

Well as mentioned before, we are talking about The League of Scoundrels, which considers itself to be the paramount elitist group, and it is the elitist groups who demand, and usually get, the highest priority in service and attention.

In countries where police, health care and public education services are provided by the state, they have become known as the 'Cinderella' services. All too often poorly trained, poorly equipped and poorly paid.

In consequence of this, albeit with a few very welcome exceptions in all three services, the public at large does not receive the quality of service to which it is entitled and for which it pays.

Those who suffer the greatest are those who cannot afford to pay for services provided by the private sector.

Many adults become permanent victims of unemployment and poverty, striving desperately to ensure their children receive sufficient levels of education, enabling them to gain access to sustainable employment and income later in life. Knowledge is wealth and wealth ensures life and survival in the human jungle.

South Africa's public education policy is unlikely to fulfil that dream and aspiration.

Education is such an important issue and one that would receive absolute priority as part of my proposed World Governance Standard, as indeed would matters such as public protection, health care and confronting the perils of global warming and climate change.

As in many countries around the world, South Africa has a very serious and worrying youth problem. Undisciplined behaviour at home, at school and within their communities is becoming increasingly stressful. Youngsters are gaining easy access to alcohol, drugs, guns and other life-threatening weapons and forming anti-social gangs in large numbers.

Some parents can no longer control their children in the old traditional ways because the children can now bring charges against them, claiming themselves to be victims of parental abuse and corporal punishment. Indeed a complete stranger can bring charges against a parent seen to slap his or her child.

The old saying: "Spare the rod and spoil the child" is being proven and many children are doing more or less whatever they please.

So, why can't the Constitution be refined to be more representative of the best interests of society in general and the nation as a whole?

Perhaps it could, but the process would probably be very protracted and time consuming.

As noble, honourable and well intentioned as the country's Constitution might well be, it is becoming increasingly perceived by the public at large as being more favourably inclined towards the perpetrators of criminal acts rather than to the victims of crime, rendering the much needed and desirable course of social justice and community building increasingly difficult to achieve – if at all. Criminals demand human rights!

It is generally believed that a revision of education policy will go far to change the attitudes of the country's youth.

I researched this subject when it was originally tabled as a South African Department of Education document entitled Interim Policy for Early Childhood Development (ECD) which was an extract from a full report produced in 1996.

It was accompanied by a letter to president Thabo Mbeki dated 16 October 2000, from Prof. Kader Asmal, who was Minister of Education at the time.

At first sight the report appeared to have been influenced by a refreshingly 'new vision' of the fundamental needs of society in general and the business sector in particular. One particular point in an overview of the ECD programme stated the intention to emphasize 'critical thinking' and 'problem-solving' skills as essential life skills for children.

The paper was not intended to prescribe the content of curriculum frameworks. It said that:

"prescribing a single, core curriculum for all users of the education and training system would ignore any initiative and creativity. Because a core curriculum is prescriptive and often rigid, it tends to over emphasise uniformity at the cost of innovation."

"The overall goal of the curriculum is to provide opportunities for children to grow and develop as active citizens contributing constructively to the building of a democratic, non-racist and equitable society."

This was followed by an equally refreshing consideration relating to the development of life skills for children. It opined that:

"the importance and interrelatedness of all the following areas of development need to be emphasised as necessary for learning for life. An integrated programme that builds on children's strengths and which gives sufficient time and encouragement for children to develop in all areas, will build from the earliest years essential life skills such as love of learning, resilience, self-reliance, assertiveness, respect for self, others and the environment, responsibility, critical thinking, questioning skills, informed decision making abilities, problem-solving abilities, co-operation, conflict resolution and negotiating skills, and the creative use of leisure time."

"The over-arching goal of language development is effective communication. The focus will be on the improvement of children's listening, speaking, reading and writing skills."

Amongst the categories of children targeted for ECD was one captioned "children at risk (0-5)" which was not explained.

However, I recalled this description from research into American education policy, as perceived by American published author Beverly Eakman.

She has published a number of books questioning education policy in her country including *"Cloning of the American Mind: Eradicating Morality through Education*$_8$," which I believe has relevance to South Africa's Outcomes Based Education dilemma.

Her findings troubled me because I could detect so many similarities of mind bending techniques in her description of the American teaching system, to those prepared for South Africa's children.

Relating to the "children at risk" targeted for ECD, she raised this during an address she gave to parents:

'With license to inspect every 5-year-old, they claim they can identify those "at risk" of becoming unstable, anti-social and even violent. If they can just intervene soon enough, without parental interference, they say they can turn these youngsters around.

Policymakers and the media like the prevention message!"

Another point proposed for South Africa's Early Childhood Development stated it should *"form part of a comprehensive national community development strategy…"*

To make sure it works according to plan:

"the establishment of representative consultative structures ….. to guide policy development and implementation."

Under the heading, "A policy in respect of policy development structures" were the enabling mechanisms by which progress towards globalisation might be turned on:

> *"In respect of the elaboration of ECD policy, the White Paper of Education and Training instructs the establishment of an inclusive statutory consultative body that must be representative of all sectors in the ECD field.*
>
> *"The establishment of such a body was regarded as a priority by the Department. Proposals in respect of the terms of reference, powers and functions, composition and the procedures for the establishment of such a body were being tabled for discussion.*
>
> *"It is envisaged that the process for continuous policy consultation and development between stakeholders and the Department of Education will be given a considerable boost when the Statutory Council is established."*

Most people might have read something quite different into these words, regarding them as a form of insurance that ECD would be dedicated to achieving the best possible tuition and facilities to prepare children for their future adult lives and for the nation as a whole.

My cautious scepticism told me there might be something more sinister afoot.

When discovering that the Curriculum Framework was described as *'a philosophical and organizational framework ….. which best meets the needs of those they are intended to serve'*, I asked myself: who exactly are "they" who are to be served?

The framework *"specifies essential, generic outcomes...."* and: *"suggests approaches to be adopted in evaluating learner progress and/or assessing learning outcomes."*

I found the word "generic" a little worrying because it applies or refers to a whole class or group.

The noun "genus" implies a class or group of individuals who can be divided into two or more groups with similar characteristics.

This suggested there may be a deliberate intention to "stream" children into groups of individuals, possessing characteristics preordained through a strategy of deliberate psychological brain washing.

Looking at comparisons in the American version, Beverly Eakman's words revealed:

"The EQA had 375 questions covering attitudes, worldviews and opinions. Most involved hypothetical situations and self-reports.

There were also 30 questions on math and another 30 covering verbal analogies. Just enough academic questions to appear credible!"

She then gave an overview of some of the questions, one of which asked:

"There is a secret club at school called the Midnight Artists. They go out late at night and paint funny sayings and pictures on buildings.

I would JOIN THE CLUB when I knew . . .

[a] my best friend had asked me to join; [b] Most of the popular students in school were in the club; [c] my parents would ground me if they found out I joined."

The next shocker was the scoring mechanism. It revealed points given for what was called a "minimum positive attitude."

For example, on the "Midnight Artists" question the preferred response was "b - Most of the popular students in school were in the club.

Why "b"?

The Interpretive Literature which is off limits to the layperson tells us why.

The EQA's creators were testing for: the child's "focus of control;" his "willingness to receive stimuli;" his "amenability to change;" and his inclination to "conform to group goals."

In English this means: Where's the child coming from? Is he easily influenced? Are his views firm or easy to change? Will he submit to group-think and "go along to get along?" The preferred answer to the Midnight Artists question reflects a willingness to conform to group goals."

Continuing with Prof. Asmal's description:

"Curriculum frameworks are not to be regarded as learning programmes. Rather, they are to be regarded as philosophical and organizational frames of reference with a dual purpose: they provide norms and standards for curriculum development and design but, at the same time create opportunities for innovation, allowing the development of flexible, relevant learning programmes and materials which will take cognisance of particular needs, constraints and realities."

When read in conjunction with what appeared to be highly desirable aspects of the report, this paragraph had some relevance. However, it also has relevance when aligned with the big picture of globalisation.

I was once again drawn to Beverly Eakman's words:

"Schools (in USA) today inundate pupils with psychological and demographic questions - a combination long known in the world of advertising as "psychographics data-gathering."

Prof. Asmal's report then moved onto National Qualifications Framework (NQF) which inclines dangerously close to Education Quality Assessment (EQA) that was introduced in the United States and widely discredited because of its "Big Brother" connotations.

Prof. Asmal's report stated that the:

"Inextricable link between the NQF, a Curriculum Framework and ensuing curriculum documents is spelt out in the White Paper on Education and Training, which states that:

"An integrated approach to education and training, linked to the development of a new National Qualifications Framework (NQF) based on a system of credits for learning outcomes achieved, will encourage creative work on the design of curricula and the recognition of learning attainments wherever education and training are offered."

Very worrying parallels between the discredited and abolished American system and that which was being proposed for South African children were detectable.

Perhaps Prof. Asmal's report was a soundly intentioned strategy for our children's future education but would enable our children to enjoy higher education standards?

Having read it back in 2000 I had my doubts at that time and with some justification they persist today. I am bound to believe the new education programme will fail our children and the nation at large.

Before telling you why, let me first explain for the benefit of non-South African readers what happened to the nation after its first fully democratic elections in 1994.

When the ANC gained power under Nelson Mandela, other prominent people within the upper echelons of the "Freedom Struggle" awaited their promised positions of power within the new political dispensation.

This was always going to be problematic because there were fewer prominent positions available to accommodate everyone. This dilemma gave rise to a solution of questionable wisdom being adopted.

The number of provinces in the country was increased from the historical four to a hugely extravagant nine. Each province necessitated a provincial premier and attendant retinue, a provincial government with all the conventional positions similar to those of a national government, and a predominantly black empowered civil service structure, which was largely unskilled at the time, to manage the day-to-day provincial administration. This meant there had to be local government structures and Municipalities.

Almost over night South Africa was transformed into a complex nation with nineteen seats of government comprising eighteen levels of provincial and local governments and a conventional national government attending to the administration of a population of less than 40 million souls at the time.

South Africa's first steps down the road to democracy became a succession of exposed corruption, power struggles and confused political and administration shuffles, which have in general remained corrupt, confused and dysfunctional ever since.

Prof. Asmal has generally been perceived as a Minister who genuinely believed in what he was trying to achieve for his fellow South Africans. He was now having to confess to the country's president that delivery of the intended benefits of a revitalized education policy was unlikely to succeed, due to the inefficiency of those charged with the responsibility to make it happen.

Here are some extracts taken verbatim from his report:

"The way various stakeholders play out their respective roles in education has a material impact on whether or not the environment is conducive to effective service delivery."

Having explained that some provinces were showing slight improvement, he then said:

"However, their contribution to effective service delivery in some instances is less than optimal and will require concerted effort in nurturing and developing. There is an urgent need for a higher degree of commitment and professionalism. This must be attended to at the political level."

"Far too many of our (ANC) *comrades have accepted their positions, salaries and benefits, while lacking the training and skills to perform their responsibilities, having previously removed those* (whites) *qualified to do so. If we are to achieve the desired results, these people will have to go and we must outsource the work to the* (white?) *private sector."*

His apparent concerns that effective service delivery would become a non-starter were clearly expressed and have since been vindicated.

He was admitting that inefficient blacks had ejected experienced whites from important policy enabling positions and had failed to perform efficaciously in their stead.

So now it has become necessary to outsource to the (white?) private sector at additional and wasteful cost to the economy and acutely embarrassing to the ANC.

On the subject of capacity for effective management and administration one could detect a level of barely suppressed frustration worrying the Minister:

"... a few provinces continue to suffer the burden of very serious shortcomings in capacity across the system. Many of the present problems have their roots in the intractable shortcomings inherited from the former homelands and 'independent' states. Without in any way minimizing the complexity of the shortcomings, it is clear that present problems revolve around poor development and implementation of systems for management and administration".

"The poor state of management and administration effectiveness begs an important question:

Why, six years after the first democratic elections [in 1994], *do the weaknesses and shortcomings continue to persist?"*

What a disturbing and worrying admission!

He concluded:

"In the provinces where the above problems are most acute, indications are that the present shortcomings in management and administration result in accumulated backlogs, which in turn, place additional pressure on already weak system performance. The result is a vicious cycle of administrative breakdown and a cumulative decline in capacity."

From this it could be reasonably assumed that nobody at service delivery level had the competence to do their jobs efficiently. Administrative tasks and problems would be transferred to colsultants.

It is ironic to remember that Prof. Asmal's dreams for the ECD Programme, to transform society in such a way as to, inter-alia, "emphasise the development of critical thinking and problem-solving skills as essential life skills," when considering other extracts from his letter:

"Too often, problems and challenges in education invoke conditioned responses without sufficient analysis of the nature of the problem and feasibility of solutions."

This appears to clearly imply that when management is called upon to explain non-delivery, their inarticulate and unrelated response shows an utter and complete lack of understanding of the fundamental aspects of the work they are charged to perform."

He also stated:

"There is an over-reliance on workshops and consultants that respond to quick and ill-conceived briefs. Although there is very little hard data available, evidence suggests that the impact of these projects is less than satisfactory thus far."

These management shortcomings are synonymous with the classic action of functionally illiterate public servants finding themselves completely out of their depth in positions of employment they have been given, rather than earned.

Such actions clearly show an absence of the essential developmental life skills of critical thinking and problem-solving abilities to which Prof. Asmal alluded.

One might reasonably presume the people responsible for the delivery of education policy decisions and services fit this category. A fact that had not escaped the notice of the Minister.

Lacking the necessary qualifications and skills the incumbents were unable, and perhaps unwilling, to take deliberate steps to improve their capabilities. Their positions in the political hierarchy would enable them to employ expensive consultants to solve problems for them. However, they lacked the competence to provide clearly defined and documented briefs to enable the consultants to do so.

One should not be surprised by this since they are clearly attempting to define problems in a manner intended to divert attention from their own inadequacies.

One must assume that highly paid and poorly instructed consultants would fail to produce practical and implemental conclusions and solutions.

One of the many penalty costs of governmental incompetence and the relentless and blind pursuit of affirmative action and BEE/BBBEE.

Notwithstanding the planning and production of a Policy for Early Childhood Development (ECD) document, budget allocations for education were not sufficient to ensure the success of its intended implementation, nor indeed of any other alternative education policy.

An article by David MacFarlane in the 20 July 2007 edition of the *Mail & Guardian* confirmed that prediction.

Unesco's "Education for All" Global Monitoring Report 2007 surveys the progress made by 164 countries towards reaching the six goals they agreed upon in Dakar, Senegal, in 2000.

Expanding and improving ECD provision for the most vulnerable and disadvantaged children is given special attention in the report.

About 5.2-million children under seven years of age are not catered for in South Africa's ECD programmes.

Whereas 11.1 percent of the 2000/01 ECD budget was allocated to children, MacFarlane reported that only one percent of the 2006/07 R104-billion education budget is allocated for ECD, representing a reduction by about 90 percent.

One might be excused for concluding the core objective of South Africa's education policy, perhaps greatly influenced by a covert globalisation strategy, was intent upon levelling education standards downward in the hope of ensuring a much needed elevated percentage of examination pass rates.

If so, South Africa succeeded in reducing the standards but failed to improve the pass rates. They actually dropped countrywide, even to zero percent in certain locations.

The inevitable ripple effect of a failed education policy would sooner or later become manifest at the employment coalface.

This was made starkly apparent in June 2007 by the Centre for Development and Enterprise (CDE) when they undertook a survey amongst forty businesses, conducted and analysed by Professor Lawrence Schlemmer and colleagues.

Interviews with senior company officials confirmed that shortage of skills is one of the most costly and troublesome issues affecting the management of South African businesses over the last two years.

CDE director Ann Bernstein said:

> "In order to confront the full reality of our skills crisis we have to face the fact that South African education and training is in deep trouble. Fixing this will take a generation. But the question no one wants to deal with in the current discussion on the skills shortage is: What do we do in the meantime?"

Bernstein pointed out the findings of the survey provided immediate options for addressing the skills crisis.

> "While we are grappling with fixing our struggling education and training system, immediate responses available are the speedy restoration of the apprentice system, opening up of immigration and a government re-think on the pressures for employment equity."

The survey included a cross section of forty businesses and only CEOs or other senior company representatives were interviewed.

Nearly half (19) of the businesses surveyed were in manufacturing with the remainder spread across mining, retail and services.

One quarter (10) had fewer than 100 employees; three had more than 10 000 employees, with the rest spread fairly evenly in size between these extremes.

The responses of these businesses clearly showed the South African economy was becoming more skills intensive. Two thirds said that more than half of their staff fell into the category of 'scarce skills'.

For the majority of businesses in the sample the greatest shortfall is in experience and breadth of judgment, as well as people with social skills.

The shortages felt by business are occurring in an increasingly competitive global skills market, where pressures are exacerbated by emigration, ageing and promotion of skilled staff.

Moreover, government's insistence on ambitious transformation goals is constricting the skills market further, driving competition for skilled black staff in a situation where whites - the largest available pool of skilled people - are no longer freely employable.

Difficulties reported in recruiting skilled black staff included problems of poaching, as well as the salary premium required to retain skilled black personnel.

These reported problems suggest the skills shortage is being driven, in part, by the unintended consequences of (Black) empowerment policies.

The most significant finding of the report was that skills shortage was primarily driven by the failure of the public education system at all levels to deliver quality consistently and in enough quantity.

Most companies surveyed found Sector Education and Training Authorities (SETAs) cumbersome to deal with, assessors poorly trained, training too theoretical or not relevant to their training needs.

The old five-year apprenticeship system was seen to have been more effective in producing the levels of workmanship required in modern business.

Longer term responsibility for skills development remains the preserve of schools and of technical and academic universities.

While views on tertiary education were mixed, businesses predictably had little or nothing good to say about the South African schooling system.

Indictments included:

- a decline in the quality of school leavers' competence in science, maths and language;
- failure to cultivate a work ethic;
- little capacity for school leavers to be trained;
- low and declining standards;
- no discipline;
- the absence of a culture of learning in South African schools.

In short, despite pockets of high performance the responses built a picture of a South African education system that:

- did not provide for future skills needs;
- was not building capacity;
- had poor teaching standards;
- suffered from a shortage of competent teachers.

Businesses in South Africa have reacted to skills shortages by paying more for scarce skills, providing in-house training, outsourcing specialized functions and recruiting abroad.

Bernstein concludes that:

> "Unless there is strong leadership to recruit, retain and utilize all the skills available to us in the domestic as well as the global markets, the private sector will struggle to expand capacity and the South African economy will be held back."

Coincidentally, on the same day I read this report I also learned that 200 000 South African university graduates, the majority of who were non-white, were unable to find employment.

The misgivings I harboured 6-7 years earlier, about the inherent flaws I suspected were buried deep in Prof. Asmal's proposed education policy, were certainly vindicated by the CDE survey.

CDE director Ann Bernstein has stated it will take a generation to overcome the unsatisfactory education problem, but recovery is dependent upon an improved policy being put in place and its date of implementation.

From later surveys of the effects of South Africa's public school education on school leavers, Bernstein revealed 80 percent are considered as being dysfunctional. For more information relating to CDE activities go to: http://www.cde.org.za.

We are not even at the starting gate in the race against time while continuing to churn out half a million or more economically worthless school leavers every year.

The long term consequences for South Africa's economic growth endeavours and growing unemployment statistics are likely to be devastating.

Not only are the poor bound to get poorer and probably increase in numbers, but the present economically advantaged might find the grass on the other side of the international fence greener for employment opportunities.

Failed education systems in so many countries have predictably neglected the need to prepare children for the real world. An essential clear understanding of money and fundamental home and personal money management is missing from childrens' lives.

A process of financial education should begin in primary school and continue throughout all stages of learning, enabling children to be fully competent in an understanding of money on a global basis.

They should be taught the principles of banking; of credit card systems; of savings and investments; of taxation and all else of a financial nature in order that they will understand the principle of living within their means before stepping out into the real world.

The absence of these fundamental aspects of basic education undoubtedly contributes to rising levels of illiteracy, of unemployment and poverty, and of the consequential escalating crime statistics worldwide.

This is starkly underscored in an extract from the message contained in "The Making of a Myth": South Africa's Neo-Liberal Journey 15th March 2006, by Dr. Dale T. McKinley, who is an independent writer, lecturer, researcher and social movement activist.

A 2003 survey conducted by the Community Agency for Social Enquiry, (which included more than 6 000 people in 60 South African poor communities) found the following:

- 55% of unemployed and 32% of employed said they were unable to afford food;
- 54% of jobless and 43% of employed could not afford basic services;
- 46% could not afford rent or bond (mortgage) payments;
- 68% earn less than R500 (US$70.00/£38.00) per month whether working, self-employed or unemployed;
- 86% are looking for work;
- 1 in 8 (12,5%) among self-employed said they earned enough to live on.

Other research conducted by the Development Bank of South Africa in 2005, revealed the number of South Africans in poverty (with the national poverty line for 2002 being benchmarked at a miserable R354.00 (US$50.00/£27.00) per adult per annum in all population groups, increased dramatically from 17 million in 1996 to 21 million in 2003, which was a depressing revelation nine years after the nation's first fully democratic elections.

At the ANC's conference in Polokwane in December 2007, Thabo Mbeki revealed that 42 percent of South Africans were living below the poverty line.

Compounding the problem, a review of poverty released in November 2007, revealed that levels of poverty throughout South Africa had doubled over the period 1996-2005, with poverty still being determined by the international benchmark of people trying to survive on less than US$1.00 per day.

According to a Report of the Committee of Inquiry into a Comprehensive System of Social Security for South Africa, 55 percent of South Africans live in poverty and 60 percent of the poor receive no social security transfers and/or grants whatsoever.

A 2006 report by the University of South Africa - 'Projection of Future Economic and Socio-political Trends in South Africa up to 2025' - put South Africa's unemployment rate at "between 30 and 40 percent, depending on which definition of 'unemployed' is used," and concluded that "the economy is not creating jobs - to a large extent it's jobless economic growth."

This is not a pretty picture, is it?

Not at all and as implied earlier, many will say that while the previously disadvantaged black communities now enjoy the so-called benefits of social freedom, an increasing number have actually become more disadvantaged financially and socially than they ever were during the dreadful years of apartheid.

This unfortunate fact was affirmed by Zwelinzima Vavi[9] general secretary of the Congress of South African Trade Unions (Cosatu).

He was addressing a gathering at the 20th anniversary celebrations of the South African Municipal Workers' Union in Cape Town.

He said unemployed and casual workers were better off under apartheid than now, adding that inequality had widened in the past thirteen years with a minority of capitalists and bureaucrats getting richer.

> "Many of the millions who are unemployed, or whose jobs have been casualised, are even worse off than under apartheid. About 20-million of our people are still mired in poverty. We still face many challenges and the task of transformation is far from complete" he said.

The reason for highlighting these unsightly blemishes upon my country's countenance is to show that we are right down there with other socially disadvantaged nations of the world. I see this as an abject failure of the long established conventional political system. The politicians at the controls have failed to provide basic, fundamental and equitable social service delivery to the people they have sworn to serve and to protect.

As a parting shot on the question of protection, particularly defence of the country's borders, consider this disturbing state of affairs:

Reports in 2006 indicated the South African National Defence Force (SANDF) could no longer be regarded as a fighting force because as little as 5 percent of some battle units can be deployed due to ill health, amongst other things.

A combat-readiness report made it clear the SANDF could not meet and repel a serious conventional threat.

The situation was no better four years later.

In November 2010, DA's David Maynier told the National Assembly the morale of troops in the SA National Defence Force is so low it could pose a threat to state security.

"The defence force, and the men and women who serve in (it), are in deep trouble. But rather than sharing information... with the people's representatives, information about the defence force has been hidden" he said.

"And just so we know how serious things have become, let me begin by quoting from the conclusion of this report, which reads:

'There is a clear need for a wide variety of matters to be attended to. Some of these matters, if not addressed immediately, are likely to further affect the morale of troops and could even threaten state security'.

"Now how is it that we are in a situation where the military itself could threaten state security?"

According to a SAPA article relating to SANDF peace keeping duties in foreign countries in 2007, hundreds of South African soldiers had been accused of killing, torturing and assaulting the very people they are supposed to protect - and South African taxpayers might have to fork out almost R1 billion in civil claims, the Johannesburg *Star* newspaper reported.

SANDF members were the accused in 287 serious criminal cases, recorded incidents of murder, shooting, assault and torture.

Add to this a list including 26 charges of murder, 22 of attempted murder, 15 of assault with grievous bodily harm, 25 of common assault and 31 of reckless and negligent driving and one has to wonder how confident the continent's AU leaders are about African Renaissance.

According to the Defence Department's financial statements, the army faced civil claims of R978 million with motor accident claims amounting to an additional R3.7 million.

Things have not been too rosy for British defence force capabilities either.

In a 'Restricted' memorandum prepared by Gen. Sir Richard Dannatt, Britain's Chief of the General Staff (CGS) dated 11 June 2007, he told senior commanders:

"Our reserves to meet the unexpected (as well as for current operations) are now almost non-existent, and we now have almost no capacity to react."

It appeared at the time that various combat units were either training for the wars in Iraq and Afghanistan or already engaged in operations there or on leave.

There was only one battalion of 500 troops called the Spearhead Lead Element (SLE) available on home soil for an emergency, such as a major terrorist attack or for rapid deployment overseas.

One can only assume that if this Lead Element had to be deployed to counter a terrorist attack or other disaster, there would be no troops following close behind their lead.

In 2011, Network54 reported that officers claimed British forces would struggle to mount small military intervention. They have also warned that the chances of an operation to rescue civilians from a conflict in a foreign territory would become remote as more and more equipment is pushed out of service under defence cuts.

Their warning came after military chiefs warned the Prime Minister that cuts to Harrier jets and aircraft carrier Ark Royal would put personnel at considerable risk.

Returning to South Africa's national problems, the government, the Minister of Finance, big business, financial consultants and economists have, in my opinion, been lying to the nation and to the world at large by saying the country's economic and administrative fundamentals are firmly in place and that ambitious growth targets are attainable.

Let's look at some of the fundamentals working against growth:

- the country is presently experiencing a potentially devastating power generation problem, due to the lack of planning, maintenance and expansion of long established facilities;
- the country's potable water supply is fast approaching disaster status;
- the failed education system exacerbates the ongoing shortage of academically prepared children entering the work place;
- in January 2008 the Democratic Alliance released its 2007 report analysing the levels of vacancies in national government

departments. Across all 29 departments, there was a general vacancy rate of 10.4 percent (or 40 594 posts). Of the 204 039 highly skilled posts available, 12.9 percent (or 26 257) were vacant - 200 more than in 2006. Excluding the three biggest departments - Safety and Security, Correctional Services and Defence – which account for 77 percent of all posts, the general vacancy rate jumps to 21.9 percent (or 18 865 posts) across the remaining 26 departments, while the highly-skilled vacancy rate increases to 31.2 percent (or 13 645 posts),

- The public sector health system is in a shocking condition. Doctors and nursing staff are grossly under-paid, equipment is under serviced, hospital pharmacies and clinics are under stocked and many are unclean and poorly maintained;
- Pollution of waterways, dams and wetlands has already reached dangerous levels.

As a parable, one could say the good ship "*South Africa*" is steaming ahead and the presidential officer of the watch and his parliamentary companions on the bridge can see no obstructions ahead.

The First Class passengers appear to be enjoying the voyage, even though they could not really afford the trip and had to buy their tickets on credit.

There have been a few irritating complaints from those in third class, demanding the level of service they were promised even though many cannot afford to pay for it, and refuse to do so anyway.

Meanwhile, down in the engine room a situation is developing.

Leaks are appearing in the bulkheads, the turbines are not running optimally, the electrical power generators keep failing and the air conditioning system is fouling up.

The passengers and some of the crew have complained to the Captain on many occasions in the past, but on the rare occasions he bothered to reply he insisted conditions were not as bad as alleged.

There is every reason to suspect the ship will not reach her intended destination but the Captain, suffering from an attack of acute denial, is attempting to navigate a crippled ship manned by an untrained and unskilled crew. A shipwreck appears to be inevitably imminent!

This short parable brings into focus the crumbling foundations upon which South Africa's economic growth aspirations are balancing.

The fundamental needs of people have been all but abandoned, and the nation's unattended infrastructure has been deteriorating steadily for years.

The underlying problem has been that the old infrastructure was originally created to serve the needs of a much smaller and productively active population. Its foundations were laid in colonial times and its growth became concomitant with the growth and expansion demands of the predominantly white population it was largely intended to serve.

Generally speaking servicing and maintenance of that old and expanding infrastructure was planned and executed in a reasonably efficient manner for years and it worked.

Since 1994 however, demands have increased on a yearly basis but the nation's new leaders failed to maintain what they inherited and failed to improve it to meet future demands.

Although economic fundamentals may appear to be robust at the macroeconomic level, they will fail completely if conditions at the microeconomic level are not serviced and maintained.

There has been no deliberate policy of planned and monitored improvement in service delivery at the microeconomic levels, where a high percentage of human resources live and are employed to fuel the increasing demands for economic growth at the macroeconomic level.

If service delivery continues to fail at the human resources residential level, retaliation could have grave consequences for economic growth.

Are you then saying that a failure to address the needs of people at the lower and poorer levels of society's economic chain, will adversely affect the country's overall economic growth potential, driven by those at the middle-to-upper levels?

In my opinion, when it runs in tandem with a failure to maintain and improve the national infrastructure, it becomes a guaranteed recipe for economic collapse and long-term recession.

Politicians the world over tend to regard infrastructure in purely material terms, with little or no apparent conception of the vitally important role played by the human components, those who most need it, use it and pay for it.

If their needs and resource deployments are not included in the equation, the long term consequences could become disastrous.

In South Africa's case, an early and deliberately planned strategy to stay one step ahead of increasing demands upon infrastructure and service delivery, would have been measured in millions of rand.

Playing "catch up" will now be measured in many billions of rand, and other needy social service issues are bound to feel the consequences arising from a diminishing availability of funds.

This might be an appropriate moment to really understand the difference between a million and the commonly used American billion.

A million days equals 2 740 years.

A billion days is 2.74 million years, which is roughly how long mankind has been on planet Earth!

The billions spent on preparations for the 2010 Soccer World Cup will have no long-term economic benefits for the entire nation.

Billions more spent on the construction of the Gautrain Rapid Rail[10] project, which provides a high speed rail link between Pretoria and Johannesburg, a distance of only 80 km (50 miles) linking in the national airport, is a very expensive and limited service.

The track is custom built for its own specialised rolling stock and is incapable of linking into the full national rail network. It is difficult to imagine it ever becoming self-sustaining and profitable.

When the initial novelty has worn off, it will probably become a social service to be subsidised by taxpayers in general, and by Gauteng ratepayers in particular for many years to come and perhaps eventually abandoned.

You really are sounding like an old "stick-in-the-mud" sceptic, constantly looking for reasons to undermine new and exciting developments in your country.

I'm simply questioning the wisdom of these particular developments and their real long-term benefits to the entire national society, measured against the enormous costs involved and the short-term employment opportunities they represented for those engaged in the construction work.

I welcome all developments around the world that provide sustained benefits to, and serve the best interests of the maximum number of people.

The two I have just covered do not, in my opinion, meet those prerogatives. Indeed, I predict ongoing maintenance of soccer stadia will become prohibitively expensive and financially unviable.

From a much wider perspective, as said before, it worries me greatly that politicians in general and many national leaders in particular, appear to have lost touch with the fundamental concerns and needs of the people they are supposed to serve.

Multinational prerogatives are regularly prioritised under the guise of being beneficial to the cause of globalisation, with little or no regard for the adversities so frequently created for the world's financially disadvantaged masses.

I perceive the human race as a single species, albeit with a variety of appearances and cultures, millions of who are in desperate need of upliftment.

> ***Fair enough, but I was not intending to raise any racial distinctions in what you are saying. However, since you have made your point, I have to ask whether a non-white point of view would have added some objectivity to your story. After all, you have given your own assumptions about their feelings but, you are a white man and, with respect, you don't really know how they feel.***

That's a very fair point.

Although I have in fact incorporated points of view from non-white folk in my book, notably Prof. Kadar Asmal and the controversial view expressed by Cosatu general secretary Zwelinzima Vavi, I have also incorporated others on the promise of anonymity.

Many black South Africans are bitterly disappointed by the manner in which they are being neglected, or badly treated by their ethnic brothers and sisters who promised faithfully to lift them up from oppression.

Some have told me, in whispered voices, they no longer support the ANC but are too frightened to say so openly and equally frightened to vote for an alternative party. They are fearful of intimidation and even of being killed. It's an African culture thing.

I have respected their wishes without questioning the validity of their fears. I have given my word and deliberately declined from making any reference whatsoever to those particular sources of information that have shaped certain things I have said.

On the flip side of the coin, I have been very fortunate to receive permission to include a very interesting article I read in *Mail & Guardian* written by a black African woman by the name of Mmatshilo Motsei.

She describes herself as a feminist and is the author of the book, *The Kanga and Kangaroo Court: Reflections on the Rape Trial of Jacob Zuma.*

Her article was captioned: *Will SA descend, drift or wake up?*

With Mmatshilo's kind consent I have reproduced it in its entirety:

The political tale of South Africa is one of noble leadership. It is a story scripted by powerful and humane beings from the times of Langalibalele Dube, Tshekiso Plaatjie, Pixley ka Isaka Seme and Mvumbi Luthuli. They are part of a long list of men and women from different political persuasions who crafted the story and lived their lives in a way that did not clash with the script.

Njabulo Ndebele has described these remarkable individuals as people who were not only honoured for their positions but also for the way they enhanced the dignity and stature of those positions. They achieved this by striving to create a complementary relationship between official and personal attributes.

After years of political exile, this nation emerged in 1994 with one thing in mind: transformation.

Taking the baton from his predecessors, Rolihlahla Mandela led us along the stormy path of transforming an archaic and repressive legal framework and writing a new Constitution.

Thabo Mbeki focused his energies on new legislation and policies, and on reviving the African sense of self, based on a cultural revolution driven by a vibrant economy.

Thirteen years later our story is one of triumph and despair. In spite of achievements outlined in endless government reports written in a language and format that most cannot access, read or understand, the state of the nation is one in which a handful of economic and political captains sail on a sea of appalling poverty, disease, death and environmental destruction.

Thirteen years into democracy, government reports a booming economy alongside rampant fraud, corruption and violent crime

Fathers rape their daughters in the name of African tradition, grandsons abuse their grandmothers for pension money, husbands kill their wives and wives hire assassins to kill their husbands, burglars kill with vicious impunity.

Having returned from political exile, the nation is faced with an act of inner exile referred to by Wole Soyinka as "internal severance".

Society's moral fibre is in shreds; our respect for life is dead and buried in a heap of self-destruction.

As a country we cringe at the mention of the word morality, yet we fail to cultivate civility and honesty, even as we make a lot of noise about crime.

In spite of knowing that education is a field on which we grow human beings, we fail to equip families and schools with the financial and cultural back-up they need to produce humane people. Instead our education system is largely geared towards servicing the capitalist economy at the expense of cultivating a healthy sense of identity.

How can we expect to harvest corn and wheat when we have planted tobacco?

Indeed, it took a mere 13 years for our democracy to be overshadowed by an intense contest over who should lead, as opposed to which direction the country should be taking after three terms of office steered by two democratically elected African presidents.

The succession race is reduced to personality cults focused on two or three men cast in a race for position, while the nation is cast in a race to free its knowledge from cultural and spiritual demise in a world dominated by colonial thinking and practise.

It is time we ask questions that we have not asked ourselves before.

What does the making of a leader in post-apartheid South Africa entail? Does a gallant freedom fighter make a great leader or statesman?

What role does African culture play in the conception of democracy and leadership

How can we promote the will not to do crime in the midst of empty stomachs, ignorant minds and diseased souls?

Do morality and spirituality have any role to play in political leadership, or should this question be limited to debates on who will succeed Archbishop Ndungane?

Like morality, spirituality has over the years been confined to the narrow practise of organised religion. Of course, religion can embrace both the moral and the immoral.

A politician whose beliefs are grounded in religion can lead to life as much as he can lead people to destruction.

I have encountered self-proclaimed non-believers whose morality matches the immorality of certain religious leaders

As Ndebele points out: "The sacred can be abused for ends that have very little to do with sanctity."

Much as we prefer to separate the personal and the political, much as we would like to believe that what happens in a leader's personal life should be of no interest to the public, the reality is that a leader of questionable personal character uses the same head space to make public and private decisions.

Nothing operates in a vacuum. Psychological, moral and spiritual factors have a role to play in the political and economic decisions we make. A spiritually awake politician will know that transformation is about more than putting people in positions of power. It includes changing the mindsets of those persons and those with whom they interact.

Many of government's policies are crafted by people whose views, beliefs and philosophies are rooted in a foreign culture, irrespective of whether those who craft the policies are black or white.

As far as our education is concerned, when Europeans get an education, they become more rooted in their culture.

When Africans get educated, they become indifferent to their culture.

Practising spiritual politics requires a degree of moral courage. Talking about moral courage in a capitalist society may seem like a pipe dream. After all, everyone wants to succeed, and at this point success is measured exclusively in monetary terms

Because a capitalist society tends to reward those who cooperate with it and punish those who resist or oppose it, this makes it difficult for most people to lead a moral life, let alone to exercise moral leadership.

In the end the question is not so much who is fit to govern but whether we are on the right track.

The choices we make in the here and now need to be inextricably linked to the bigger project of rewriting the story of Africa. After all, what happens in Polokwane in December [2007] will reach far beyond Limpopo -- and far beyond 2009.

Delegates should choose a leader who will not only create jobs but also commit to growing human skills that can help build a new psychological space - and these are not limited to intellect and technology.

This takes time, patience and determination. It is not about instant wealth, fame or power. Choosing this path will prove difficult for any leader, because after decades of being robbed by their oppressors and fellow comrades the majority of people prefer instant outcomes.

One hopes the ANC can move beyond the well-rehearsed rhetoric of creating a better life for all. Such words will remain hollow until we all seek the courage to take a public stand against all forms of economic injustice, especially those from which we benefit.

As people move into their respective "camps" in preparation for the much-awaited time of reckoning, it is hoped they will ask themselves this question: How does being part of this camp contribute to building a humane, healthy, self-respecting and prosperous nation? What material and non-material legacy am I leaving for my children's children?

As we move towards the political crossroad, Ben Okri also asks: What will we choose?

Will we allow ourselves to descend - into universal chaos and darkness?

A world without hope, without wholeness …

A world breeding mass murderers energy vampires, serial killers with minds spinning in anomie and amorality with murder, rape, genocide as normality?

Or will we allow ourselves merely to drift - into an era of more of the same…

Or might we choose to make this time a waking-up event a moment of world empowerment?

As an African woman, I am aware that this article, like most that address the [ANC leadership] succession race, is silent on the role of women in leadership. Rather than collude with the lie of men's exclusive and natural predisposition to lead, the omission is intentional. The story of African women leaders and warriors is complex and big. It calls for its own time and space.

I have read this article many times and am moved by the deep emotional sense behind it. I feel the disappointment that others have also expressed.

I sense the frustration of an intelligent woman who, like so many of her peers, knows that so much more could, and should have been done, and still remains to be done for a nation of previously oppressed Africans and particularly the children.

Thank you Mmatshilo I feel humbled and privileged to carry your words in my book.

In all my travels to various parts of the world and from the research I have conducted, I have yet to find a nation filled to the brim with fully contented and fairly treated citizens. A nation to which I would do everything possible to emigrate in the knowledge that my remaining years would be spent peacefully and securely in financial comfort, with all essential services ready to leap into efficient action when called upon to do so.

You are looking for Utopia, which unfortunately does not exist.

You're right it doesn't exist, but something infinitely better could and it would be known simply as Planet Earth.

But definitely not under prevailing conditions.

The masters of politics, religion and their companions associated with multinational greed, money manipulation and territorial xenophobia will do everything within their collective powers to prevent it from ever happening.

Make no mistake, they certainly have the power, the resources and reason to prevent change occurring other than by their own design and dictates. They have been enormously successful in controlling our lives and destinies for centuries and would become seriously outraged if we attempted to control them ourselves.

Regardless of political assurances of fair and just governance, we have become painfully aware that matters directly affecting our security and welfare receive the greatest amount of lip service and the smallest amount of practical action.

It would be naive to assume this is an unfortunate administrative accident. We are the victims of a conspiracy that has endured for centuries. We have obediently accepted our allocated human resources working station in life and been grateful for what we receive in return.

Unfortunately millions of people throughout the world never attain a social station greater than "work fodder," in much the same way that foot soldiers years ago were sent into battle as "cannon fodder" to use up the enemy's ammunition.

This sorry state of affairs has to be changed.

There has always been a need to provide sustainable job opportunities for people the world over, but neither the private nor public sectors have been able to do so on a sustainable basis.

The need has become increasingly urgent and desperate over the past couple of decades, as unemployment figures continue to rise globally with no signs of relief in sight.

I don't believe relief will ever materialise under prevailing economic conditions and a failed world monetary system. Both have run the course and collapsed at the finish.

The pool of gainfully employed 'haves' has been evaporating in volume while that of the 'have nots' has been deepening exponentially.

The process, fuelled by the incessant demand for infinite economic growth is eroding the quality of life for increasing numbers of people at an alarming rate.

What can be done in the immediate term to alleviate this trend?

One area of massive manual employment opportunity requiring basic entry level training, with lifelong employment and advancement potential, is staring nation leaders in their collective faces.

With the need to react to the challenges of climate change becoming unavoidable, the need for environmental and ecological recovery, maintenance and protection work becomes increasingly essential.

Whereas my proposed World Governance Standard would gainfully employ a total global force of possibly one billion people, there are many opportunities available now for foundation laying worldwide.

By adopting a proactive stance now, nation leaders could immediately embark upon the creation, or radical upgrading, of dedicated environmental rejuvenation authorities, geared and equipped to train and employ presently unemployed human resources.

A carefully planned and managed strategy with strong legislative authority could bring immediate relief to existing environmental degradation, plus advanced preparatory measures to deal with the consequences of advancing climate change conditions.

South Africa alone could gainfully employ at least 500 000 people expressly for this purpose, enabling trickle down benefits for perhaps another two million or more.

I am not an economist or costing analyst but I imagine Ministers of Finance would be hard pressed to authorise the allocation of funding for such a hugely expensive project running into billions of rand per year.

Well, although it would not be a problem in my proposed cashless society, I believe it is actually within reach of present budgetary capacity now. The yearly cost would be a fraction of the total allocation for the 2010 World Cup Soccer spectacular.

Also, there are large pools of potentially "paid for" human resources in prisons having no hope whatsoever of gaining employment upon release, who might welcome the opportunity of guaranteed employment in environmental maintenance.

We already have approximately 250 000 youngsters with drug dependency problems that are costing South African taxpayers R10 billion a year.

On the management side, I have little doubt there are people with the right experience and qualifications able to supervise an environmental maintenance operation with military precision.

It could become a venture producing enormous financial benefits to national economies in terms of environmental and resource asset protection and rejuvenation. It would greatly improve the conditions of a nation's valuable assets, not least of all its essential and presently endangered potable water and wetlands. South Africa's potable water sources are expected to come under severe pressure by 2015.

An environmental work force of this nature needs to be planned for now, well in advance of the time when world governments will become forced to fully train and equip their own forces.

Savings derived by the economy from a repaired and recovered ecology and environment, together with cleared pollution from dams, waterways, wetlands and illegal dumping sites, would cover a major percentage of costs, not least of which would be the billions of rand saved in the reduced treatment of illnesses caused by pollution.

Pollution offenders, who would become more easily identified and prosecuted by the existence of such a large and dedicated environmental policing force, would become contributors to the operating costs. The total work force's disposable income spending power would release new cash-flow into the consumer market.

If needs be, a very modest "Green Tax" levy could also be introduced on stock exchange share trading volumes – which run into billions of rand on a daily basis - and on banking transactions where paperless automatic electronic transfers could be enabled with the minimum of human intervention.

Another equally essential specialised unit, also drawing upon suitable members within the poor and unemployed sectors, as well as from the rapidly expanding pool of unemployable school leavers, would be in an expanded and equipped national disaster management and prevention force, trained in all its many and varied disciplines.

Both groupings could provide lifelong employment for their members.

Climatic conditions often play a major role in the creation of disasters so there would be a very close synergy between the disaster management and environmental preservation units.

In the years ahead, climate change is expected to play an enormously powerful role in the disaster creation department, so a dedicated national management unit would be fully occupied in ways we have never seen before and can barely imagine.

There will be no tactical advantages gained by losing any of the battles fought against the onslaught of climate change. Every battle will have to be planned and fought to be won. It rather depends, of course, how the battles are planned and how many millions of lives will constitute an acceptable collateral loss factor.

Are you trying to say we are going to lose the war against global warming and climate change, and that millions of lives are going to be sacrificed in the process?

Man has never, and will never, win a war against Mother Nature particularly the major unstoppable one we know is gathering power right now.

An initial plan for combating the anticipated effects of climate change might be to extend the lead time for as long as possible, by slowing down the flow of carbon emissions.

However, that idea may be a lost cause in view of the huge volumes of methane gas and CO_2 working towards a serious 'burping' session in the Arctic Circle and possibly elsewhere around the world.

Determinations by China, India and South Africa to press ahead with environmentally unfriendly economic growth plans will undoubtedly add to the problems.

As far as can be determined thus far, even a complete shut-down of our greenhouse gas emissions will not halt the climate change phenomenon we started. It might, at best, assist in slowing the process down a little, in order perhaps to gain a little more time to salvage, and possibly restore, sufficient of the natural life support elements we need for survival.

A rapid conversion of the present global monetary system to my proposed alternative system would certainly remove the traditional financial constraints from a survival programme.

Conventional fossil fuel energy sources might then be more deliberately and efficaciously used for essential emergency services.

I fear that if we await a conventional political survival plan, requiring the cooperative agreement of all nation leaders, we shall find ourselves waiting forever.

Under such conditions an aspirant world domination nation, or consortium of nations, might take the initiative and opportunity to take control of the situation, militarily and economically. Whether or not this might lead to conflict expanding to a global scale remains to be seen. If it does, then we can anticipate an acceleration of global warming and climate change with rapid and disastrous consequences for all life on Earth.

My goodness you are moving into extremely alarmist territory now and probably going over the top more than a little bit.

Are you suggesting that a military conflict might be brewing and that the human race is possibly at risk of being hit by the consequences of climate change much sooner than currently expected?

I'm not suggesting we should be preparing for a World War III scenario but, from time to time I detect politically inspired manoeuvres of a worrying nature.

Man's history has been punctuated by wars and armed aggression in the eternal quest for power and domination. Throughout my long life I cannot recall a single year free of armed conflict occurring somewhere around the world and nothing has changed today. In fact it has actually worsened over the years.

We currently have a pile of conditions bubbling away that could lead the world into some very dangerous waters.

Crude oil is going to dominate our lives to increasing extents in the years ahead, so perhaps a better understanding of the role it plays in all our lives won't go amiss.

I'm sure we all understand enough about oil to appreciate its historical and present importance to us. We are also aware of the growing interest and research in alternative energy sources. There is even talk of removing CO_2 from furnace coal smoke emissions to make energy from coal more environmentally friendly.

You are absolutely right, but there is growing evidence to expect that climate change conditions will impact adversely upon many, if not most, of those alternative energy generating options, particularly when all forms of food become increasingly scarce as is happening already.

Remember also, crude oil provides us with much more than fuel for motor vehicles, aircraft and ships at sea. It provides derivatives such as lubricants, plastics, fertilisers, edible fats, pharmaceuticals, cosmetics and many other essential items.

The alternatives you mentioned are not immediately available on the enormous scale necessary to replace crude oil and coal for energy generating purposes. Also CO_2 is not removed from coal smoke, it is captured and stored somewhere.

Crude oil and its many derivatives is a natural resource that probably touches more lives directly and indirectly on a global basis than most others, so it warrants taking a look at its long-term availability to us and the consequences we face when it runs out.

Easy oil – how long will it last?

'Easy' relates to oil that is pumped directly from an underground reservoir or oil well.

World oil production estimates over the period 1930 – 2050, prepared by estimators Colin Campbell and Jean Laherrère, using a methodology employed by M. King Hubbert, who accurately predicted the peak in U.S. oil production, showed total production will have peaked in 2004 at approximately 71 million barrels per day (b.p.d.) but that all known global supply sources will have peaked individually prior to that date as shown below for the major sources alone.

Their results were published in *Scientific American* ("The End of Cheap Oil?") back in March 1998:

U.S.A. and Canada, 13.7 million b.p.d. in 1970;
Persian Gulf, 20.5 million b.p.d. in 1977;
Former Soviet Union, 13.7 million b.p.d. in 1985;
UK and Norway, 8 million b.p.d. in 2000.

Campbell-Laherrère forecasted total world production, excluding Persian Gulf, would have peaked at 49.3 million b.p.d. in 1998 and by the year 2050 total world production will be down to 13.7 million b.p.d.

With the USA alone taking about 7.3 billion barrels per year (20m b.p.d.) in 1998, being forty percent of major world production at the time, and that world demand will increase annually, the Campbell-Laherrère forecast suggests there will be insufficient world production of easy oil to meet the needs of the USA alone long before 2050.

It begs the question therefore: what will the super power do to overcome this dilemma? Or perhaps more to the point, what plans might have already been put in place for that inevitability?

That is one of the many scenarios focusing upon the world's long-term oil supply prospects.

In the search for expert opinions, I was particularly impressed with a very informed report by Peter Maass, published in the *NY Times Magazine* August 21, 2005 which I received as a subscriber to *South African New Economics* (SANE) network two days later.

The following extracts taken from his report bring a down to earth perspective into the whole debate surrounding the supply of oil from the prime Middle East region.

The largest oil terminal in the world, Ras Tanura, is located on the eastern coast of Saudi Arabia along the Arabian Gulf.

Peter Maass visited the location with his escort, Aref al-Ali from Saudi Aramco, the giant state-owned oil company, who mentioned to him: "One mistake at Ras Tanura today, and the price of oil will go up."

Some oil experts voiced concerns that Saudi Arabia and other producers may, in the near future, be unable to meet rising world demand.

The producers are not running out of oil yet, but their decades-old reservoirs are not as full and as geologically spry as they used to be, said Maass, and they may be incapable of producing, on a daily basis, the increasing volumes of oil the world requires.

"One thing is clear," warns Chevron, the second-largest American oil company in a series of new advertisements at the time, "the era of easy oil is over."

One needs to know whether the Saudis, who possess 22 percent of the world's oil reserves, can increase their country's output beyond its 2005 limit of 10.5 million b.p.d. and even beyond the 12.5 million b.p.d. target it had set for 2009.

According to Saudi statements world consumption is about 84 million b.p.d. which equates to 30.66 billion barrels a year.

Saudi Arabia is the sole oil superpower. No other producer possesses reserves close to its 263 billion barrels, which is almost twice as much as the runner-up Iran with 133 billion barrels.

It should be remembered, however, that neither the Saudi nor OPEC reserve assessments are made available for independent audit checks.

New fields in other countries are discovered now and then but they tend to offer only small increments.

The most exciting of these is the 3 to 4.3 billion barrels of undiscovered, technically recoverable oil reported to be in an area known as the Bakken Formation, in the North Dakota and Montana regions of the USA.

(Details http://www.usgs.gov/newsroom/article.asp?ID=1911)

Some fundamental calculations based upon the information from Peter Maass's report suggest that if world consumption remains at 84 million b.p.d., and if the stated reserves of Saudi Arabia prove to be accurate, their 22 percent contribution to world demand, pumping at 12.5 million b.p.d. would last 57 years to 2062.

Pumping at the same daily rate, Iran's would run out of capacity much sooner after 29 years by 2034.

At 15 million b.p.d., capacity might last only 48 (2053) and 24 (2029) years respectively.

If the remaining 78 percent of essential incremental oil reserves dry up at the world's smaller wells during this period of time, which would appear to be an industry expectation, a rapid and disastrous total global economic collapse is assured.

According to Maass, demand-driven scarcity has prompted the emergence of a cottage industry of experts who predict an impending crisis that will dwarf anything seen before.

Their point is not that we are running out of oil per se, although as much as half of the world's recoverable reserves are estimated to have been consumed already, and about a trillion barrels remain underground. Rather, they are concerned with what is called "capacity" - the amount of oil that can actually be pumped to the surface on a daily basis.

These experts - still a minority in the oil world - contend that because of the peculiarities of geology and the limitations of modern technology, it will soon be impossible for the world's reservoirs to surrender enough from oil reserves to meet daily demand, says Maass.

Some oil experts refer to oil recovery at wells as having a peaking date in their lives.

According to Maass, the reference to "peaking" is not a haphazard word choice - peaking is a term used in oil geology to define the critical point at which increasing amounts of oil can no longer be produced from reservoirs. This tends to happen when they are believed to be about half-empty.

Peak oil is the point at which maximum daily extraction from a well is reached. Afterward, no matter how many pumping points are drilled into the ground, the sum total of daily extraction from the reservoir begins to decline.

Saudi Arabia and other OPEC members may have enough oil to last for generations but that is no longer the issue. The eventual and painful shift to different sources of energy - the start of the post-oil age - does not begin when the last drop of oil is sucked from under the Arabian Desert. It begins when producers are unable to continue increasing their output to meet rising demand. Crunch time comes long before the last drop.

(Typically, with today's technology, only about 40 percent of a reservoir's oil can actually be pumped to the surface.)

Reverting to my personal opinion, this throws a lot of question marks at the stated reserve figures for Saudi and Iranian wells and at the incremental sources.

It also brings into question the realistic number of years the world can rely upon sustainable crude oil supplies.

It is critically important to note that Maass's report was prepared in 2005 when it was stated oil costing more than $60 a barrel hasn't caused a global recession. We are now at a time when – at the time of writing – oil had already touched $100 a barrel briefly and global recession has definitely become a reality.

Returning to Peter Maass's report:

Although higher oil prices could still happen, it can take a while to have their ruinous impact. The higher above $60 a barrel the price rises the more likely a recession will become.

High oil prices are inflationary; they raise the cost of virtually everything - from gasoline (motor fuel) and lubricants to jet fuel to plastics, pharmaceuticals and fertilizers - and that means people probably buy less and travel less, which means a drop-off in economic activity.

So after a brief windfall for producers, oil prices might begin to slide as recession sets in and once-voracious economies slow down, oil would become less used.

Prices have collapsed before. In 1998 oil fell to $10 a barrel after an untimely increase in OPEC production and a reduction in demand from Asia, which was suffering a financial crash.

Saudi Arabia and the other members of OPEC entered crisis mode back then, adjusted for inflation, oil was at its lowest price since the cartel's creation, threatening to feed unrest among the ranks of jobless citizens in OPEC states.

During his visit to Saudi Arabia, Peter Maass had a meeting with a man who he believes knows more about oil than anyone else. His name is Sadad al-Husseini, who retired in 2004 after serving as Aramco's top executive for exploration and production. They spoke for several hours.

According to Maass the message he delivered was clear. The world is heading for an oil shortage. Husseini explained that the need to produce more oil is coming from two directions.

Most obviously demand is rising. In recent years global demand has increased by two million b.p.d. (Current 2005 daily consumption was about 84 million b.p.d.)

Less obviously, oil producers deplete their reserves every time they pump out a barrel of oil. This means that merely to maintain their reserve base, they have to replace the oil they extract from declining fields. It's the geological equivalent of running to stay in place.

Husseini acknowledged that new fields are coming online, like offshore West Africa and the Caspian basin but he said their output isn't big enough to offset depleting reserves and growing needs.

"You look at the globe and ask, 'Where are the big increments?' and there's hardly anything but Saudi Arabia," he said.

"The kingdom and Ghawar field are not the problem. That misses the whole point. The problem is that you go from 79 million b.p.d. in 2002 to 82.5 in 2003 to 84.5 in 2004. You're leaping by two million to three million a day each year and, if you have to cover declines, that's another four to five million."

In other words, if demand and depletion patterns continue, every year the world will need to open enough fields or wells to pump an additional six to eight million b.p.d. - at least two million new b.p.d. to meet the rising demand and at least four million to compensate for the declining production of existing fields.

"That's like a whole new Saudi Arabia every couple of years," Husseini said.

On the question of increased production targets, Husseini said that 12.5 million b.p.d. is just an interim marker, as far as consuming nations are concerned, on the way to 15 million b.p.d. and beyond - and that is the point at which he believes problems will arise, says Maass. According to his assessment, experts like Husseini are very concerned by the prospect of trying to produce 15 million b.p.d.

Even if production can be ramped up that high, geology may not be forgiving. Fields that are overproduced can drop off in terms of output quite sharply and suddenly leaving behind large amounts of oil that cannot be coaxed out with existing technology.

This is called trapped oil because the rocks or sediment around it prevent it from escaping to the surface. Unless new technologies are developed, that oil will never be extracted. In other words the haste to recover oil can lead to less oil being recovered.

"You could go to 15, but that's when the questions of depletion rate, reservoir management and damaging the fields come into play," says Nawaf Obaid a Saudi oil and security analyst who is regarded as being exceptionally well connected to key Saudi leaders.

"There is an understanding across the board within the kingdom in the highest spheres, that if you're going to 15 you'll hit 15 but there will be considerable risks . . . of a steep decline curve that Aramco will not be able to do anything about."

Husseini, for one, doesn't buy that approach.

"Everybody is looking at the producers to pull the chestnuts out of the fire as if it's our job to fix everybody's problems," he told Maass.

"It's not our problem to tell a democratically elected government that you have to do something about your runaway consumers. If your government can't do the job you can't expect other governments to do it for them.

"Back in the 70's, president Carter called for the moral equivalent of war to reduce our dependence on foreign oil; he was not re-elected."

Since then few politicians have spoken of an energy crisis or suggested that major policy changes are necessary to avert one.

The energy bill signed earlier this month (August 2005) by president Bush did not even raise fuel efficiency standards for passenger cars.

When a crisis comes - whether in a year or two or ten - it will be all the more painful because we will have done little or nothing to prepare for it," he concluded.

Unlike some reports which tend to sensationalise world oil supply issues, Peter Maass's report stayed tuned to the observations of on-the-spot experts who are intimately associated with every aspect of oil and its recovery from under the ground.

Having considered the observations gathered from both sides of the availability question, a persistent thread of common agreement suggests that supply capacity to meet increasing world demand is now measured in decades. The burning question is – how many?

Oil Sand

There are alternatives to easy oil and the world's largest reserve is reportedly wrapped around grains of sand in the Canadian boreal forest of Northern Alberta.

It is said between 1.7 and 2.5 trillion barrels of crude oil, of which only 300 billion are expected to be recoverable, are spread across thousands of square kilometres of Alberta's forest and tundra.

However, these much-contested reserves in the Alaska National Wildlife Refuge are believed by Saudi sources to amount to about only 10 billion barrels, or just a fraction of what they possess.

There is a big drawback for oil sand's development which is the high production cost associated with extracting the heavy gooey bitumen - a petroleum product that can be refined into petroleum or other products - stuck to every grain of sand recovered.

Production costs, estimated at the time to range from $18 to $20 or more per barrel of oil sand bitumen, which was considerably more expensive than producing conventional Arabian Gulf light crude, which at that time was costing less than $2 a barrel to recover.

Although billions of dollars have already been invested in development proposals from companies like Imperial Oil, Petro-Canada, Suncor, Syncrude, Shell, Chevron and Conoco, full scale commercial production beyond 600 000 b.p.d. (only 219 million barrels per year) had not yet taken place during the period of my research.

Expectations at the time were for more than two million barrels of oil per day whereas, according to Allan Ross, an energy analyst based in Calgary, 20 million barrels a day would be needed to satisfy their next-door neighbour alone, the energy-hungry United States.

The whole recovery operation is environmentally damaging and requires huge volumes of water throughout the whole process.

From this and other oily scenarios, all manner of speculations may arise when the depletion of global reserves are weighed against the eternal needs for crude oil and its many derivatives.

As the world moves deeper into recession the price of crude will move accordingly. But as climate change takes a stronger grip on weather conditions and global agriculture, the demand for crude derivatives will surely grow before it falls off.

It is said that an army moves on its stomach. It also moves on full fuel tanks and guaranteed reserves. This principle will become increasingly pertinent in the minds of nation leaders in the years ahead.

Sadly, the world remains weighed down with a multitude of problems against which only the very wealthy are presently able to immunise themselves, albeit with limited protection.

The common denominators missing from global problems are politically inspired sustainable solutions.

At present, world leaders engage in regular meetings, endless talks, volumes of recommendations and resolutions, but no deliberate action. G8 leaders give assurances and make promises with the ease of skilled confidence tricksters.

The promises proclaimed at the Gleneagles meeting in 2005 remained unfulfilled four years later in L'Aquila, Italy. Sadly, and predictably, world leaders cannot be trusted to take climate change issues seriously. They cannot be trusted to act responsibly and decisively on any issues affecting the best interests of the global population who, sooner or later, will be forced to do so themselves.

Early manifestations of climate change will see foodstuff of every description becoming increasingly difficult and expensive to produce, to distribute and to buy, exacerbated by increasing crop failures. The starving millions will continue to starve and increasing numbers will join them.

The food security problem

There are almost a billion undernourished people in the world today and their plight has been acknowledged in the Intergovernmental Panel on Climate Change (IPCC)[11] published 16 November 2007, extracts of which vindicate my own concerns:

Under the heading:

Adaptive capacity is intimately connected to social and economic development but is unevenly distributed across and within societies.

"A range of barriers limits both the implementation and effectiveness of adaptation measures. The capacity to adapt is dynamic and is influenced by a society's productive base including natural and man-made capital assets, social networks and entitlements, human capital and institutions, governance, national income, health and technology.

Even societies with high adaptive capacity remain vulnerable to climate change, variability and extremes."

The shortage of available food will give rise to heightened crime, territorial conflict and food related corruption, as evidenced throughout Zimbabwe in 2007/08 and more recently exposed in South Africa relating to cartel fixed pricing for bread, milk, fertilizer and other products.

Religious fanatics might start blaming each others' faiths for the damnation being wreaked upon humanity by various divine orders. As mooted earlier, militarily advantaged nations might feel compelled to bring enormous pressures to bear in manoeuvres to gain optimum access to, and control of oil production and refinement, and bio fuel sources.

As already said, money presently rules our lives.

If conditions on earth deteriorate to the degree I have suggested, money will reign supreme for a while before becoming completely worthless. If that is allowed to happen terminal global recession will become unavoidable and uncontrollable.

Obviously things do not have to become so brutally unbearable and no effort must be spared to ensure they do not. I remain unconvinced, however, that conventionally structured political processes will carry us through the turbulent years ahead. They have failed the entire human race in the past and will, I am sure, fail us now and in the future.

You might be right but what about the United Nations? It's a body already in existence, geared to provide a forum through which world leaders can confront the severity of climate change and its predicted effects upon mankind's very existence and work together to deal with it.

Well, the United Nations was founded with such noble principles in mind and the body's members were, from the outset, obligated to protect their collective economic integrities and the well-being of their citizens with the assistance of facilities established within the UN for those purposes. This is underscored by the Mission Statement of The Department of Economic and Social Affairs of the United Nations Secretariat, which is a vital interface between global policies in the economic, social and environmental spheres and national action.

The Department works in three main interlinked areas:

- it compiles, generates and analyses a wide range of economic, social and environmental data and information on which States Members of the United Nations draw to review common problems and to take stock of policy options;
- it facilitates the negotiations of Member States in many intergovernmental bodies on joint courses of action to address ongoing or emerging global challenges;
- and it advises interested Governments on the ways and means of translating policy frameworks developed in United Nations conferences and summits into programmes at the country level and, through technical assistance, helps build national capacities.

Regrettably, so many of those political members have failed in their responsibilities and allowed the United Nations, with a few notable divisional exceptions, to deteriorate into a virtually ineffective entity. The victims of this travesty are predictably the citizens of the entire world, not just those of UN member nations.

Strikes, riots and civil commotions are becoming regular occurrences in an increasing number of countries around the world, sparked by deepening poverty, escalating unemployment, spiralling cost of living expenses, devaluation of disposable incomes and failures in fundamental service delivery.

At the elitist political and commercial levels, nations are being formed into their own select blocs.

The European Union is the first that comes to most minds. Then there is the North American Union formed by the USA, Canada and

Mexico in 2005, who are alleged to be planning to create a new American Union currency called the Amero.

Next in line will probably be the African Union, rich in minerals, precious metals and diamonds. Then the two fast growing economies of India and China will join to become the Asian Union.

The United Nations has not failed completely in its mission statement objectives and continues to play a number of important and effective roles in humanitarian aid and assistance when it can.

In fact it could be said the United Nations as an entity has not failed at all. Its component parts, the political leaders of member nations, have failed to faithfully follow the plotted course towards global unification and peaceful co-existence. Too many have sacrificed that challenging voyage, and their duties within an international leadership crew, at the altar of their own private agendas and personal career aspirations.

So in the final analysis, politicians and their variously designed and dysfunctional political structures are to blame for the sorry state of failed global governance. They have gone far beyond their respective 'use before' dates and must now be replaced by something refreshingly new, something healthy and something durable and long lasting.

And you have that 'something,' about which I trust you are about to tell us and to give us a little advance taste?

Yes, but before doing so I beg forgiveness from the very special, rare and unique breed of career politicians who do not fit into the generalised mould of corrupt power seekers I have been depicting.

I know only a few personally and greatly respect their sincerity, integrity and their genuine endeavours to serve their constituents honourably. I salute them all and trust they will remain committed throughout their careers.

Meanwhile, I hope I have shown sufficient reason to dispense with the present forms of fragmented and corrupt international political governance, in order that you can clear your mind and prepare to receive and consider my proposal for a single form of world governance, of the people, by the people and for the people.

In closing this chapter on politics and politicians, I give you a couple of quotations to think about.

First, the words of US Senator, Daniel Webster (1782-1852) which he penned June 1, 1837. They reveal why education of the masses has been withheld for so many years:

"I apprehend no danger to our country from a foreign foe ...

Our destruction, should it come at all, will be from another quarter. -- From the inattention of the people to the concerns of their government, from their carelessness and negligence, I must confess that I do apprehend some danger. I fear that they may place too implicit a confidence in their public servants, and fail properly to scrutinize their conduct; that in this way they may be made the dupes of designing men, and become the instruments of their own undoing. Make them intelligent, and they will be vigilant; give them the means of detecting the wrong, and they will apply the remedy."

And finally, Thomas Jefferson, referring to the American Declaration of Independence July 4, 1776:

"We hold these truths to be self-evident, that all men are created equal, that they are endowed by their Creator with certain unalienable Rights, that among these are Life, Liberty, and the pursuit of Happiness.

That to secure these rights, Governments are instituted among Men, ...

That whenever any Form of Government becomes destructive of these ends, it is the Right of the People to alter or to abolish it."

Chapter 6

A History of Religion

Matters of faith – and questionable fact

Politics is a creation of man which can, in the words of Thomas Jefferson be "altered or abolished by the right of the people."

This chapter considers religion, another of man's creations.
It attempts to determine the original intention and purpose of religion and whether it ever made any credible contribution towards the well-being of the world's people.

For the majority of people religious belief is a very sensitive, emotionally charged and private matter. Many prefer not to debate it, nor consider opinions on religion that differ from their own, which is a little sad perhaps, since such perceptions might give credibility to those who say knowledge is the enemy of faith. I do not believe this. I believe knowledge is the very essence of faith, in whatever matter it is vested provided the knowledge is soundly based upon fact.

> ***Allow me to come in here. I can understand your argument for a changed monetary system and a different form of governance in a new world order, particularly for preparing to meet the huge and worrying challenges of climate change. I accept that money and politics and, for that matter, climate change are man made and that man has the right to change them. However, I do not believe religion is man made and I hope you are not about to say it must be altered or abolished.***

Rest assured, I have no intention of suggesting religion should be abolished. On the contrary, I believe my proposal for a new world order could provide religion with new and invigorating roles to play in shaping the future. I shall, however, propose that religious leaders review certain aspects of doctrine to consider changes that many believe would be more appropriate for the twenty-first century and beyond.

As in previous chapters, I shall give reasons for my proposals, which I hope will be considered with an open mind. My reasons will also explain why I regard religion as being a subject for constant review under a new world order of survival.

As to my assertion that religion is man made, the results of my research certainly support that opinion. After all, what is religion? I would characterise the fundamentals of most religious faiths as being pronouncements that their ancient scriptural doctrine must be accepted as being unquestioningly factual, and that proof with supporting evidence is deemed to be completely unnecessary. That is the very essence of faith, albeit misguided in my view.

One of the fundamental objectives of some religious doctrine appears to be an attempt to give reason, meaning and purpose for man's presence on planet Earth. The course of enlightenment includes, inter alia, proclamations of how man and Earth and all other celestial bodies came to be.

Faithful believers are given assurances of attaining peace and happiness throughout their lives on Earth, by obeying the rules of scripture and by conducting their lives according to alleged divine commandments. The ultimate reward for the faithful after death is the promise of life everlasting in Heaven. The alternative is endless torturous suffering in Hell.

It could be said that a divine arrangement between man and his God, containing such attractive benefits for the faithful, gives new meaning to "having one's cake and eating it." It is certainly a "win/win" arrangement that might prompt sceptics to think it is too good to be true.

But, does it really matter what sceptics think? Certainly not.

One is bound to assume that an arrangement such as this, promising heavenly rewards in the life hereafter, will fill the world with happy, loving and God fearing people.

The evidence of reality tells us this is clearly not so, I am inclined to assume a large majority of people, particularly alleged believers, have little or no respect for, or belief in, divine commandments.

The religious differences of opinion that contribute so violently to the growing culture of worldwide conflict, vindicate my assumption.

The secular World Governance Standard that I propose will have terms and conditions that might be likened unto a global Constitution, upholding and protecting the fundamental rights, interests and privileges of every human being in the world, irrespective of religious or cultural doctrines. No religion or culture would be permitted to alter, or to have conditional influences over, those rights interests and privileges.

Religious doctrine should not be permitted to practice religious law that places conditions, restrictions or prohibitions upon people's access to Constitutional rights. Attempts to do so would be deemed a violation of those fundamental Constitutional rights.

If I can come in again, I guarantee you will experience huge resistance from the entire religious community if you attempt to tamper with any aspect of their doctrines, particularly the Islamic religious leaders and their followers.

Society has to be tolerant of all religious orders and customs.

I agree there are bound to be many objections raised but I am confident the proposed future World Governance Standard architects and religious leaders will find ways to resolve them. After all, there would be no intention to deliberately obstruct religious worship or to interfere unreasonably with the teachings of fundamental religious beliefs. It might become desirable to define 'fundamental.'

You mentioned that society has to be tolerant of religious doctrines and customs. As true as that is, society must rightfully expect tolerance and understanding to be exercised by religious orders towards society, which remains conspicuous by its absence in many parts of the world.

I have a vision of a new World Governance Standard being created from the collective input and consensus of the entire human race. The point of departure should, I believe, begin with the protection and care of every new born child's fundamental right to life.

Despite popular belief of extremists, babies are born without religious or cultural genes in their little bodies. They come into the world as the consequence of copulation. The upbringing of children should, I believe, be governed by a law prohibiting parents or guardians from compelling children to become involuntary members of a particular religion or culture.

I also believe children's years of schooling should include comprehensive education about every known culture, religion and religiously inclined ideology in the world. Let their eventual future spiritual and cultural decisions be informed by the wisdom of unbiased knowledge and comprehension.

Throughout our history, religion should have become a catalyst for creating peaceful and harmonious coexistence between different congregations, and between societies at large regardless of religious and cultural differences. This did not occur.

If deliberate steps are to be taken now to pursue that desirable course, scriptures and religious doctrines will, I believe, need to be deliberately revisited by theologians and religious scholars. They will need to determine what ancient historical perceptions and interpretations deserve to be reviewed and deliberated upon, in the light of mankind's more informed awareness of his home planet and of the endless depth of space in which it resides. For example, the Roman Catholic Church used to condemn to death those who proclaimed Earth was not the centre of the Universe.
Assessors will be advised to determine what revisions of scripture might strengthen doctrine credibility without diluting the fundamental reasons for and purpose of worship.

A strong credibility in the pursuit of love, respect, tolerance and peaceful coexistence is more likely to strengthen the hearts and minds of believers and to attract respectful understanding from non-believers.

I am Agnostic and it is my understanding that all religious believers, regardless of their particular faiths, share a common philosophical opinion relating to creation, proclaiming it to have been by the will of a supreme form of divine power, obviously greater than man.

From my own assessment of religious teachings, I detect flaws in them all, some more glaring and serious than others. But this is of no consequence whatsoever, because believers will believe whatever they choose to believe and I respect their absolute right to do so.

In matters relating to the survival of the species, to which believers and non-believers alike clearly subscribe, revised religious doctrines could provide such a valuable contribution to enriching the humanity segment of mankind's psyche.

Religious doctrine derives, inter alia, from the translations and interpretations of ancient folklore and story tellers. Collectively, some folklore stories attempted to convey meaning and understanding of commands that were said to have been delivered by an unseen supreme source to one or more chosen people. Those early interpretations originated in times when human knowledge and understanding of worldly and celestial phenomena was, at best, extremely limited.

Over the years, more translations of translations will have been accompanied by revised interpretations, perhaps embellished by the addition of new words and expressions thought by interpreters to enhance the tales.

As we know so well, the more often a fisherman's story is told, the larger in size and fighting spirit of the fish that got away tends to become!

Religious leaders should be encouraged and persuaded to review their doctrines in search of those embellishments and interpretations that no longer sit comfortably in a modern and more enlightened global environment.

I believe we should consider culture as a living, growing and ever changing reflection of a society's evolving lifestyle choices.

Many cultures were created in the dark and distant past and have never been revised to changing times. They remain rooted in the past having little or no relevance in the present. They might become completely lost and meaningless in the future.

Whereas religions demand unqualified acceptance of, and unerring faith in ancient doctrine, many people prefer to be informed and guided by irrefutable evidence whenever possible, or by convincingly credible and logical argument when it is not. Proclamations of commands and instructions emanating from ghosts and spirits, both good and bad, have no credibility for me at all.

Having come to terms with the enormity of the Cosmos, the physics of the space-time continuum, of distances measured in light years, and of what I perceive to be the inevitable and awesome reality of infinity, it is my belief that space and all it contains has always been there, and will endure in ever changing arrangements and composition eternally.

Well, that's a rather bumpy start for your religious readers, many of who will have a completely different conception of how the Universe and everything in it was created.

Absolutely, but I haven't said I am right and they are wrong.

I have simply stated what I believe to be the truth, which I accept as being supported by very credible and well documented scientific research and discovery.

While religious believers may choose not to believe in infinity, while preparing themselves for the miracle of "everlasting life after death," they might at least acknowledge a plausible parallel of probability, and I shall talk more about probability later on.

While I do not believe in the existence of any of the many gods and spirits that abound throughout the catalogue of religious faiths, I do not categorically say they do not exist because, in common with those who believe they do, there is absolutely no proof, one way or the other to support either opinion. I simply believe the balance of probability regarding the existence of divine powers is non-existent and completely outside my vision of credible acceptance.

I am compelled to add, I would not kill those who do not support my point of view, which sadly appears to be the manner by which differences of religious beliefs and opinions are settled by a shocking number of fanatics in some so-called religious groups.

Such behaviour should, and hopefully does, raise a number of worrying questions in the minds of the religious faithful and their leaders.

The need for a cultural renaissance

A global renaissance should ideally include a revision of the psyche and culture of the entire human race. As mentioned before, the complete removal of illiteracy, poverty and starvation from our planet must be given a much higher level of proactive attention than has been the case thus far. Religious faiths and ancient cultures have sadly failed to achieve this desirable objective.

Having regard for the divergence of religious and cultural doctrines that have emerged over the millennia, and for those who do not subscribe to any of them, the foundations of a secular global governance policy would prioritise and focus upon issues common to all members of the human race. Issues such as the right to life, access to education, to health care, to employment, to food and to a roof over one's head. Unfortunately, these and other essentials will not be provided through prayer. They will only be realised through deliberate and dedicated human intervention.

Everyone must be guaranteed assurance and protection of their personal dignity and their entitlement to equal opportunities. They must receive freedom from discriminatory marginalism and persecution of every kind.

These might appear to be straightforward and fundamental rights for everyone requiring no special focus whatsoever. However, attention should be drawn to the existing plights of many women and children and the treatment they endure through the enactments of religious fundamentalist doctrines. Also acts carried out by certain witch doctors, traditional leaders and of so-called cultural healers, notably throughout much of Africa, the Middle East and the Far East.

For example, there are a number of cultural healing practises conducted in my country which are quite horrific. They entail the collection of selected items of mhuti – the name for various body parts of the human anatomy - prescribed for people wishing to be cured of various ailments or disorders, or to simply enable them to gain courage or strength of mind and body for a variety of reasons.

Various forms of mhuti are even used by some professional South African football teams, under assurances by their particular witchdoctors, they will play brilliantly and win important matches. There is no evidence to support the efficacy of such bizarre claims but presumably the winning sides will be convinced. A drawn result might be interpreted as an equality of mhuti power used by both teams.

Male and female genitalia, lips and eyes are popular in the quest for virility, hearts for strength and power, and other body parts for a number of other purposes. Parts extracted forcibly from unwilling donors whilst still alive are highly favoured, because it is believed the screams of unbearable pain emitted by the victims bring forth their spirits into the part being removed, thereby ensuring great potency for the recipient.

Black women in rural localities, assumed by their fellow villagers to be witches for whatever obscure reason, are stoned and driven from the village, or more often burned to death.

Horrendous activities of this nature may take many generations to erase from the cultures that practise them. Hopefully a concerted renaissance might accelerate the process.

It will be desirable that the founding members of the proposed Global Administration will comprise, amongst others, theologians and experts in the sciences of historically traditional and cultural practises across tribal, ethnic and religious grounds.

The paramount objective of the proposed form of global renaissance will be to provide the entire human race with a unique opportunity to write its own new cultural lifestyle rule book. A culture that will ensure a full and rewarding life for every human being on Earth. A life to be lived without fear of assault on mind or body under the protection of a single nation world leadership, elected by all the people, from amongst all the people, dedicated to the best interests of all the people.

People's minds can then become freely focussed upon the recovery, improvement and maintenance of the world's environmental, ecological and habitable condition for themselves and all future generations. A world where opportunities will abound for all and where mankind will exist as one race – the human race.

In a money-less environment all religious institutions will need to review their doctrines to ensure compliance with revised worldwide democratic conditions. For example, the contractual obligations of the global community and the Global Administration, produced as a Constitution, will permit only one rule of law to obtain worldwide. The fundamentals thereof shall be to declare all men equal before the law. Their defined rights will enable them to live their lives to the fullest extent within the prescribed social behavioural parameters which shall be common to all.

Objectives of the Global Administration would be targeted, inter alia, at the removal of homelessness, poverty, starvation and the cruel indignities of human exploitation and abuse. It is hoped the removal of money and its historical influence as an instrument of temptation and corruption will go far towards achieving peaceful coexistence worldwide.

For these and many other beneficial reasons, it would become incumbent upon religious leaders to support these noble endeavours, with the assurance that their continued spiritual roles might be perceived as value added benefits to the world at large and to their followers in particular. After all, many of them are more informed and aware of universal truth than their ancestors, while being a little less informed than those who will follow.

I might be wrong but, I am getting the impression you are suggesting that religious leaders in the past took advantage of the illiteracy of their followers, which gave rise to doctrines that are no longer in tune with present conditions.

That is a fair analysis of the situation as I believe it to be. I also believe that many religiously inclined people today are compelled to adapt prescribed religious lifestyles to prevailing conditions, in the knowledge that ancient religious lifestyle prescriptions have become unworkable in modern times.

The majority of married women no longer stay at home, tending the vegetable patch, spinning yarn and weaving cloth to make clothing for their family. Many are second, and sometimes sole breadwinners for the family.

Notwithstanding the enormous strides that mankind has taken to inculcate literacy around the world, there are still many millions who are sadly completely illiterate, and many more who are functionally illiterate. They might know what to do but lack the intellectual ability to do it.

Illiteracy throughout the global masses was fairly widespread as recently as 500 – 600 years ago and considerably more so in earlier times, which we tend to forget. Yet even today I have personal experience of people who still cannot apply their minds to the simple reality of time differences around the world. When told it is today in one part of the world and tomorrow in another they simply don't understand it.

I recall telling my dear old Zulu house maid years ago that astronauts had landed on the moon. The following morning she told me she had "looked very hard and very long" but could not see the men on the moon! I tried explaining how far the moon was away from Earth and how much smaller it appeared to be up in the sky but, bless her heart, she just stood there shaking her head unable to grasp that explanation at all.

If things like this cannot be understood by so many people today, while surrounded by an abundance of technological wizardry, how could people hundreds or thousands of years ago have been capable of comprehending Earth's creation by any way other than through the will of a powerful god?

Well clearly that is what many did believe and still believe today, as evidenced by the enormous following that religion enjoys around the world right now.

I accept what you say about people believing but, as I shall explain later on, many years ago those beliefs were expressed under the duress of some very nasty consequences befalling those who openly declared they did not believe. Recall what I said earlier about Earth being the centre of the Universe. This is what I regard as the essential "fear factor" of religions that has prevailed throughout time right up to the present.

It is not dissimilar, I suppose, to the fear factor of a spanking that parents traditionally applied to keep their mischievous children in line. In modern times however, I find it quite amazing, and equally ridiculous, that small acts of corporal punishment delivered to mischievous children by their parents, like a slap on the arm or leg, can give rise to criminal charges being raised against the parents. Too ludicrous for words in my opinion and I believe it is becoming a cause of so much societal delinquency and indiscipline throughout much of the world today.

When measured against a religious proclamation that an eternity of pain and suffering will befall the spirit of a person after death, simply because he or she chose not to believe in a god, I have to wonder who is more deserving of being criminally charged, the arm-slapping parents or the fear mongering religious leaders?

The fear factor undoubtedly contributed greatly to the historical size of congregational attendances, although there have apparently been noticeable declines on a global basis over the past fifty years.

To what has this been attributed?

I haven't researched the subject so am unable to provide a qualified reason. I can only assume that people may have become more aware and better informed about the scientific history of Earth, the endless expanse of our known universe and the shear enormity of the Cosmos and infinity, and measured this knowledge against the messages contained in ancient astronomically disadvantaged scriptures. It might have led them to question the early assumptions relating to creation and decided modern science provides more credible probabilities.

Maybe, but it would still have been a probability not a scientifically proven fact.

Perhaps, but as I mentioned earlier 'probability' is an interesting word and we cannot dismiss it as being meaningless. It found its way into scientific equations and calculations a long time ago in quite extraordinary ways.

For example, many of the wonderful technological advances achieved over the past seventy years or so, can be attributed to the application of the quantum theory in one form or another, which relies in no small part upon the science of probability.

This was born out by French physicist Prince Louis Victor de Broglie's 'Wave Mechanics Theory' and German physicist Werner Karl Heisenberg's 'Uncertainty Principle,' which won him the Nobel Prize for physics way back in 1932.

The great Albert Einstein who gave the world his theories of relativity, the one more popularly known relating to space, time and uniform motion and the perhaps lesser known one dealing with acceleration and gravitation, wherein probability and uncertainty each play a role.

We all know of course, he gave us his famous $E=MC^2$ which scientists regard as being the formula by which it can be proven that pure energy produced Earth, the stars, suns and planets in the Cosmos.

This also supported the "Big Bang" theory that suggests our universe was created from exploding energy which eventually converted into matter.

It is believed this particular theory, as well as the quantum theory, troubled Einstein somewhat.

He was not, as far as I could determine, a religious person but believed, like millions of others, that a god or supreme power would have created everything in a deliberate and orderly manner.

He believed that abstracts such as probability and uncertainty could never have featured in such a precise process of divine creation and uniformity. He actually devoted the latter years of his extraordinary life trying to prove this by working diligently on his 'Theory of Everything.'

Those who knew him well became inclined to believe his endeavours failed to provide credible support for his theory. On the contrary, they kept bringing him closer and closer to proving the quantum theory.

It has been suggested, with much truth I imagine, that he became increasingly convinced of the non-existence of a god or supreme power, seeing his own calculations producing a high 'probability' that neither existed. He died in 1955 without completing his years of work.

I must confess I was completely unaware of all this intriguing information, particularly this last part about Einstein trying to prove God's existence. Amazing.

Is this what influence you to become an Agnostic?

Goodness no. I only became aware of all this scientific knowledge relating to probability and uncertainty during the last 25 years or so.

As to becoming an Agnostic, that came about much earlier when I was in my late teens and had been in the Royal Navy for three or four years.

My religious persuasion at the time was Church of England and I had given it and other religions some thought for quite some time. I was not particularly happy with the C. of E. denomination, passed onto me by my parents, because of my intense dislike of the manner in which it was man-made by the infamous King Henry VIII for his own self serving interests.

I read quite a lot and had discussions with various Naval Chaplains, trying to come to terms with what I perceived as people's bland, nonchalant and unquestioning acceptance of God and the whole amazing subject of creation.

Whereas I considered, at the time, God's creation to be the most incredible thing ever, I could never understand why others seemed to take it all for granted without question.

When discussing creation with other believers, it became very clear that none of them appeared to have the slightest idea or conception of its shear magnitude and magnificence. Eventually I began to wonder if I was perhaps the only person in the world who actually believed it all.

More reading, more research and more chats with Chaplains and I gradually came to believe that perhaps I had been a misguided believer in a wilderness of divine indifference.

The more I read and the deeper I delved into history, the clearer it became to me that religion had to be one of the oldest, most cruel and expertly managed commercial deceptions of all time.

I was bitterly disappointed, and I suppose a little relieved, to realise that science was a more dependable path to follow when searching for the truth.

Having abandoned a belief in any of the many alternative gods on offer, I had to decide how to define myself if asked to do so.

Atheism didn't quite crack it because there appears to be a popular, albeit completely unfounded, belief that atheists were evil, having an inclination towards the devil. I opted for English biologist Thomas Huxley's 1869 definition of agnostic:

"one who holds that only material phenomena can be known and knowledge of a superior being or ultimate cause is impossible."

OK. So now we know a little more about you, what you believe in – and don't believe in – and how you propose religious leaders should review their doctrines for the future.

You lost faith in your own church and you say you considered alternatives. Did you come close to accepting one and what on earth gave you reason to call religion a commercial deception?

I am perfectly happy to answer your questions but it could take some time.

That's OK, I imagine like many other people, I shall be particularly interested to see how you explain your commercial deception statement.

Fair enough.

When I set about gathering my thoughts and organising material for my book, I was reminded of a quotation attributed to our late departed Professor Albert Einstein:

"There are problems in today's world that cannot be solved by the level of thinking that created them."

Although his mind was probably focused upon his insatiable love of mathematic and scientific problems at the time, I believe his words are equally germane to the very worrying social, cultural, financial and religious problems confronting mankind throughout the world today. The very problems we all seek to resolve today will indeed call for a different level of thinking to that which created them in the first place.

Many were created through a level of ancient thinking that could not possibly imagine the impact they would, and did have upon civilizations centuries later.

Research took me back to the time when man's psyche evolved from basic instinctive aspects of self survival, to a realisation that he was acquiring the ability to think and to make decisions based upon those thoughts.

I reached the time when man took the evolutionary quantum leap that propelled him to unassailable heights above all others in the animal kingdom. This was when he created and controlled fire about 250 000 years ago. As important as that event was, I believe it was his ability to think about it first, then work out how to do it that was the most significant aspect of the discovery. This was a huge and sudden evolutionary leap forward which I still do not understand.

So you think the ability to create fire started man's thinking abilities?

No, I'm sure he had learned to think long before that, over and above his natural instincts which were mainly for the purpose of survival.

Man was suddenly rushing from pure instinctive reaction into the proactive wonderland of cognitive problem solving. His ability to think about and to create fire on demand probably enabled him to mature his thinking abilities to do things with it. For example, he could create lighting and central heating for the communal cave and provide cooking facilities for the women. He could have fires burning at the entrance knowing they would act as a deterrent against dangerous animals wandering in.

While physical strength and energy had always been the essential prerequisite for man's survival, certainly for becoming the leader of the pack, many years later it was the thinking leaders who won prominence.. They gathered other thinkers, as well as guards and troops around themselves and were able to survive the longest.

The ability to think beyond the instinctive fundamentals will have marked one of those first amazing leaps towards enabling knowledge and functional literacy to come into play.

Perhaps it was the physically weaker male members of the clan who learned how to develop imagination and to improve upon their instinctive qualities of animal cunning. They might have become able to provide specialised counselling to the leader in exchange for certain privileges within the pack.

Enter the quid pro quo era and the early dawning of politics and inventive ingenuity!

> ***This is all assumption, with a lot of perhaps' and maybes on your part and you have no solid evidence to support what you are saying.***

You are right, I don't, but I have found no credible evidence to disprove or dismiss my assumptions, which I believe are reasonable when measured against the little we know about man's evolution. We know even less about how the power of mass domination unfolded throughout history. After all, there had to be an ancient evolutionary dawning for man's departure from the pure animal instinct with which he started to the point he has reached now.

With the passing of time man's cognitive capabilities will have expanded in step with enlarged community settlements and the setting of territorial boundaries. Thought processes will have probably become more directly focused upon whatever daily activity occupied the greater part of their time.

But within those communities there might have been one or more special thinkers, possibly with more developed brains and lateral thinking capabilities.

It was probably from their numbers that the foundations of manipulative power sources were laid, manifested in the different layers of mass leadership positions that appeared in society over the years that followed.

Whatever those early thinkers might have lacked in terms of physical stature and prowess, would surely have been more than compensated for by their ever-maturing skills in the arts of convincing persuasion, negotiation, and the subtleties of manipulative cunning.

What do you mean by "manipulative power sources," and what are the "layers of mass leadership positions" to which you refer?

Manipulative power sources are leaders who have complete decision making powers over the lives and destinies of the people they rule.

Other thinkers will have developed abilities to subliminally influence those who actually ruled. They became the "behind the scenes" rulers.

In more recent history the rulers will have comprised monarchs, emperors, war lords and the like. The power of rule was administered by force, often quite terrible, directed by the military commanders appointed by the supreme leader. These military commanders were some of the "layers" of leadership to which I was referring and there would have been other layers or rankings above and below them.

Meanwhile, back in the main powerhouse of rule, the supreme leader will have surrounded himself with military and civil advisers, counsellors and a retinue of other characters upon whom he might need to call for advice on specific issues.

These will have become more of the various layers of empowered people of influence within the leadership elite, amongst whom will have been those able to exercise subliminal influence over the leader.

Perhaps the early stages of reverse psychology were developing at that time.

But those examples, many of which can be found in recorded history, will have arrived long after the much earlier pre-historical time I was considering. The time when the foundations of mass leadership will have been laid and built upon over thousands of years, enabling the types and titles of power to evolve and to become firmly established and entrenched within the fabric of global societies and their young cultures.

I was searching for that illusive point in time when man, or at least certain men, became consciously aware of how positions of leadership could be ordained by them and applied in a number of ways to ensure obedience and compliance by the masses, thereby ensuring sustained and absolute rule.

My research took me into the hallowed territory of psychologists, anthropologists and Palaeolithic archaeologists who, being far more skilful than I, devote their lives in the search for truth.

I've never quite understood what anthropology is all about. What is it exactly?

Anthropology is the study of man, his origins, his physical characteristics, institutions, religious beliefs, social relationships, and how he has evolved in so many different ways in various parts of the world and under a variety of circumstances.

Research for the beginning of early mass leadership was inconclusive but it certainly goes back thousands of years. It nevertheless became clear there were three predominantly powerful forms of mass leadership and control in man's early history. They were, and remain, territorial rule, military rule and spiritual rule, all of which included the essential fear factor.

Whereas certain religious leaders have since dispensed with their participation in territorial rule, some have converted it into a major function within their religious governance institutions, such as Islam.

Religious leaders in most non-Islamic countries remain largely respectful of the authority of their territorial rulers.

Research nevertheless revealed a synergy existing between territorial and religious leaders, designed to ensure their combined strength and power would guarantee their iconic existence for all time. An enduring arrangement that might be colloquially expressed as: "you scratch my back and I'll scratch yours and together we shall rule the world."

As I see it, you are suggesting that national and religious leaders have colluded in some way to hold power over the people they are supposed to serve and to protect. That sounds a bit outrageous to me. How did you arrive at that conclusion?

Yes, it certainly is outrageous, but according to research it appears to be so and to have happened thousands of years ago, back in the time of our early entrepreneurial thinkers, back to the time before the mysteries and awesome powers of spiritualism were created and introduced to the illiterate peasant-stock masses.

In the early days the two power sources were probably not always evenly matched in terms of predominance, although the territorial power usually had the greatest influence over the mobilisation of people in matters of production and war.

The religious power would generally stand firmly and overtly beside the other, extolling the divine support for whatever the people were required to do, and the divine rewards they would eventually enjoy.

As strong as these two controlling and collusive powers undoubtedly are, the territorial leaders were constantly at risk of being replaced. Not only by forces from within their region of rule, but also by other regions through invasion and occupation.

The religious leaders generally became subjected to a lesser degree of risk except, perhaps, in that earlier period of different forms of pagan worship.

It became increasingly clear that those ancient entrepreneurial religious practitioners must have become endowed with excellent survival abilities, because religion has become the longest surviving influence of power over the minds of men.

But how and when did this stroke of genius occur? When, where and how did religion start? There are no definitive answers to such questions because nobody appears to know.

My research revealed a number of hypotheses, some of which were founded upon various assumptions and interpretations relating to artefacts collected over the years, many of which were thought to have religious or spiritual connections. Such assumptions are invariably the easy choice when imaginations are limited to conventional causes.

Some suggested, with very sound reasoning, that visitors from outer space, many thousands of years ago, may have influenced primitive man to believe that 'gods' had come amongst them. Primitive man would have known nothing about 'gods,' so I believe the word has been applied gratuitously by modern assessors as an assumption of what was assumed they 'might' have thought.

The 'visitors from space' hypothesis is well supported by many ruins discovered in Chile, Peru, Bolivia and other parts of the world. Many could only have been designed and produced by the use of modern skills and tools.

For more information go to:

http://www.theruthlesstruth.com/2010/08/20/tiwanaku-bolivia-crystalinks/.

As intriguing and very plausible as the hypothesis of extraterrestrial visitors is, I chose to look elsewhere for answers, which probably lay buried some 40 000 years ago in our own ancient evolutionary history. It became increasingly obvious it would be very difficult to find them. Not surprising really since people have been lost for answers to questions arising from events that occurred more recently than that.

For example, who decided to build Stonehenge on Salisbury Plain in Wiltshire, England approximately 4 210 years ago, and why?

Was it the ancient English at a time when they were moving from the Stone Age era into the Iron Age? Or was it the ancient Welsh whose skeleton bones have been discovered close to the site, and from whose region in Preseli Hills in south Wales, some 240 km from Salisbury Plain, the inner circle of huge blue stone rocks originated?

It is recognised as being one of the most important megalithic monuments in Europe but for years nobody appeared to know who thought about it, designed and built it and for what reason.

Without the collection of missing pieces from the larger picture of that period of time in history, experts have been obliged to put forward suggestions based upon their interpretations of what they perceive.

Some people suggested that Stonehenge might have had religious and astronomical purposes but there is no irrefutable proof to support this. It was definitely erected well before the Druids arrived on the scene, even though present day Druids claim it has relevance to their solstice celebrations.

Stonehenge has been standing there, clinging to its secrets and defiantly challenging anyone to unravel the mystery of its purpose and creation for centuries. In the absence of any definitive proof we were left with intelligent guesswork and interpretations of all available evidence.

But further research eventually triumphed.

Project leaders Professors Timothy Darvill and Geoffrey Wainwright believe Stonehenge was a centre of healing. They have compared the monument to a "Neolithic Lourdes," to which sick people travelled from far away hoping to be healed by the stones' powers.

Prof. Darvill was reported as saying: "Stonehenge would attract not only people who were unwell, but people who were capable of healing them. Therefore, in a sense, Stonehenge becomes the 'A & E' (Accident and Emergency) centre of southern England."

If true, this would push religious attachments to Stonehenge right out of the picture. Or would it? Will we ever know the full truth about Stonehenge? (http://www.nationalgeographic.com/history/ancient/stonehenge.html)

It has become apparent to me that even the most popular religions practised today were founded upon unsupported word of mouth stories, and interpretations, largely by people who actually wanted to believe them.

I was unable to find definitive answers to my questioning research relating to the birth of religious belief so, in much the same way as many others, I had to make my own interpretations and to draw my own conclusions from available information, then factor in the opinions of specialists before making my own informed assumptions.

In so doing I endeavoured to think like those early thinkers and to imagine the conditions under which they were living and how those conditions might have influenced their thought processes and actions.

Perhaps being advantaged by their now finely tuned sense of animal instinct and cunning, they were able to devise a plan to convince their respective leaders, and other community members, that their thoughts and counselling abilities were uniquely valuable assets to the entire community.

The plan would have to be bold, convincing and unassailable. It would have to be presented in a manner that would raise a measure of fear of the unknown in the minds of community members. What is more, it had to work first time. There would be no second chance because failure would have probably ended their ambitions for status and positions as counsellors and advisers. It might also have ended their lives.

Those thinkers may have been carefully studying their peasant stock communities, comprising hunter gatherers and perhaps semi-agricultural workers.

The hunter-gatherers will have been accumulating knowledge of their own, gaining an understanding of animal habits and migratory patterns, while the farmers would have been wholly reliant upon their abilities to predict weather conditions prevailing at seasonal times of change to ensure sufficient water for irrigation and a warm sun to ripen their crops.

The thinkers may have acquired an understanding of the fundamentals of hunting, gathering and crop growing to be comparable with those who engaged in such a way of life. They might even have been hunter gatherers or crop growers themselves at some time during their lives. But being dedicated thinkers with an urgent personal empowerment mission to accomplish, they will have looked beyond the fundamentals of those activities and studied all preconditions that would favour or militate against intended results. It's what thinkers tend to do.

This is particularly so in our world today where knowledge and information are highly valued and marketable assets, so I believe this is a reasonable assumption to make.

My hypothesis suggests the successful thinkers, whose lives and habits later contributed to the trail of material evidence that modern science has been able to accurately evaluate, chose a denominator that was common to all activities, coated it with a liberal shroud of mystique and added the essential element of fear to get the people's undivided attention.

The sun would have been a brilliant choice because it affected all aspects of life directly or indirectly and indeed continues to do so.

Archaeological records show us the sun was a very popular and predominant icon of early pagan worship.

One of our thinkers might have embellished his assumed power by proclaiming to possess a unique form of communicating relationship with the sun, by which he exclusively received commands and instructions that had to be obeyed and followed without question by the people. To make quite sure the message was clearly understood by the community, he possibly added the warning from the Sun God that failure to do so would be met with punishment of great suffering or even death for the offender.

There is sufficient scientifically collected evidence to prove that death by execution and sacrifice was frequently performed as part of many paganistic ceremonial events, notably during the period of sun worship.

Our thinkers, brimming with confidence and assurance, and having become firmly proclaimed and accepted by the people as their High

Priest of the Sun God, ably assisted by aspirant candidates for entry into the newly created pagan order, together with a few well chosen handmaidens, would have encouraged and convinced the territorial leader to declare his formal and public approval and adoption of the Sun God Deity.

The quid pro quo for the leader would have been the guaranteed assurance of absolute loyalty from the entire community who were clearly seen to be firmly supportive of the High Priest, through whom he would enjoy a consequential strengthening of his leadership rule.

Such a newly forged co-operative governance deal could have resulted in the self-proclaimed High Priest deriving more that a fair share of the ruling power for himself, directly through his pagan ministry and indirectly through his increased strength of leadership counselling. This form of power sharing between national and religious leaders has been very apparent throughout history in many parts of the world and prevails even today.

In some of our present day nations the influence of religious power in matters of state is overtly apparent, while in others it has become absolute.

I believe it is reasonable to assume, as mentioned earlier, that the foundations of all religions were created by mankind, those early entrepreneurial, visionary and laterally thinking members of the human race. Those early pagan religious faiths probably became the templates for the more mysterious spiritual religions that followed much later.

So, are you trying to tell us that the more popular religions of today all came about because of the pagan rituals of sun worshipping? I don't think people are going to buy that one.

No, I am not suggesting that at all. I am, however, suggesting that the ability of paganism to attract such enormous support from communities, may have encouraged the creators of other forms of worship to proceed with high expectations of success.

The example of sun worship is one of the most commonly known forms of paganism to which people of today can relate. There are many other pagan icons known to man, such as various birds, animals, mountains, trees, rivers, the moon and other celestial bodies.

Paganism is the longest running form of worship known to man and is still practised throughout the world today. Like all other religions, it relied entirely upon those three essential core principles – mystery, obedience and fear – to attract and to hold its followers, to consolidate and expand its power base and to amass wealth and power for the preachers.

The mystery principle appears to have been, and still remains, one of the most important of the three in many of the religions practised today. It is the shroud of invisibility covering that which is proclaimed to be the magnificent substance of truth, which can never be unambiguously described or credibly revealed to those who yearn to know and to see. They simply have to have faith and believe.

Then there is the principle of fear which, when related to a number of both ancient and modern Deities can be quite dreadful. In generalised terms I believe the fear factor was created to ensure obedience to the Deity by revealing to potential detractors the dreadful fate that awaited them after death and sometimes just before.

I continue to wonder what has enabled religious belief to become such an ingrained part of the human psyche. Why has such a powerful influence over the minds of people always been shrouded in secrecy, mystery and fear. Why have people permitted themselves so willingly over centuries, to savagely slaughter their fellow human beings in the name of the faith and the god in which they happen to believe?

Are we to assume they simply had blind faith in what they have been told and in what they have been persuaded to believe?

This might be the case as far as paganism is concerned but you can't paint the more formalised and widely accepted religions with the same brush. I assume you researched them and were able to give them your stamp of approval.

Yes, I did further research on a number of religions, but only those which I thought to be more popularly known by the majority of people. Until such time as at least one of the many gods and alleged creators of our universe makes an appearance in my lifetime, religious institutions will never receive my stamp of approval.

Researching any subject can be a lengthy and time consuming exercise. Studying and assessing the results of research takes even longer. I really wanted to get a reasonably accurate arrival date of religious worship into the human psyche.

And did you?

No, but I discovered that many people, much wiser than me and with far more sophisticated resources and networking facilities at their disposal, were also unable to put more than an educated guess on a period of time when religion may have begun.

As far as I can determine there are two scientific time scales relative to the history of mankind: the Neolithic and the Palaeolithic which is divided into the lower, middle and upper Palaeolithic.

The full Palaeolithic stretches from approximately 3 million – 12 000 B.C. and man's migration from the Cradle of Humanity in South Africa started only 100 000 years ago.

The Lower Palaeolithic covers 3 million – 70 000 B.C.; the Upper covers 40 000 – 12 000 B.C., and the Middle is obviously the period in between.

The Neolithic is categorised as the South West Asian (9 000 – 6 000 B.C.) and the North European is (4 000 – 2 400 B.C.).

That was a huge number of historical years in which to dig around to search for answers to any questions, let alone those for which you were searching.

Indeed it was, but it's hardly any time at all compared to the life spans of many other species on the planet. The humble and much despised cockroach, for example, has been around for approximately 127 million years. Man's time on Earth is but a very brief moment by comparison, which leaves the door wide open for those who put forward quite compelling and reasonable arguments for the visitors from outer space hypothesis.

Meanwhile, there was a need to find that particular time in history when one man's thoughts could be conveyed with authority to other men, in a way that could be clearly understood and accepted. In other words the time when we stopped grunting and became able to converse with each other.

Rudimentary forms of language are thought to have started in 48 000 B.C. and I had estimated pagan worship to have started about 40 000 B.C.

A member of the archaeological science, Prof. Trevor Watkins, (http://www.arcl.ed.ac.uk/arch/watkins/watkins.html) delivered a paper at the Liverpool conference of BANEA, (the British Association for Near Eastern Archaeology) in January 2001, and I reproduce passages from his paper enabling you to compare professional and expert opinions and estimates with my own.

Under the heading 'The Upper Palaeolithic Revolution,' Prof. Edwards wrote:

"The idea that hominid cognitive faculties and their evolution, are at least as important as changes in cranial morphology and brain size, has been gaining ground in recent years."

He reviewed the opinion that Homo sapiens and Neanderthals had co-existed for tens of thousands of years in south west Asia, until the latter disappeared rather abruptly.

He mentioned the cranium and brain size of Homo sapiens have remained virtually unchanged from approximately 100 000 years ago up to the present time, and that Homo sapiens developed cultural faculties which advantaged them over the Neanderthals.

"So we can infer that the competitive advantage began to show only at the very end of the middle Palaeolithic," he said.

I have assumed that to be about 40 000 years ago at the time when man had reached a new phase in human evolution.

He then said:

"Linguists interested in the evolution of language, believe that the first modern language – that is, a language that is as complex and powerful as any language you can find in the modern world – would have been evolved around 50 000 years ago."

Interestingly it is believed that artistic capabilities evolved in tandem with language, and that art was probably used as a symbolic method of depicting certain verbal expressions into descriptive visual records.

For example, paintings of people hunting and slaughtering an animal might have been a visual artistic record of an actual event having taken place, that concluded in a welcome feast for all concerned.

While it might be reasonable to suggest this heralded the beginning of writing, the experts believe that writing – or as they call it: "the externalised symbolisation of language expressions" – did not occur until only 5 000 years ago, e.g. about 3 000 B.C. which is not very long ago.

It is not surprising, therefore, that the search for evidence of the beginning of religion has to be conducted during a period of time extending over thousands of years, when word of mouth was the only form of communication, punctuated perhaps by reward for believers and grievous bodily harm for dissenters!

Important events such as commands and proclamations had to be committed to memory, much of which will have been crafted into stories and fables, which became embellished legends woven into the cultural fabric of early societies.

We all know how the essence of stories can change when relayed by word of mouth, person to person, even over a very short period of time. An embellishment here, a new word there and a sprinkling of additional bits and pieces thrown in for good measure. It's a normal human trait.

The reliability of many ancient artefacts and much of the centuries-old folklore, has been found to be extremely questionable. Experts in such matters will endeavour to interpret the meaning and substance of what is before them and share their findings with peers in a bid to find consensus. The outcome will be an opinion of experts based upon their collective expertise, albeit unsupported by irrefutable proof. There appears to be evidence to suggest that artistic impressions of events, people, commands and icons of worship occurred at some point during this time.

While there is good reason to presume that religion began during that era, an accurate starting date cannot be determined. Prof. Watkins emphasised this point in his paper:

"In fact, we know as little about the origin and evolution of religious representations as we know about the origin and evolution of symbolic representation in terms of material culture.

"The problems start with the cross-cultural, general definition of religion.

"In days gone by, most people in this country *[England]* would have claimed experience of religion, but overwhelmingly it would have been experience of Christianity. We would not say that someone brought up to speak English was ipso facto knowledgeable about linguistics, and it would be as illogical to presume that someone brought up in a particular Christian faith could, by the same token, claim expertise in comparative religion.

Ironically, we are almost the first generation to have access to such a wide variety of evidence about the world's religions, and yet many people today have no experience of religion at all."

You can better understand the problem with which I was confronted.

His paper concluded with a very definite and professionally motivated statement:

"In short, there is no single, convincing account of the nature of religion and religious experience, and there certainly isn't an account of the evolution of religious representations. And there won't be one, at least until the relevant prehistoric archaeological material is investigated in appropriate ways.

There are two important and related projects here: the investigation of the cognitive evolution of symbolic culture, and its application to the problem of the evolution of cosmological thought and expression.

I think that that is one of the most exciting challenges for archaeologists in the years to come."

So although my search for reliable and dependable evidence was in vain, I was at least comforted by the knowledge that experienced experts have been equally unsuccessful.

All very interesting but what does it actually prove? Although you have quoted an expert's opinion and interpretation, it is still only an interpretation, not a statement of fact.

Exactly so, and all available evidence relating to the more popular religions researched, predominantly those practised by millions of people around the world today, can be similarly rated as having derived from interpretations of less than reliable stories and folklore, all lacking any dependable substance or evidential truth whatsoever.

So what did you find from your research of major religions?

I decided to begin with the oldest and longest running religion and work my way through to a younger faith.

The Hindu Faith – a brief overview

Hinduism, which is deemed by many to be the oldest spiritual religion in the world, having an enormous and devout following, seemed to be an appropriate starting point.

Some experts believe Hinduism began with the Vedas, who are said to have preceded universal creation and described as being the breath exhaled by the Almighty Brahma (God/Creator.)

Such a proclamation required a great deal of knowledge and understanding to comprehend.

Being disadvantaged in that regard, I searched for someone with the competence to explain the history of Hinduism in words that would be understood by the majority of people, particularly myself. After comparing the presentation and content of a number of web sites, I finally decided upon the one dealing with what was said to be the 'True History and the Religion of India[12]' according to His Divinity Swami Prakashanand Saraswati.

Whereas Saraswati contends Hinduism began at the time of creation of our entire planetary system by Brahma 155.52 trillion years ago, other Hindu experts also believe it started at the time of universal creation, alleged by them, however, to have been only 2.8 billion years ago.

Certain Vedic scholars say it started later still, at the time of creation of the human race itself, which they put at 1.34 million years ago, while their Vedas counterparts say that Hinduism is only 50 000 years old.

Most Indian historians suggest 10 000 years is closer to the truth, while Western researchers and scholars put it at 6 000 years, started by the Aryan invaders of the Indus Valley.

Not a very good start, I told myself, but typical of the confusion I had come to expect. Not only is the age, the origin and the creative purpose of Hinduism shrouded in mystery and confusion, but I had difficulty understanding the fundamentals of the religion itself. It appears to comprise a number of different Deities with many different gods and goddesses and, as with all other religions, I could find no reliable or credible clues to suggest why and how any of them came to be. The seemingly essential ingredient of mystique found in all religions is very apparent in Hinduism.

The scholastic minds of Hindu specialists have apparently been unable to find consensus regarding the launch date of the faith, and Swami Prakashanand Saraswati's proclamation that it all started trillions of years ago may be regarded by many, including myself, as unbelievable. Hindu specialists could not put a reliable starting date on the faith, which applies to several others.

Since religion is universally immersed in a sea of confusion and deep mystery, realistic interpretations of scriptures and the composition of doctrines remains suspect.

Buddhism

If I was spiritually inclined I believe this is the philosophy to which I would be attracted.

I have not researched it to any great depth, but the little I know reveals it to be a philosophy of love, respect and peaceful coexistence, rather than a religion.

Aspects of the philosophy that appeal to me are respect towards parents, elders, teachers, friends and servants; behaviour that accords with the advice given by the Buddha, who encouraged generosity to the poor and to friends and relatives.

During earlier research, looking for people in history who sought to turn people away from selfishness, conflict, brutality and the many other disturbing aspects of life that caused so much unhappiness and intolerance, I came across King Asoka[23]. He was the third monarch of the Indian Mauryan dynasty and regarded as one of the most exemplary rulers in world history.

However, Buddhist literature preserved the legend of Asoka as having been a cruel and ruthless king who, in his early years of rule slaughtered thousands of his subjects, seemingly for no particular reason whatsoever. During one such act of genocide he apparently became overcome by remorse and stopped it immediately.

He converted to Buddhism and thereafter established a virtuous reign. It was only in the nineteenth century that a large number of edicts, in India, Nepal, Pakistan and Afghanistan came to light, which revealed how King Asoka changed his life so completely. They showed how this powerful and capable ruler attempted to establish an empire founded upon righteousness.

His reign became one that made the moral and spiritual welfare of his subjects his prime objective.

According to Ven. S. Dhammika, the spiritual director of the Buddha Dhamma Mandala Society in Singapore, Asoka encouraged harmlessness towards all life forms.

I was attracted to this statement because it aligned with my own beliefs that all life forms, including mankind, had the right to share space together on the planet. Earth and its abundant resources are not the exclusive property of mankind. More precisely, they are not the property of elitist minorities within our species.

In conformity with the Buddha's advice, Asoka also considered moderation in spending and regarded the habit of saving to be good. Treating people properly was much more important than performing ceremonies that were supposed to bring good luck and favours from divine domains.

I was particularly pleased to learn that Asoka desired that people should be knowledgeable and respectful of other people's religions, which is sadly lacking in the world today, and something I believe should be vigorously promoted in global education systems.

The Jewish faith

Searching for what I hoped to be a faithful and unbiased record of the Jewish religious history, I decided upon a work by Flavius Josephus[18] because of the historical date of his writings.

It is believed Josephus wrote seven books in about 75 A.D. covering the war between the Jews and the Romans and eighteen years later (93 A.D.) he wrote his "Antiquities of the Jews," which included the constitution of government and Jewish law, translated from Hebrew to Greek, and more recently translated into English and other languages. It was written during the time of the Roman Empire, close to the birth of Christianity and long before Islam.

He would estimate it to be about 3 931 years ago (from 2006), since Moses the legislator lived and brought forth the word of God.

In the preface to his work Josephus goes to some considerable lengths to make excuses for the misinterpretation of Jewish law by some post-Moses legislators. It would appear there was an old, and even today, irresistible tendency for Jews to 'bend the rules' to suit any number of circumstances, particularly in matters relating to financial transactions between Jews and the almost mandatory adherence to the profit motif.

The fundamentals of the Jewish religion begin with the Old Testament which Josephus draws upon to explain all creation according to Moses.

Whereas modern philosophers argue amongst themselves what the duration of one day might have been at the time of creation, it is said the entire project took six days, as proclaimed in the well known book of Genesis. However, I could find no reference from Moses to say when the actual date of creation was thought to have been.

Most people throughout the world are familiar with one or other of the Genesis versions of creation. This is the one that Jewish people believe according to Josephus.

He wrote that Moses recounts that on the first day, when God created the heaven and the earth, it was shrouded in thick darkness. So he commanded that there should be a period of darkness and of light and that the darkness shall be called night and the light period shall be day.

Apart from failing to say what "the heaven" was, he shows confusion about the processes that enable light and darkness, day and night. Neither of these would have been possible four days before the appearance of the sun, the moon and all other celestial bodies.

Nevertheless, on the second day Moses tells us God placed the heaven over the whole world keeping them separated from each other.

On the third day he made the land and sea to appear and commanded the plants and trees to spring out of the earth.

On the fourth day he placed the sun, the moon, and the other bodies in the sky above, arranging their motions and courses so that seasons could be signified.

On the fifth day he produced the living creatures which would live in the seas and those that would fly in the sky, sorting them into species and endowing them with the ability to procreate in order that they might increase and multiply.

On the sixth day he created the four-footed beasts male and female, and he also formed man.

I believe this is an early point in the Old Testament when one of the many predictable religious confusions makes an appearance.

There are two versions of creation in Genesis and, according to Josephus, Jews accept and believe the familiar Adam and Eve version in Genesis 2.

But let us first consider the Genesis 1 version of what happened on the sixth day.

Here is a verbatim extract of Genesis 1 verses 24-31 taken from the 1980 sixth impression of the Good News Bible, which compares similarly with my own, much older Holy Bible printed in London by British and Foreign Bible Society prefaced with the words:

> "Containing the Old and New Testaments translated out of the original tongues and with the former translations diligently compared and revised by His Majesty's special command, A.D. 1611. Appointed to be read in Churches."

On the sixth day:

> "Then God commanded, *'Let the earth produce all kinds of animal life: domestic and wild, large and small' – and it was done. So God made them all and he was pleased with what he saw.'*
>
> Then God said:
>
> *'And now we will make human beings, they will be like us and resemble us. They will have power over the fish, the birds, and all animals, domestic and wild, large and small.'*

He created them male and female, blessed them, and said:

> *'Have many children, so that your descendants will live all over the earth and bring it under their control. I am putting you in charge of the fish, the birds, and all the wild animals. I have provided all kinds of grain and all kinds of fruit for you to eat; but for all the wild animals and for all the birds I have provided grass and leafy plants for food.'*

And it was done. God looked at everything he had made and he was very pleased. Evening passed and morning came – that was the sixth day."

So, in this version we are told God created human beings (plural), making them to be like himself and some others ("like us"). He and his assistants created a number of human beings, male and female to take control of all other living things.

This version favours the plausible hypothesis that Genesis is a confirmation that extraterrestrial visitors probably created or genetically modified mankind. Genesis 6: 1-2 records that:

"When mankind had spread all over the world, and girls were being born, some sons of God saw the girls were beautiful and took some for their wives."

Could it be that those early scribes trying to interpret the stories of Moses, chose to believe that a being descending from the 'heavens' could have only been a God, when in fact he might have been a visitor from space? The reported "sons of God" might have been other crew members.

The whole event has possibly been recorded by ancient and uninformed scribes, as a misinterpretation of what might have been a highly advanced form of genetic engineering.

Nevertheless, in Genesis 2:7 we are given another version which, according to Flavius Josephus, is the one found in Jewish history.

In this version we are told God took dust from the ground, formed it into the shape of man, inserted a spirit and soul inside, breathed life-giving breath into his nostrils and called him Adam, which is a Hebrew word signifying one that is red, because the colour of the dust was red.

He then created the Garden of Eden for Adam and planted all manner of fruit trees, telling Adam to cultivate and guard the garden.

Then God said:

> *"It is not good for the man to live alone. I will make a suitable companion to help him."*

God then took some soil from the ground and made all sorts of animals and birds and introduced the creatures to Adam and it was he, Adam, who gave them the names by which they are known, even today!

Was it God's intention to create Adam as the 'Lone Game Ranger' of his huge game park we call Earth? Was he to ensure the creatures worked and multiplied according to the divine plan?

According to Josephus, Moses said God "suddenly noticed" that Adam had no female companion and corrected his 'mistake' by making a woman thus:

'When God saw that Adam had no female companion, for there was no such creation, and he realized that Adam could not procreate like all the other creatures, God put Adam to sleep.

While he was in this state, God took away one of Adam's ribs and formed it into a woman.

When God brought the woman to Adam he knew her instantly and acknowledged that she was made from himself."

Although the Hebrew word for woman is Issa, Genesis 3:20 tells us Adam named her Eve, which signifies the mother of all human beings.

I detect a situation here where Moses has cast God in the role of an "absent-minded professor" while simultaneously introducing his audience to the wonders of genetic engineering from body parts.

This somewhat confused, and undoubtedly unkind attempt to explain woman's creation, nevertheless brings into debate the whole question of genetic engineering as we understand it today.

Dissidents who condemn the practice, put forward a number of reasons for so doing, including on religious grounds.

Protagonists might argue that no greater authority than God has already established a biological, genetic and ethical precedent.

As the Greek proverb proclaims: "If God be with us, everything that is impossible becomes possible."

Nevertheless, Josephus wrote that Moses recorded that on the seventh day God rested and Jews call this day the Sabbath which denotes rest in the Hebrew tongue.

The "after thought" and bizarre creation of Eve is actually very worrying in my opinion. In so many global religions women have always been considered inferior to their male counterparts and the measure of inferiority can vary quite dramatically.

It begs the question, therefore, to what extent has the inferior status of women throughout the world today been supported through the observance of outdated cultural, religious and mystical doctrines, such as the Adam and Eve story?

After all if, as in Genesis 2:22, God forgot to create Eve alongside Adam but had remembered to provide all other living creatures with female companions, this reduces Eve to something of an after-thought in the entire assortment of living things on Earth. Accordingly, all females who followed after her spare rib creation were destined to become beasts of burden for men and the convenient bearers of children in the painful pursuit of procreation. The painful aspect is discussed further on.

Nearly 4 000 years ago, the reason for womens inferior position in society would not have been a debatable issue. It was a given, as indeed it remains in some parts of the world today.

The social standing of women in Moses' time was practically zero. They certainly had little or no control over their personal destinies.

As Moses relates in Exodus 21:7, a man can sell his daughter as a slave, whereafter she could not be set free as a male slave could.

A male baby would have a position of greater importance within the family and society than his mother, which is indeed the case today in a number of other religions and cultures. In Swaziland for example, the legal status of women only overtook that of a male minor as recently as 2006. A national survey on violence experienced by female children and youths in that country found that two-thirds of women are beaten and abused, with sixty percent of females being coerced or forced into their first sexual experience.

Not surprisingly a shocking 49 percent of Swazi women aged between 25 and 29 are HIV-positive, reflecting the low status and high sexual abuse of women in that shameful Kingdom territory.

Moses certainly pulled no punches when describing the reasons for all women to be utterly beholden to men for their very presence on Earth. Then he rubbed salt into the wound by blaming Eve for leading the virtuous, and clearly very gullible Adam up the garden path of temptation to evil.

Moses says in Genesis 2:8:

God planted a paradise in the east (Eden) wherein there was a tree of life and a tree of knowledge for an understanding of good and evil and he commanded them both to take care of all the plants.

He also commanded them they should eat of all the plants but to abstain from the tree of knowledge which, if they touched it would prove their destruction.

If it was so dangerous why plant it?

Now at that time a serpent lived with Adam and his wife.

(A strange domestic pet!)

Moses tells us it had an envious disposition towards their happy living and their obedience to the commands of God.

With malicious intent the serpent told them they should taste the fruit of the tree of knowledge and obtain the understanding of what was good and what was evil, and they would lead a happy life.

Eve tasted the fruit of the tree and being pleased with it persuaded Adam to taste it also.

Moses has clearly excused Adam – and all men thereafter - for not taking control of the situation and for breaking the trust that God had placed upon him to manage the affairs of all living things, including his cloned woman.

Every man today who accepts this account of creation should be carrying the lion's share of shame and blame arising from Adam's weakness and disobedience.

Moses tells us what happened next:

"Immediately they both became conscious of their nakedness and were ashamed.

They tied fig leaves together as clothing to cover themselves which made them more comfortable before each other.

When God came into the garden Adam ran away. This surprised God because Adam usually enjoyed talking with God.

When he realized what had taken place he punished Adam and his wife."

We should be surprised they were both naked because, in Genesis 3:21, we are told that God had made clothes out of animal skins for them after creating Eve. More religious confusion.

Once again the omnipotent and omnipresent God must have known what had happened. Why does Moses persist in belittling God in his story by saying he was "surprised" when Adam ran away?

> *"He told Adam that plants would no longer grow freely from the soil, and that he would have to plant and tend his crops and that some might grow and others might not.*
>
> *He told Eve she would in future be inconvenienced in breeding, and would endure sharp pains in bringing forth children because of tempting Adam to taste the fruit of the tree of knowledge.*
>
> *He removed from the serpent the ability to speak and placed poison in its mouth so it would become an enemy of mankind.*
>
> *He also removed its legs and forced it to slither along the ground.*
>
> *He then removed Adam and Eve out of the garden into another place."*

I have difficulty commenting dispassionately upon these words of Moses. For what possible reason would God create evil and why would he, by the use of a talking serpent with legs, tempt his young inexperienced and illiterate humans into disobedience of his will? Was Moses once again, in his own inimitable and uninformed way, trying to give comprehendible reasons to his followers for the difficult conditions under which they lived at the time?

Was he adding to the inherent guilt complexes of women, divine reasons for them to be subservient to men? Was he explaining to them the reasons why childbirth was painful and in some cases fatal, by blaming it all on the temptress woman Eve? Was he trying to tell men that a woman had duped them into suffering an interminable existence of lifelong toil and hardship, and that men were innocent victims of Eve's impropriety?

In other words, was he actually composing a fictional fable to vindicate the culture of his time, and women's subordinate place in it, rather than a serious account of creation?

Neither Moses nor Josephus ventured to say what the equivalent ages of Adam and his cloned wife were on their creation birthdays. With such responsibilities placed upon him, I imagine Adam would need to have the mental and administrative capabilities of a 30-year old man.

Nevertheless, Josephus tells us the couple had two sons, Cain and Able and that Cain murdered his brother and that God "cast him out of the land."

Adam and Eve had previously been cast out from the Garden of Eden, so to which other deserted region of the world would Cain have been sent? Nevertheless, after travelling over many 'countries' he and his 'wife' (who must have been his sister!) built a city named Nod.

Rather than settle down and attempt to mend his ways to regain the trust of God, Cain continued his wicked ways.

According to Josephus, Cain decorated his home with things of great wealth stolen from other people and eventually became the leader of equally wicked men. He set boundaries about lands and built a fortified city called Enoch after the name of his eldest son.

Incredulously, in the deserted part of the world to which he was banished, hordes of other people are conjured up from thin air by Moses. Countries – that could not have existed – allegedly full of people who materialised from nowhere, with valuable possessions they could not have possessed, keep cropping up all over the place.

Did they all derive from Adam and Eve? Were they more of God's cast offs? The mystery continues – as usual and quite predictably.

Here comes a real Moses masterpiece according to Flavius Josephus:

> *"Nay, even while Adam was alive, it came to pass that the posterity of Cain became exceeding wicked, every one successively dying, one after another, more wicked than the former.*
>
> *They were intolerable in war, and vehement in robberies, and if anyone were slow to murder people, yet was he bold in his profligate behaviour, in acting unjustly, and doing injuries for gain.*
>
> *Now Adam, who was the first man, and made out of the earth, after Abel was slain and Cain fled away, was solicitous for posterity and had a vehement desire of children, he being two hundred and thirty years old, after which time he lived another seven hundred and then died."*

What can one say?

If we are to believe that Adam lived for 930 years and at the tender age of 230 was still able to produce children, it was obviously the age of supermen and superwomen, albeit a wicked bunch! Or should we question Adam's alleged great age in view of the words in Genesis 6: 3 which state:

"Then the Lord said: 'I will not allow people to live for ever; they are mortal. From now on they will live no longer than a hundred and twenty years."

Also, was Eve still alive and bearing children, presumably with more pain and discomfort than modern women could possibly imagine, or was Adam committing incest with his two daughters and presumably their daughters ad nauseam? If so, how could Moses come up with his statement in Leviticus 18:6 "do not have sexual intercourse with any of your relatives."

If Adam and Eve had applied that edict, then clearly their children would have been the first and last human beings on Earth and our species will have become extinct rather quickly.

Extinction of the species was addressed by Moses in his incredible story about the great flood, starring Noah - who was tenth from Adam - and the magnificent Ark.

He tells us in Genesis 6: 7 God decided to wipe out all living things, including the entire human race, saving Noah, his wife and sons and their wives. They were commanded:

> *"…. put into the ark not only other provisions, to support their wants there, but also sent in with the rest all sorts of living creatures, the male and his female, for the preservation of their kinds; and others of them by seven pairs of two."*

I have to ask why God couldn't get it right first time? Is he actually fallible?

> ***You know, we are all familiar with the story of Noah and the Ark, and I imagine like myself, most people regard it as just that, a story rather than a record of fact.***
>
> ***Do you really think it is worth while spending time picking it to pieces?***

An interesting and very reasonable observation, but not quite as accurate as you might imagine.

The story of the Flood is followed seriously by Jews, Christians and Muslims alike, and large numbers of people believe it to be an integral part of their overall belief in creation, as opposed to evolution.

There is a general belief the Ark came to ground after the flood somewhere on Mount Ararat in Turkey and people have devoted years searching for signs of its remains.

Apart from a couple of stupendous hoaxes some years ago, when alleged findings were reported, my research has revealed no reliable proof of the ark's existence whatsoever.

I have provided some website addresses – for and against the Ark Theory[19] – in the Annexure for those interested.

If it was simply a fairy story that nobody took seriously it would have no place in my book. As it happens, Noah's maritime adventure is believed by millions of people and I have to question their ability to really understand the magnitude of the task he was set.

For example, how did he overcome such things as selecting and felling trees suitable for an ark; converting them into boat building materials; designing a craft to accommodate a wide variety and number of life forms, with space for food and water? All this had to be accomplished using manpower as the only source of energy, with no tools other than those shaped from pieces of stone.

How many field workers would be required to select and round up thousands of land based life form species, and sort them into the requisite seven pairs of two?

And what about the fate of all those field workers who had so diligently and lovingly collected all the animal, reptile and insect passengers? They would not be on the passenger list so what was going to happen to them?

Nevertheless, we are told:

> *"The flood, which lasted for forty days, occurred on the twenty-seventh day of the second month of the six hundredth year of Noah's life."*

That period of time was 2 656 years after Adam, and according to Flavius:

> *".... the time is written down in our sacred books, those who then lived having noted down with great accuracy, both the births and deaths of illustrious men."*

My goodness, that is quite a revelation. Let's check those words again:

> *"... those who then lived having noted down...."* etc.

Is Flavius telling us that Jewish people believe Noah also took aboard a number of learned scribes, together with their volumes of instant history books to record events of the time?

Is he also telling us that language and writing – or "the externalised symbolisation of language expressions" as we learned earlier – as well as writing instruments and materials had already been invented, long before the flood actually occurred?

Perhaps we should overlook such things. We wouldn't want truth and reason to spoil the intriguing plot of a story.

I shall venture no further into the story because I am satisfied it has no relevance in mankind's history of evolution. Those with opposing views will be aware of the whole story, including the post-flood antics of Nimrod; the tower of Babylon; the emergence of the Greek civilisation and the creation of countries around the world.

Josephus makes the point by inference that all mankind, notably from the period after the Flood, derived from Noah and were destined, without reason or logical explanation, to become Jewish.

Those who are called Hebrews are, according to Josephus, so named from their progenitor Heber, not from Abraham the Hebrew as appears to be popularly believed.

According to Flavius Josephus' history of the Jewish people, he gives us an insight into how some apparently believe the universe was created, and how the Earth and its full complement of resident life forms came to be.

For those who are struggling to come to terms with the life spans of characters in the story, let me close with this statement from Josephus:

> *"Let no one, upon comparing the lives of the ancients with our lives, and with the few years which we now live, think that what we have said of them is false or make the shortness of our lives at present an argument that neither did they attain to so long a duration of life, for those ancients were beloved of God, and made by God himself and because their food was then fitter for the prolongation of life, might well live so great a number of years."*

Whatever it was they were eating in those days would certainly have exciting commercial prospects today.

Remember also, God had punished Adam 2 656 years earlier, telling him crops would not grow easily. He would have to tend them himself and some would fail.

A Jewish opinion of Jews

I shall now fast-forward a few thousand years and introduce Professor Israel Shahak (1933-2001) to you. He wrote a book entitled "Jewish History, Jewish Religion"[20] which contains some interesting observations concerning his Jewish peers in general and Israel in particular.

He casts a satirical eye upon the confusions, like those I have covered, found in any religion that tries to promote credibility for that which is discreditable or to justify that which is unjustifiable.

Professor Shahak was an Israeli Jew whose political activities began in 1965-66 with a protest that caused a considerable scandal at the time.

He had personally witnessed an ultra-religious Jew refuse to allow his landline telephone to be used on the Sabbath, in order to call an ambulance for a non-Jew who happened to have collapsed in his Jerusalem neighbourhood. (Cell phones had not yet been invented!)

Shahak arranged a meeting comprising rabbis nominated by the State of Israel asking them whether such behaviour was consistent with the interpretation of the Jewish religion.

They replied that the Jew in question had behaved correctly, indeed piously and backed their statement by referring him to a passage in an authoritative compendium of Talmudic laws, written in the twentieth century, to the effect that a Jew should not violate the Sabbath in order to save the life of a Gentile, unless the consequences would have put a Jewish life in danger.

I asked myself why an Israeli Jewish citizen would deny possible life-saving assistance to another Israeli citizen who was not Jewish, on the Sabbath, or indeed any day of the week?

If a white Christian man acted similarly against a black man in South Africa, his actions would be deemed outrageous, unforgivable, un-Christian, unconstitutional and racist. What is so different about Jews in the State of Israel?

Professor Shahak:

> "Let me begin with the official Israeli definition of the term 'Jewish', illustrating the crucial difference between Israel as 'a Jewish state' and the majority of other states.

By this official definition, Israel 'belongs' to persons who are defined by the Israeli authorities as 'Jewish', irrespective of where they live, and to them alone."

"On the other hand, Israel doesn't officially 'belong' to its non-Jewish citizens, whose status is considered, even officially, as inferior."

"This means in practise that if members of a Peruvian tribe are converted to Judaism, and thus regarded as Jewish, they are entitled at once to become citizens of Israel and to benefit from the approximately 70 percent of the West Bank land (and the 92 percent of the area of Israel proper), officially designated only for the benefit of Jews.

All non-Jews (not only all Palestinians) are prohibited from benefiting from those lands. The prohibition applies even to Israeli Arabs who served in the Israeli army and reached a high rank."

"The case involving Peruvian converts to Judaism actually occurred some years ago. The newly created Jews were settled in the West Bank, near Nablus, on land from which non-Jews are officially excluded."

"All Israeli governments are taking enormous political risks, including the risk of war, so that such settlements, composed exclusively of persons who are defined as 'Jewish' (and not 'Israeli' as most of the media mendaciously claims) would be subject to only 'Jewish' authority."

I suspect Jews in the USA or Britain would regard it as anti-Semitic if Christians proposed their nations should become officially 'Christian states,' belonging only to citizens officially defined as 'Christians.'

My goodness, that would put the cat amongst the pigeons. So, how does one define who is Jewish and who is not?

Prof. Shahak answered this for us:

"According to Israeli law, a person is considered Jewish if either their mother, grandmother, great-grandmother and great-great-grandmother was a Jewess by religion; or if the person was converted to Judaism in a way satisfactory to the Israeli authorities, and on condition that the person has not converted from Judaism to another religion, in which case Israel ceases to regard them as Jewish."

Now we know a little more about how a Jew is officially defined and even created in various parts of the world. This would make it evident that the State of Israel comprises a nation of advantaged Jews and disadvantaged non-Jews

This phenomenon of ethnically defined societies living in the same country is not unusual throughout the so-called civilized world, where the people share a common identity of nationality. However, they generally contribute to and share the social benefits. Why has Israel decided to be so different?

In his book, Prof. Shahak highlights many differences which distinctly benefit Jewish people and which are blatantly discriminatory against non-Jewish residents of Israel.

One glaring example is the ID card which everyone is obliged to carry at all times.

The carrier's 'nationality' can be recorded as 'Jewish', 'Arab', 'Druze' and the like with the significant exception of 'Israeli'.

This would appear to clearly imply that the country is not an 'Israeli state' at all but a 'Jewish state.'

Quite so, and it becomes very apparent when considering the circumstances of those citizens of Israel who left the country for a time and subsequently immigrated back, either in or out of accordance with the 'Law of Return'.

Those who ethnically comply with the definition of being Jewish and can therefore benefit from the Law of Return, are eligible for generous Customs benefits at the time of re-entry into Israel, to receive subsidy for their children's high school education and to receive either a grant or a loan on easy terms for the purchase of an apartment, as well as other benefits.

Returning non-Jewish citizens of Israel get none of these benefits.

Information on the Law of Return can be found at:

http://www.jewishvirtuallibrary.org/jsource/Immigration/Text_of_Law_of_Return.html.

The more I learned about Israel and its predominantly advantaged Jewish component, the more I became inclined to predict that a Middle

East settlement of international acceptability is unlikely ever to occur in that troubled region.

It also appears unlikely that national stability and true democracy will ever become a reality in Israel for all its citizens. I am of the opinion there are too many imponderables and far too many overtly discriminatory regulations to enable Israel to become an open and truly democratic society for all.

There is even confusion in many minds about the territorial boundaries of Israel.

According to Prof. Shahak there are a number of discrepant versions of the nation's Biblical borders, including one that encompasses areas within all of Sinai and part of northern Egypt up to the environs of Cairo; in the east all of Jordan and a large piece of Saudi Arabia, all of Kuwait and part of Iraq south of the Euphrates; in the north all of Lebanon and all of Syria together with a large part of Turkey up to lake Van; and Cyprus.

One can assume these boundaries are unattainable in today's world but, it is often stated by seemingly informed sources that Jewish power and the means by which it can be wielded, can be extremely effective in a number of the world's political circles.

Since the unforgivable horrors of the Nazi holocaust, after which the present state of Israel came into being, while riding upon the crest of global empathy and emotion, the Jewish political machinery has been running in overdrive working for international recognition and support.

We often hear, for example, that presidential elections in the USA are not won without Jewish influence and the inevitable quid pro quo. Predictably, I could find no evidentiary proof to support this.

Resistance from any global power, other than the USA, towards Israel's expansion of its territorial borders would be of little or no consequence in the grand scale of events.

It is important, therefore, that Israel secures and retains the support of the USA in all its endeavours by whatever means available. It must avoid becoming a liability for the USA, rather than the friendly asset it is generally regarded to be.

Although the Suez War in 1956 is buried in history, it should not be forgotten that in the Knesset on the third day of the war, David Ben-Gurion (1887-1973) announced the reason for the war was "the restoration of the kingdom of David and Solomon" to its Biblical borders.

There is every reason to assume that goal probably remains the long-term objective of the legislators of the Jewish state of Israel.

Remember also that Israel is an atomic power with an extremely dedicated, proficient, and oft quite brutal military force.

Judaism is perceived as having no regard for the lives of Gentiles and the military force might consider it a divine obligation to kill as many as possible under any conditions, particularly in times of unrest and war.

Israel appears to be a living example of how religious discrimination influences the lives of a country's citizens.

If Prof. Shahak's account was correct at the time and the same conditions prevail today, one is inclined to ask: what influences devout Jews to zealously support and follow such a racist and discriminatory religious faith? Is it an irresistible decision to accede to peer pressure to be an accepted member of an exclusive power collective, or is it a decision influenced solely by absolute fear of assumed alternatives?

To conclude my brief coverage of the Jewish religion and to bring further informed perspective into the subject, I give you the following passage from Prof. Shahak to think about:

> "Therefore, the real test facing both Israeli and Diaspora Jews is the test of their self-criticism, which must include the critique of the Jewish past.
>
> The most important part of such a critique must be a detailed and honest confrontation of the Jewish attitude to non-Jews.
>
> This is what many Jews justly demand from non-Jews: to confront their own past and so become aware of the discrimination and persecutions inflicted on the Jews.
>
> In the last [at the time] 40 years, the number of non-Jews killed by Jews is by far greater than the number of Jews killed by non-Jews.
>
> The extent of the persecution and discrimination against non-Jews, inflicted by the Jewish state with the support of organized

Diaspora Jews, is also enormously greater than the suffering inflicted on Jews by regimes hostile to them.

Although the struggle against anti-Semitism (and of all other forms of racial discrimination) should never cease, the struggle against Jewish chauvinism and exclusivity, which must include a critique of classical Judaism, is now of equal or greater importance."

Finally, in his book "After the Party – A Personal and Political Journey Inside the ANC," Andrew Feinstein includes a chapter captioned "On Being Jewish." It was written some years after Prof. Shahak's death.

In it, he quotes Sara Roy, the daughter of Holocaust survivors:

"*...in the post-Holocaust world, Jewish memory has faltered – even failed – in one critical respect: it has excluded the reality of Palestinian suffering and Jewish culpability therein. As a people we have been unable to link the creation of Israel with the displacement of the Palestinians. We have been unwilling to see, let alone remember, that finding our place meant the loss of theirs.*"

Is hers another voice in the wilderness or are there other like-minded Jews around the world?

Christianity

Some religious orders have created shameful histories for themselves.

The Christian military Crusaders of the 11th, 12th and 13th centuries for example, are believed to have slaughtered more people than were murdered during Hitler's holocaust.

The Roman Catholic Church's shameful 588 year period of Inquisition from 1232-1820, founded to hunt down people identified as being religious heretics and to slaughter them, generally by being burned to death at the stake, is yet another shameful piece of Christian history.

One well=known person who suffered this horrific form of death was France's historic heroine Jeanne d'Arc (Joan of Arc) who was executed thus in 1430. In what I perceive as a disgraceful attempt to redeem itself, the Catholic Church canonized her 490 years later in 1920.

The Catholic Church has recently suffered very expensive embarrassment running into hundreds of millions of US dollars in damages, arising from the sexual assault upon children by a number of their Priests.

I like to believe it wasn't Catholicism or Christianity that shamefully assaulted those children. I am more inclined to believe the priests were the sole offenders.

There are many horrifying records of religiously motivated brutality, directly and indirectly attributable to those who have sworn to preach peace, love, forgiveness, tolerance and the strict observance of all that is morally and spiritually right. It is the perpetrators who must be blamed, not necessarily the fundamentals of religion itself.

In one way or another religious influence has managed to force its way into the lives of people throughout the world for years. The conversion of "savages" in Africa to Christianity by missionaries is just one disgraceful example. , regardless of their religious persuasions.

The Power of Fear

In my opinion one of the cruelest applications of fear has been religion's promised punishment of eternal pain, suffering and damnation after death in a place called Hell, for those who fail to accept and adhere to religious doctrine.

This particular fear was, and largely remains, an essential weapon of most religious faiths and cultures. It has successfully bound many congregations to their particular churches for centuries.

The mythical domains of heaven and hell are essential elements of the full set of accoutrements, without which the business of religion would have no meaning, no power and ultimately no purpose.

Like any other well structured business, the terms and conditions published by the executive will encourage loyalty, with the promise of attractive rewards for the faithful, and a variety of unattractive penalties for those who disregard those terms and conditions.

With some reluctance I agree that cruelty has become a trademark for certain religious groups. With equal reluctance I accept that certain doctrines might be regarded as cruelly outdated by modern standards. But those who believe in their faiths do so through their own convictions and freedom of choice. Those, like yourself who are non-believers will not be affected or influenced in any way at all.

I accept and endorse what you say about the right of people to believe in, and to follow, any religious faith of their choice, provided it has no detrimental affect upon themselves or others. For example, the children of devoutly religious parents are given no choice in the adoption of a faith. They are obliged, as was I, to do as their parents tell them, which is actually undemocratic.

Contrary to what you say about non-believers, they can become affected, and sometimes gravely disadvantaged, by certain religious doctrines that regard non-believers of their particular faith as evil beings. Teaching Christianity in Islamabad, for example, is reported to be punishable by death under Islam's Sharia law. According to the same law, a student in Afghanistan accused of downloading a report on women's rights from the Internet faced the death penalty.

I wonder what the repercussions of Muslims living in a Christian country might be if that country's government proclaimed the same punishment for people accused of teaching Islam or any other non-Christian religion in that country, or for downloading material from the Internet deemed unsuitable by Christian standards?

There are irrefutable records proving religious intolerance and bigotry having wreaked pain, suffering, wars and death upon the human race for centuries. Indeed, religious intolerance continues.

Although religion itself might not be entirely to blame, the accusing finger can be more appropriately pointed at the people who interpret scriptures and folklore and write the rules and act upon them according to their own personal interpretation.

The apparent ease with which acts of aggression are inflicted by religious zealots upon non-believers, or those of different faiths, can so often be linked to doctrine. It becomes so natural to use violence when punishment is an essential part of deity doctrine. It has been successful in securing obedience from congregations and for killing detractors for centuries. Some religious philosophies appears to proclaim - if it works don't fix it!

When religious precedents have been firmly established, they quickly become an integral part of the psyche and culture of practitioners and followers alike. They become part of the common template used for designing the fundamental structures of most religious doctrines.

Punishment has been firmly established in that template and its nature and form, as introduced by non-pagan religions, became harsher over the years. Perhaps this was a consequence of many translations and interpretations of early scriptures and cultures.

I am of the view that the punishment factor is entirely unnecessary. It has a history of getting so dreadfully out of control, often with horrifying results. I believe it is evil.

The Islamic Faith

Having considered the Jewish faith in some depth earlier, and being aware of the long enduring Middle East culture of conflict between the Jewish and Palestinian communities, I considered a research of the Islamic faith to be appropriate and necessary.

Before imparting the results of my research on Islam, I believe it is important for me to first express my personal opinion of this particular faith. I do not regard it as a religion in the broadly accepted understanding of the word. I regard it more as a totalitarian ideological culture of hatred, committed to the pursuit of Jihad and world domination.

Nevertheless, I believe there is good reason to try and learn more about Islam because it has become so often associated with violence and terrorism by the media, by non-Islamic people and by a number of political heads of state.

I believe we should ask ourselves whether all the reported acts of violence by Islamic extremists were executed strictly in terms of Islamic doctrine, or were they attributable to a deliberate misinterpretation of the faith's objectives, in pursuit of the perpetrator's own selfish agendas? I hoped research would provide satisfactory answers.

Unfortunately, as with Hinduism my research of Islam was factually disappointing.

It begins with Muhammad, who was born in Makkah (Bakka, Baca, Mecca) in the year 570 A.D., the son of Abdullah of the family Hashim, the chief of the pagan worshipping tribe of Koreish

He was completely illiterate all his life, unable to read or write from birth to death.

The tribe worshipped idols at sunrise, noon, and at sunset and they faced the direction of the idol black stone and the Kaaba which, for reasons I could not determine, became the most sacred site in Islam.

Research led me to Drs. Zahoor and Haq[13] which assisted me to learn a little more of Muhammad's transition from paganism to an alternative form of religion of his own creation.

They record that angel Gabriel was said by Muhammad to have visited him as commanded by Allah revealing Ayat (meaning signs, loosely referred to as verses) in the Arabic language.

The first revelation was given to him while in a cave called Hira when he was 40 years old (610 A.D.). Further revelations continued over a period of 23 years to 633 A.D. He died that year at the age of 63.

He said the revelations he received were sometimes a few verses, a part of a chapter or the whole chapter. Some revelations came down in response to an inquiry by non-believers.

There are, however, conflicting accounts relating to the very important first revelation.

According to Sir. William Muir[15] (1819-1905), the Sunni version states:

Gabriel bade Muhammad to "read" the verses presented to him:

"Read in the name of thy lord and cherisher who created: Created man out of a clot of congealed blood. Read! And thy lord is most bountiful, He who taught the use of pen, taught man that which he knew not".

The appearance of Gabriel surprised Muhammad and when he was ordered to read he said "I cannot read."

This happened three times, and each time Muhammad declared his inability to read the angel pressed him hard to his bosom in a futile attempt to make him read.

Eventually, Muhammad memorized and repeated the five verses whereupon the angel released him and disappeared.

This Sunni version also says he contemplated suicide upon his return home, believing his first encounter with Gabriel had actually been a visit from an evil spirit.

However, according to the Shia Muslims, far from being surprised or frightened by the appearance of Gabriel, Muhammad welcomed him as if he had been expecting him. They also say he would never have contemplated suicide.

The customary religious confusion persists.

I find the 23-year period of time to memorize the Qur'an puzzling.

Clearly, if Gabriel did actually deliver the revelations, but was not enabled by divine powers to transform Muhammad into a literate person with instant reading and writing skills, surely Muhammad's scribes could, over such a long period of time, have applied their joint efforts to achieve such a desirable result with his own encouragement.

Also, why spend 23 years teaching him the Qur'an in preparation for a massive global crusade then take his life in the last year of tutorship?

Experts who have studied the revelation issue thoroughly, remain doubtful about its authenticity, saying that if a spirit or angel actually did visit Muhammad in Hira, and later in other locations, it could not have been Gabriel[17].

After all, why would Gabriel use force upon Muhammad in an attempt to make him read? Gabriel is known to have been a great calming influence over people such as Mary, such as Zacharias the father of John the Baptist, such as the prophet Daniel.

Was this really Gabriel?

I also have difficulty believing Gabriel brought something with him for Muhammad to read. The omnipotent God would have known Muhammad could not read so I am sure he will not have sent Gabriel with reading material for presentation purposes, which leads to another anomaly. If Gabriel actually did present verses of the Qur'an for Muhammad to read, we must assume it already existed in printed form. Are we then required to accept that the printed version could not be made available to Muhammad or his scribes for duplicating purposes? I continue to be mystified by the apparent confusion relating to such an early stage in the story of Islam.

But then, according to information in the Islamic Library[14], a contrary opinion regarding the delivery of verses to Muhammad says he received them while he was alone in the mountain cave, suggesting there were no scribes in attendance at the time. This seems reasonable to me. If he was simply meditating in the cave, perhaps on pagan matters, with no expectations of a heavenly visitor, why would he need to be accompanied by scribes?

Apart from the clear confusion between the Sunni and Shia Muslim interpretations, and the mystery of what, if anything, was shown to Muhammad, I am compelled to wonder which particular god Muhammad might have thought his visitor was representing at the time of the alleged encounter. After all, he was a devout pagan worshipper at the time, so it is not unreasonable to assume he might have thought he had been visited by a messenger of the pagan icon of his faith.

Nevertheless, in one way or another, the verses were taken down over many years and the Qur'an was allegedly completed. However, I have been unable to find out where the original is located.

It is said that two copies of the copied text of the original, which was said to have been authenticated by Muhammad, do exist. One at the museum in Tashkent in Russia and the other at the Topkapi Museum in Istanbul, Turkey. But these are only copies of copies, not copies of the original. So where is the original?

With limited research skills and facilities at my disposal, I decided to compare my results with those of dedicated professionals. I browsed a number of sources and finally settled for Bible Probe[16], which proclaims to be a non-denominational site for Christians & Jews.

They open with the following statement which I believe is important to include here:

> "We apologize to anyone who may be offended by the history of the founder of Islam (Muhammad), and we are aware of the sensitivities involved. However, infinitely more damage has been done to Islam's "believers" by Islam's history of withholding the truth about its founder to them -- and the circumstances

surrounding its inception -- than any "damage" this true history [which followed] can cause."

The statement is followed by a great deal of information, much of which alleges to be confirmed and supported by reputable sources which I have assumed to be so.

It then turned to its opinion of Muhammad the man and the Islamic faith:

"………… Muhammad posed as an apostle of God. Yet his life is filled with lustfulness (12 marriages and sex with a child, slaves and concubines). Rapes, warfare, conquests and unmerciful butcheries."

"Also, question the 'dark side' of a religion such as Islam that requires you to only recite Selah and prayers like the Namaz, in a language (Arabic) you (possibly) do not understand."

"All Muslims, Arab and non-Arab alike, are obliged to pray in Arabic even if they do not understand a single word.

Muslims are also required to read the Qur'an in Arabic, in order to attain any graces at all from Allah."

"Ibn Tymiyyah a very well respected ancient Islamic thinker says:

"The Arabic language itself is part of Islam, and knowing Arabic is an obligatory duty."

Bible Probe then highlighted the same question I raised earlier:

"Islam doesn't even have an original Qur'an. It was made up supposedly from memory and a few scraps found under a bed.

This was about 150 - 200 years after Muhammad died at his wife Ayish's home in Medina, and he was lowered into a hole in the ground where he remains."

This suggests the original Qur'an from which, as mentioned earlier, copies of copies were allegedly made, could not have been in existence to be authenticated by Muhammad.

"Al Bukhari, a Muslim scholar of the 9th-10th century, and the most authoritative of the Muslim tradition compilers, writes that whenever Muhammad fell into one of his unpredictable trances his revelations were written on whatever was handy at the time.

The leg or thigh bones of dead animals were used, as well as palm leaves, parchments, papers, skins, mats, stones and bark.

And when there was nothing at hand the attempt was made by his disciples to memorize it as closely as possible."

"Zaid b. Thabit said: "The Prophet died and the Qur'an had not been assembled into a single place." (p. 118, Ahmad b. Ali b. Muhammad al Asqalani, ibn Hajar, "Fath al Bari", 13 vols, Cairo, 1939/1348, volume 9, page 9)"

"The next oldest Muslim manuscripts are [also] from the 8th-century.

One is written in al-ma'il script and the other in Kufic. Neither of these corresponds precisely to today's Qur'an.

Also, in 1972, construction workers who were restoring the Great Mosque of Sana'a in Yemen found a cache of manuscript scraps that differ and contradict today's Qur'an so badly, that Muslims try to hide this.

These Yemeni Qur'an manuscripts date back to the 7th and 8th centuries and are actually the oldest found and they are written in Hijazi.

Hijazi (Makkan or Madinan) script, is the script in which the earliest masahif of the Qur'an were written.

These manuscripts call to question whether the present Qur'an was delivered to Muslims in pristine form."

"Muhammad's child wife said this after Muhammad died:

"The verse of the stoning and of suckling an adult ten times were revealed, and they were (written) on a paper and kept under my bed. When the messenger of Allah expired and we were preoccupied with his death, a goat entered and ate away the paper."

References: Musnad Ahmad bin Hanbal. vol. 6. page 269; Sunan Ibn Majah, page 626; Ibn Qutbah, Tawil Mukhtalafi 'l-Hadith (Cairo: Maktaba al-Kulliyat al-Azhariyya. 1966) page 310; As-Suyuti, ad-Durru 'l-Manthur, vol. 2. page 13."

According to Bible Probe, Aisha (Muhammad's favourite child bride and only 6 when married) believed whatever Muhammad told her about his divine inspiration.

"Muhammad claimed that he used to get revelations from Allah only when he slept with Aisha.

Why is it that Gabriel did not bother to visit him when Muhammad spent nights with other wives in his harem?

Reference: ahadith from Sahih Bukhari: "Muhammad used to get divine inspiration only in Aisha's bed"...3.47.755"

"Aisha did not see Gabriel while Muhammad introduced Gabriel to her…4.54.440

Volume 4, Book 54, Number 440:

Narrated by Abu Salama:

Aisha said that the Prophet said to her:

"O Aisha, this is Gabriel and he sends his (greetings) salutations to you."

Aisha said, "Salutations (Greetings) to him, and Allah's Mercy and Blessings be on him," and addressing the Prophet she said, "You see what I don't see."

"In Sura 5:48 we are told that Muhammad is given the Qur'an as a confirmation of the bible; that is - it is meant to prove the bible's authenticity....

"And We have revealed to you the Book with the truth, verifying what is before it of the Book and a guardian over it."

"In Sura 46:12 we are told....

"Yet before it there was the Book of Moses (Torah/Old Testament) which was an authority and a mercy. This (the Qur'an) is the Book confirming it in the Arabic tongue....."

"If you are a Muslim and not praying the mandatory five times a day (in Arabic), which must be preceded by the ritual washing/ablution (Wudu), according to Muhammad you are in great danger of going to hell.

Muslims may be excused from observing the other pillars of Islam like fasting, almsgiving and pilgrimage to Mecca, but no Muslim is ever excused from mandatory five times a day prayer."

Concluding comments

Researching Islam was a very difficult, confusing and unsatisfying experience. I was left with more questions than answers.

As with most faiths researched I experience great difficulty trying to understand why penalties of pain and suffering are directed at non-believers. This appears to be particularly so with Islam, wherein I detected such great differences of interpretation of the wording and commandments of the Qur'an itself, particularly when one interpretation delivers pain, suffering, death and destruction to so many people, including fellow Muslims.

It underscored my conclusion that Islam is the ideology I mentioned at the beginning, rather than a religion in the generally accepted sense.

In his book 'The River War,' Winston Churchill, while still serving as an officer in the British army, wrote in 1899:

"No stronger retrograde force exists in the world. Far from being moribund, Mohammedanism is a militant and proselytising faith. It has already spread throughout Central Africa, raising fearless warriors at every step; and were it not that Christianity is sheltered in the strong arms of science, the science against which it had vainly struggled, the civilisation of modern Europe might fall, as fell the civilisation of ancient Rome."

(http://en.wikipedia.org/wiki/The_River_War)

To all Muslims throughout the world, particularly those on the fundamental extremist fringe, I commend to you the words of your Prophet Muhammad:

> *"The merciful are shown mercy by the All-Merciful. Show mercy to those on earth, and God will show mercy to you."*

In other words, by all means follow your faith and count the blessings you believe will be yours to enjoy in Paradise. By all means pity the disbelievers who you believe have denied themselves access to the same blessings. Do not treat them as enemies to be persecuted and murdered. By doing so, you cast shame upon yourself and upon the entire Islamic faith and upon the Qur'an.

I must say I found all that very hard going and very difficult to absorb and to understand. You've already said you believe

all religious orders need to revisit their doctrines, why not leave it at that and move on?

Having expressed a belief that religious doctrines need to be revisited, I feel obliged to explain why and to present my reasons.

Religious and territorial leadership unity

A review of ancient and modern history reveals how the combined power sharing arrangements between nation rulers and religious leaders, certainly advantaged the royal family process where it existed.

Contrary to popular belief, royalty was not created by divine proclamation, but by those who originally appointed themselves as the sole beneficiaries of the domains over which they ruled. The self appointments were accepted and graced with the celebratory approval and blessing of the territory's religious leadership.

The ruling monarch will have been publicly proclaimed and successive royal leaders will have followed in perpetuity from within the original family. The personification of comfortable accidents of birth!

Over the years, for a variety of reasons, royal families from a number of dominions became interrelated arising from the union of marriages, thus diluting the indigenous factor and "thinning the blood." For example, the British royal family of today is certainly not pure British bloodstock.

The original introduction of pagan rule which, over the centuries, gave way in part to various forms of what became the more popularly practiced spiritual worship, is the point at which religion began to affect, influence and dominate the lives of people to an ever increasing degree.

In those earlier times, spiritual leaders acquired residence within proximity to the royal court, to be close at hand for providing spiritual guidance and religious counselling to the monarch when necessary.

As their accumulation of power and wealth progressed through the ages, they built their own magnificent residential palaces, fully equipped and staffed to ensure a long and secure life of opulent comfort. To varying degrees of style and luxury the process has evolved over the years to become the standard for deities worldwide.

The emergence of evangelism underscored the financial advantages derived from commercialised religion. It opened the cash flow taps, attracting millions to pour into seemingly bottomless coffers.

Some might consider this practise to be one of duping the intellectually disadvantaged masses. As true as that might be, it has become a very profitable piece of entrepreneurial commercial wizardry worldwide.

Although differences of opinion and scriptural interpretation exist between leaders of different religious orders, they clearly share a common understanding that their positions of power and influence must, for common commercial reasons, remain firmly entrenched and intact. United they stand, divided they fall, and their fortunes would become severely compromised.

Although, as discussed earlier, research provides no reliable starting date for religion, we know that in one form or another it has become part of mankind's psyche over thousands of years. We also know religion played a significant role in compelling the masses to accede to subservience and obedience towards both territorial and religious leaders. It became the norm for their working class station in the emerging pattern of societal class distinction structures.

That unknown date in antiquity will have marked the turning point when our ancestors surrendered to the will and influence of those ancient and powerful religious and national ruling classes, fearing the inevitable consequences for not doing so.

The "them and us" class distinction syndrome took root and has endured. Those early medieval thinkers obviously knew exactly what they were hatching.

Whereas academic education for the masses was virtually unattainable in the dark ages, spiritual instruction became a largely mandatory occurrence. Pagan doctrine and worship was inculcated with great ceremony and dexterity, as depicted in ancient temple ruins and artefacts unearthed in various parts of the world over the years.

Ancient doctrine dictated that only the god, or gods of a particular nation or culture must be worshipped and obeyed. All others were declared to be false and those who worshipped them were deemed to be enemies of the real god and of the people. A trait that sadly persists in certain religious fundamentalist ideologies today.

The ancient pagan prerogatives used to be driven home very forcefully, sometimes with great ceremony by such things as the public execution of enemy prisoners of war in quite horrendously imaginative ways.

With the passage of time the steadily increasing number of deities became better organised. They grew stronger, more confident and dictatorial in their doctrines. They became exceedingly wealthy, discriminately inclined towards females and consistently cruel in their treatment of all who opposed, or were not devotees of, their particular religious orders.

World opinion has been moving away from capital punishment for murder and other serious offences. It has also questioned certain acts of corporal punishment, particularly at places of learning such as schools. Religious leaders should, therefore, be compelled to do likewise with their doctrines and preaching. After all, places of worship can be likened to places of learning and religion should be leading by example in matters of humanitarian integrity and respect.

Lip service and ineffectual disapproval of religious intolerance and violence must be replaced with vociferous condemnation, explicit prohibition and, when applicable, enforced criminal action for unrepentant offenders. Anything less would amount to tacit approval and should not be tolerated.

Religion and law

The American Constitution proclaims all men are created equal, that they are endowed by their Creator with certain inalienable rights among which are life, liberty, and the pursuit of happiness.

Although the majority of people worldwide probably subscribe to the spirit of this proclamation, millions have never enjoyed the benefits of such fundamental human rights because of political, military or religious suppression.

A responsibly composed secular global constitution would require religious laws to be reviewed, to determine their relevance and legality in terms of a supreme democratic secular law of the land.
Religious leaders would not be permitted to prescribe any form of punishment upon the mind or person of human beings. Perpetrators would become liable to arrest and prosecution.

The world's present assortment of existing national and international laws and legal systems, as well as many related components, would be modified or removed to comply with a new single nation Constitution.
A Commission of eminently qualified people would be appointed to draft the global Constitution and all laws consistent with its provisions.

With the removal of countries, and of traditional money and the capitalist system from society, and the demise of money-related crime, the drafting of new laws and a jurisprudence system common to a single nation world is expected to become much easier to accomplish. I fully expect the traditional gap between the law and justice would be removed completely.

The Commission would liaise with religious leaders for the purpose of identifying aspects of religious law that are deemed to be in conflict with, inter alia, human rights embodied in the Constitution.

With the weight of responsible social justice on their side, religious leaders would be enabled to revise their doctrines by confidently denouncing and jettisoning religious laws, considered by majority consensus, to have become outdated and un-Constitutional, and which have been tarnishing their corporate images for centuries.

I imagine congregations would be greatly relieved and comforted by the adoption of socially responsible doctrine reformation. Attendances at places of worship might increase exponentially as a consequence thereof.

Religion would be provided with a wonderful and exciting opportunity to play a significant role in a global renaissance. It would become remembered as mankind's transformation of a greatly troubled world into one where human kindness, good will, unity of purpose and prosperity for all, became normal lifestyle habits.

Do I detect that Utopian existence we discussed earlier reappearing on the other side of your horizon?

It pleases me to hear you say that. It infers you are still catching a tantalising glimpse of an appealing lifestyle that you are sure is just beyond reach. A lifestyle you would dearly like to experience and hopefully adopt, but which you perceive as fiction. Prevailing world order conditions would certainly make it so.

Such a Utopian-style experience should not be regarded as fictional. It can actually become a glorious reality.

If we had clung to the idea that space travel belongs firmly in the genre of science fiction, we would not have had men walking on the moon nor seen high definition images of the surface of Mars and other planets and constellations.

I believe the task of converting our greatly troubled planet into a world of contentment and peaceful coexistence, will be easier to bring about than were many of the technological accomplishments in man's catalogue of wonderful achievements.

Converting our cultures to enable future generations to be born in a transformed world, inhabited by a single nation of people controlling their own destinies and sharing the benefits of Mother Earth's abundant resources, is definitely within our intellectual and technical capabilities.

There would, however, be no instant guarantees of an easy life for all, with plenty of everything for everyone. In all probability it might be a difficult and hazardous life to begin with if climate change conditions worsen.

We must ensure future generations inherit from us a legacy of peaceful coexistence, participative governance, financial stability and a lifetime of endless opportunity.

It must be a huge improvement on the legacy of conflict, social unrest, debt, poverty and despair they will inherit by default if we choose to change nothing.

Changing those conditions would be so incredibly simple to plan, to organise and to accomplish but, I am fearful the conditioned and intransigent psyche of millions of the world's present population will refuse to believe it to be possible.

Millions more will remain completely reliant upon world leaders to overcome the many problems with which we are confronted.

Many others still believe, misguidedly in my opinion, that divine intervention will protect them from adversities.

> ***Just because you think divine intervention is misguided does not mean people are wrong to believe and to have faith that their God will save them. There are many millions of people throughout the world who do believe in God and believe He put them on Earth for a purpose and wants them to live their lives to the full, in order that they might prepare themselves to learn in the life hereafter what that purpose was.***

As I have said before, I fully respect people's right to believe whatever they choose to believe. I am not saying those with strong religious convictions are wrong to believe divine intervention will save them. I am simply expressing an opinion that such a belief is perhaps misguided in the absence of corroborating facts or precedence to support that belief.

Recent and early history suggests divine intervention in moments of adversity and disaster has been predominantly conspicuous by its absence.

Finally, if the reason for man's purpose on Earth is only to be revealed in an afterlife, the living will remain uninformed. Those millions of people who believe the words of Moses in Genesis, presumably believe their purpose on Earth is to take all life forms under their control and ensure they go forth and multiply. Why did mankind fail to do so?

This chapter has attempted to reveal why I perceive religion as having had damaging effects upon the psyche of mankind for millennia. I also show how I believe religious leaders could play such an essential and important role in mankind's renaissance, revival and survival.

Religion has become one of the four powerful control instruments created by man that have, in one way or another, contributed to the pandemic scourges of crime, corruption, conflict and poverty throughout the world.

Mankind must awake and acknowledge this and take bold, brave and deliberate steps to save itself, from itself, by itself.

Amen to that too!

In the following chapter I have something to say about countries to finish off my quadruplex of problems confronting mankind.

Chapter 7

Sovereign State Countries

The deliberate segregation of humanity

Unlike the other subjects under review, this one falls into a singularly unique category.

The creation of monetary systems, political rule and various religious doctrines, planned to become powerful instruments of control over the lives and minds of people, could never have come about without the creation of countries.

My goodness, that's a bold and very sweeping statement to make. How on earth can you support it?

Well, if our early ancestors had simply wandered the world, living in reasonable harmony with each other, looking after the interests of all forms of animal life as suggested by Moses, we might have evolved as intended as one large family of human beings scattered all over the planet in millions of little settlements without borders.

Each settlement might have appointed its own community leader but there would have been no need for money, for politicians or for a range of divergent religious orders.

Unfortunately, in very simplified terms, our ancestors allowed themselves to become divided, fragmented and segregated. Community leaders were enabled to become nation leaders. They set borders and extending them, invariably by force, transforming our home planet into a world of many foreign worlds.

The ordinary people of those worlds became the victims of the personification of divide and rule and have suffered the consequences ever since.

This chapter challenges the creation of sovereign countries and questions who the real beneficiaries of these bordered domains have always been.

The arrival of elitist minority imperial and religious rule, administered by their appointed political leaders functioning under a protective umbrella of military strength, marked the end of any aspirations of freedom for the global masses. Freedom quickly became an illusion and the masses were required to pay the cost of this domestic colonialism, mendaciously referred to as democracy, which kept most of them in subservience and poverty for much of their hard working lives.

With the passage of time citizens of some country 'worlds' rose up against authoritarian rule in a variety of ways. Many rulers were deposed and replaced by an assortment of others, some more tyrannical than those they replaced.

In some parts of the world citizens fought hard for what they imagined was freedom from oppression, believing they had won the struggle for democracy, gaining greater control over their lives. These were illusionary beliefs because the power of elitist leadership prevailed and the people remained entrapped behind territorial borders. They have continued paying the ever increasing costs of the so-called benefits of pseudo democracy ever since.

William Penn (1644–1718), an English real estate entrepreneur and philosopher, summed it up perfectly when he said:

"Let the people think they govern and they will be governed."

He became the founder and proprietor of the State of Pennsylvania.

In more recent times some countries have become broadly classified as first- or third-world nations, depending largely upon their economic, social and infrastructural state of development. Regardless of classification the people remain subservient to their respective ruling regimes.

The cruel reality is that peoples function in life has always been, and remains, as work fodder for the ruling elite and multinational corporations.

Money has become the life blood of the human species. Powerful multinational corporations monitor its rate of flow through the arteries of global economies, by controlling the heartbeat of the world's monetary system. They also control the pulse of politics which enables them to effectively control the world.

We examined the consequences of a flawed monetary system earlier, so let us consider the effects this might have upon the social structures of many countries.

The decreasing value of disposable incomes in the workplace has contributed to increasing levels of crime and corruption, which is tearing the very fabric of community and family life apart.

A memo in 2007, addressed to Gordon Brown, Britain's Prime Minister at the time, written by Philip Gould, a British political adviser closely linked with the Labour Party, highlighted the troubled times in Britain:

> *"There is no doubt the political landscape is changing: crime, terror, immigration and so on are now the dominant issues. Underpinning these concerns is a growing sense of the power of events beyond our control - globalised economies, international terror, community disintegration and so on. The public are increasingly aware of the forces of change that politicians find hard to effect."*

In excess of 600 000 eastern Europeans arrived in Britain since their own countries acceded to the European Union.

According to an article by Iain Martin in the Telegraph August 5th 2007:

> "....during the previous year, 53% of births recorded in London were to mothers who were not born in Britain; across England and Wales it was 22%."

Many of these mothers will have given birth in Britain's National Health Service (NHS) hospitals without charge, having contributed nothing to the National Insurance Fund, which UK taxpayers are required to do by deduction from their salaries throughout their working lives.

Martin's article continued:

"It has been estimated that in 18 years the capital's adult population will be even more diverse than now. Even modest population projections, from the Government's own actuary, puts the UK population up seven million at 67 million by 2031."

"But there is one rather large problem. There is, under our (Britain's) current arrangements with our EU partners and lack of border controls, very little the Government can do to control the flow. Tony Blair stumbled into this enormous social experiment with no plan, equating open borders with friendliness and modernity."

This state of affairs exposes the inherent flaws within the structures of multi-nationalism and globalisation, where agreements and implementation of common protocols so often fail to attain the intended objectives, causing much stress for and between national publics at large.

In South Africa, with the flood of an estimated five million desperate Zimbabweans having poured into a country that is already experiencing upwards of 40% unemployment, high fuel and food prices and widespread social service delivery problems, it becomes the indigenous public who will suffer the burdensome consequences of such a large additional volume of people in need of food, clothing, work and roofs over their heads.

Problems of this worrying nature are occurring all over the world and people are calling upon their political leaders for change. They want stricter controls. They want order brought back into their lives. They want to safeguard that which they believe is sacred to them, their homeland, and their country.

> ***Well, I can't argue with those sentiments. Why should hoards of uninvited and unwanted foreigners invade our land and be given grants from the taxes we have paid? Why should they be given privileges that our own people have difficulty getting for themselves? Why should they be given roofs over their heads while our own people remain on long waiting lists for homes?***

Why in deed? It just isn't fair, is it? So why does it happen and what can be done to stop it?

If we really want to know the 'why' and the 'how,' we should start by first reviewing the history of education given to children over the centuries, those who have since been classified as 'human resources in waiting.'

As mentioned earlier, throughout history children have been the unsuspecting victims of a conspiracy of deception that has denied them access to the empowering benefits of soundly based education policies. The school-going years of every generation throughout history, have been subjected to a conspiracy that has kept the global community denied access to informative education about money, about politics and about religion.

Let us consider in more detail the informative education we were denied.

We were taught absolutely nothing about money. We were never introduced to the workings of the global monetary system. We were never taught about the workings of the banking and insurance industries. We were never introduced to matters relating to personal finance, money management, budgeting, savings, retirement annuities, the effects of interest rates, investments, stock exchanges or other money related issues.

We were never taught about politics. We never had the distinctions between local, provincial and national governance explained to us.

While we might have been aware of the existence of different religious faiths, their different doctrines philosophies and teachings were never explained to us. Accordingly, we were never given an opportunity to make comparisons between them and to question why there were so many?

Notwithstanding the country's wide range and types of employment, and the fact we were being trained for future employment, the various types of employment were never part of our school education. If we were fortunate enough to acquire employment after our schooling, we knew we would be rewarded with the opportunity to earn money.

We were told that spending our money would help the economy to grow but we had no idea what that meant.

Sadly, when children of my generation left school they had little or no idea what they intended to do with their lives. However, work was reasonably easy to find and many fortunate children were able to become apprentices in a variety of trades.

Life for school-leavers in the 21st century is more difficult, particularly South Africans as we learned earlier.

The bottom line is that countries and their political leaders are failing to train their young generations for future employment.

I had never thought of this before, and you are absolutely right. The subjects you covered were never part of the

teaching syllabus during my school-going years. Upon reflection, it never occurred to us that we should be informed of such matters.

Sadly, and deliberately, children have never been educated in these important social issues, even in today's modern and so-called enlightened world.

In respect of money, the majority of kids generally regard money as something to have and to spend.

As far as politics and religion are concerned, they are told, in hushed tones, that these are subjects that should never be discussed because they usually lead to trouble.

Without an awareness of these fundamentals of life, the majority of children have been churned out of the world's deplorable schooling factories for centuries, as nothing better than malleable working class cretins. In the majority of cases their parents were similarly disadvantaged in their youth, rendering them ill equipped to assist their children to do any better for themselves.

But what about matters relating to one's country and patriotism?

We now move into the vagaries of subliminal subterfuge and the skilful art of mass illusion performances on a global scale.

I inferred earlier that the masters of politics, religion and territorial rule planted the seeds of loyalty and obedience into the minds of their subjects many years ago, seasoned with a liberal helping of fear.

The effect of these seeds was to produce a latent layer of feeling buried deep in the subconscious depths of people's minds which, when roused under a variety of circumstances, rushes to the surface with remarkable force and effect. It has become known as patriotism, the official meaning of which is:

"Devotion to one's own country and concern for its defence."

These words become the fuel that can drive feelings of patriotism into xenophobic acts of brutality very quickly when encouraged under carefully prepared conditions, and it is xenophobia that has become that latent layer of feeling deep in mankind's psyche.

Immediately children attain a level of comprehension the subliminal subterfuge is brought into play. They are told about their country; its name; where it is in the world; the national anthem; the flag; about the king or queen or president or whoever the head honcho happens to be, and how important it is to love, honour and obey them all.

They are taught to respect and to be proud of the leader, and to be proud of the country and all that it stands for, even though they have no idea what that actually means.

Tourists and business people going abroad are often reminded they are ambassadors of their country. Members of a country's defence force are expected to fight and to die for their country if necessary.

Remember Kennedy's words? "Ask not what your country can do for you but what you can do for your country."

Country has been made big in the minds of people.

It is not so much an inbred feeling of instant patriotism at birth. It has been a deliberate and expertly choreographed programme of indoctrination that has been superbly played out over thousands of years.

Most people will say they love their country, even though they cannot explain exactly why. They may be worried about the economic crisis, they may not have too much confidence in the government of the day, and they might see religious fanaticism as becoming a big problem for them. But they love their country!

Yes, like most people I suppose, I would go along with that. So what is your point?

I'm not surprised you would go along with that. For years I would have been right there with you. Unfortunately we have all been conditioned to accept country, patriotism, heads of state and political leaders as icons of super importance in our lives. Many of us have, as already mentioned, been denied the depth of education that would have enabled us to think differently and to see just how superficial they actually are.

So what is the truth about countries and the purpose of people in them? I remain greatly attracted to the words attributed to Moses in

Genesis 1:27-30. We can make some interesting comparisons between what he said and what we have allowed to happen.

You will recall that on the sixth day of creation when, according to the Genesis 1 version, God made many men and women and told them:

> *"Have many children, so that your descendants will live all over the earth and bring it under their control.*
> *I am putting you in charge of the fish, the birds, and all the wild animals. I have provided all kinds of grain and all kinds of fruit for you to eat; but for all the wild animals and for all the birds I have provided grass and leafy plants for food."*

He didn't tell them to go forth and create countries, into which the people must be herded and ruled over. He didn't say the people should be trained to build empires for their rulers and to do battle with others in neighbouring territories. Not at all. He simply told them to have their descendants take the world and its animal kingdom "under <u>their</u> (collective) control."

Clearly this did not happen. The people missed the plot completely and all subsequent community and religious leaders capitalised on that dreadful mistake.

Those ancient words of Moses represent the very substance of my proposed solution for the world's financial, environmental, territorial and climate change problems. The people must take control.

Allow me to re-write the words of Moses as my own interpretation of what is more appropriate to our own times.

> "Adam, I have created this planet, which is larger than you can imagine, and these fish, birds, animals and insects are going to cover it. They have all been conditioned to perform a variety of extremely important and essential functions that will enable vegetation to thrive and to keep the atmosphere clean and provide a healthy environment.
>
> Although I have provided plant life for their food, I have also conditioned many of them to feed upon others with a view to maintaining a reasonable balance and variety of work force species.

Their survival and continuous work is absolutely paramount. If that delicately balanced work force becomes unstable the whole ecological balance will become disastrously upset. That must be avoided.

This is where you come in.

I want you to procreate and spread your offspring all over this world of mine. Your purpose in life will be to take care of my work force, and ensure conditions remain suitable for them to do their intended work efficiently for all time.

You and your kin will become one very large family, settling down in various parts of the planet and enjoying a wonderful lifestyle with job satisfaction.

You must ensure your kin know how important their work force management jobs are, and they must never lose sight of the absolutely critical importance of that work.

Eventually your huge family will find ways of communicating with each other over great distances, exchanging progress reports and working together to resolve problems as they arise.

So go forth, multiply and take care of my planet."

Well I don't really know what to say. It sounds a bit outrageous to me and it might be bordering on blasphemy. I could see where you were going, and by comparing your interpretation with the words of Genesis you appear to be on the same, or at least a similar wavelength. I think I, and probably others regard your 'purpose' of man's position on Earth somewhat degrading. As you implied earlier, you portray man as being little more than a planetary Game Ranger of somewhat lesser importance than all other life forms. General consensus would argue that man has advanced far beyond the capabilities of other animals and is far superior in every way.

No, I think you will have a problem getting your interpretation accepted.

Possibly, but let us consider the alleged superiority of mankind over all other animals. You will recall that Moses said:

'When God saw that Adam had no female companion…"

Was he not implying that God did not consider man as important as all other creatures? After all, he created them all before man. They were the important workers with a lot of ground to cover and a lot of essential work to do.

I certainly agree that man has, under his own steam, advanced intellectually much further than all others. After all it was essential for him to do so in order that he might attend to the enormous responsibility placed upon him. However, at what cost to himself and to all others has man abused his intellectual capabilities and abandoned his responsibilities?

Man has endangered the ecology, polluted the atmosphere and sacrificed millions of his own species at the altar of greed and corruption. Nobody with more than two brain cells could possibly accept such actions as being representative of an intellectually superior and socially responsible species.

It matters not to me whether the words of Moses were of divine origin or inspirationally composed by the man himself. Man's non-compliance with the spirit and letter of those words goes right to the heart of humanity's problems today.

Man must return to his roots of belonging to one huge family of human beings, spanning the surface of a single nation world called Earth. He must stop thinking small in the confines of illegitimate countries and start thinking big within the expanse of a borderless planet.

Neither God nor Moses provided an instruction manual relating to the manner in which the planet should be managed, so until someone presents a better solution, I believe mine is the way to go to ensure we all reap the abundant benefits.

Man must eat the fruit from the tree of knowledge and understanding and apply his superior brainpower wisely.

Well, I must say these are unusual words to hear coming from an Agnostic. I'm beginning to wonder if you might be turning full circle in your beliefs.

Others might think you are beginning to see the light. What has persuaded you to turn to the Bible for the answers to all our problems?

I haven't actually turned to the Bible per se. A few words said to have been spoken by Moses and believed by millions, happen to correspond so closely with my own philosophy – or should that be vice versa?

Sadly, with at least one exception to my knowledge, those words appear to have made little impression upon the minds of millions of other people throughout history, particularly those who claim to be devoutly religious and who turn to prayer and the Bible for solutions. If I can find solutions why can't they?

The one exception of whom I am aware is John Onaiyekan, archbishop of Abuja, Nigeria, and a member of the CIDSE-Caritas Internationalis Climate Justice delegation.

He has said:

> "The Book of Genesis tells us the Lord created the earth and put us on it, expecting us to tend his garden. Mankind has neglected this important responsibility. I believe God made enough resources available for the whole of humanity."

I too believe there are sufficient resources, not only for the whole of humanity but for the entire complement of life forms on the planet.

Unfortunately, neither Moses nor the rest of humanity applied those words for creating a sensible, humble yet meaningful lifestyle culture for the entire human race.

Not surprising I suppose since the Ten Commandments, which are also words that make sense to me, have also been largely abandoned by man throughout his evolutionary journey through life.

I accept in principle what you have been saying about the words of Moses and how man might have made a better life for himself if he had changed his ways all those years ago. But what is actually wrong with having countries? People of the world can still unite to solve the financial problems and do everything possible to survive the consequences of climate change. We don't have to dispense with the countries our ancestors struggled so hard to create for our security and protection.

In my opinion countries offer no common protective features whatsoever for the people residing within their borders. Countries do not attack other countries. It is the rulers of countries who command their own people to attack people in other countries.

Neither our ancestors nor we have struggled to build our countries, whether for our own assumed safety and security or for the well-being of future generations. Ordinary people are neither mandated nor permitted to do so, other than by the commands of their rulers.

I hear what you say but most countries of the world have democratically elected leaders with mandates reflecting the needs of their people. On this basis a large percentage of the global community can be said to be in control of how they are to be governed. The need for worldwide democratic governance is an ongoing process and will, I am sure, be achieved eventually.

We could argue for hours about democratic governance and where in the world it does, or does not, exist.
Democracy is an interesting word.
What would your reaction be if I said a democracy is nothing more than mob rule, where fifty-one percent of the people may take away the rights of the other forty-nine?
I would say your interpretation is grossly flawed.
Really? Those words were spoken by Thomas Jefferson, US Founding Father who drafted the nation's Declaration of Independence.
Are we to assume his words are a gross distortion of what the American people believed democracy stood for? Was he actually predicting what democratic governance might degenerate into in the United States of America, and possibly elsewhere in the world?

Let us review the assumed integrity of national sovereignty which, over the years has been greatly abused.
In many cases democracy has been washed away completely by repressive governance; faction fighting; genocide; vicious cruelty inflicted upon huge numbers of men, women and children; mass starvation; religious intolerance; terrorism and other inhumane acts of savagery.

The pressing need for global unity, for social harmony and for radical change has become increasingly vocalised by people all over the world.

The Internet plays host to many interactive networks and blogging sites, enabling the flow of social problem exchanges between millions of people worldwide. People are looking for solutions and urging world leaders to provide them.

Why was the segregation of people into demarcated territories ever allowed to happen? How did fear, aggression and xenophobia become entrenched in the cultures of people in those territories?

Cultures evolved within different countries and were bound to be different from each other because their societal tapestries were woven from the threads of different social histories. The one thread that became common to all tapestries was xenophobia.

History shows us the creation of divergent tribes, clans, cults and countries, produced equally divergent and damaging effects upon the psyche of the entire human race. Within a span of perhaps 100 000 years, the ruling elite transformed a single world planet into a planet of many worlds. The rulers of each little world proclaimed the inhabitants to be indigenous to that world only, proclaiming all others to be foreigners and potentially dangerous.

Instead of remaining a single united and ever growing 'Game Ranger' family of animal carers and planet watchers, man adopted the herding instincts of his charges and lost the plot of his purpose on Earth completely. Worse still, he began hunting, killing and eating his charges and has continued doing so ever since. Creatures of the world have become increasingly and justifiably fearful of man.

Inevitably, and sadly, man was conditioned to be fearful of people in neighbouring territories across the border and of some in more distant little worlds.

Over the years, some people have become fearful of their own community members, of their next-door neighbours and even of members of their own families.

Oh, I think you are becoming excessively gloomy now. We all know there are problems throughout the world. There always have been, but problems can be solved and overcome There have been many problems in the past and political

leaders have worked their way through them. Not always to our complete liking I admit but they see the bigger picture and act accordingly.

They are working much closer together now at multinational levels, working on ways and means by which nations can be encouraged and assisted to come together to improve the lives of their people. I believe common sense will prevail. After all, politicians know how important it is to accommodate the needs of their people, and to retain their support at the polling stations. They know on which side their bread is buttered.

Quite so, but remember they are members of the League of Scoundrels who demand more than bread and butter in their diets.

Consider also, if politicians actually governed their little world countries according to the will and best interests of their people, and through a deliberate process of mutual respect and co-operation of and between their peers in all other little worlds, common sense and peaceful coexistence throughout the planet might very well have prevailed.

Unfortunately, common sense is not an abundant resource in the corridors of political power and peaceful coexistence is not to be found anywhere on the planet.

In the reality of international governance, political decisions are influenced by the powerful multinational corporations who are firmly in control of the world's economy.

The motivation of our multinational masters is to ensure infinite economic growth endures, thereby enabling the harvesting of resources and the generation of wealth to continue unabated.

Resource rich under-developed nations are required to remain economically disadvantaged and in desperate need of aid and loans. In many cases government officials of such nations receive payment for plundered resources by way of carefully crafted financial aid loan packages. The assumed benefits of such packages rarely reach the needy people on the ground, having been diverted to personal accounts and the purchase of arms. Loan repayments become unsustainable and new loans are arranged with restructured repayment terms which inevitably become impossible to honour.

The impoverished people in poor countries stay poor and in many cases become even poorer. Outstanding repayment amounts soon exceed the loan values, in some cases by as much as a factor of twenty.

To sustain this highly profitable practise, often supported by members of government, it becomes imperative that countries remain in place as essential components of the present world order. Multinationals will deploy their considerable power and political influence to ensure they do.

> ***You appear to be implying that members of government, or at least some of them, are directly complicit with multinationals in an anti-social conspiracy to enrich themselves while deliberately retarding economic growth that would greatly benefit the poor people in their countries. I find that very difficult to believe.***

If you think it is unbelievable, then I recommend you read "*A Game As Old As Empire – The secret world of Economic Hit Men and the Web of Global Corruption*" edited by Steven Hiatt, for an insight into the working parts of the multinational money generating powerhouse.

It's a collection of veritable horror stories about multinational organisations, corrupt politicians and national leaders, colluding to create wealth and power for themselves by exploiting the valuable resources within targeted countries. Meanwhile, the citizens of such countries remain burdened by poverty and starvation.

The stories were written by those who had been charged to get the deals set up and running.

Also, if such nefarious activities were not taking place, a number of NGOs established to investigate and report upon such unsavoury happenings would have no reason to exist.

One such non-profit NGO called the Tax Justice Network[21] (TJN), operates in a number of countries around the world, concentrating upon the movement of huge amounts of corporate revenue for what it perceives as tax evasion purposes.

If we look at TJN's opening declaration we get a clear understanding of what they are endeavouring to achieve:

TAX HAVENS CAUSE POVERTY

"The Tax Justice Network promotes transparency in international finance and opposes secrecy. We support a level playing field on tax and we oppose loopholes and distortions in tax and regulation, and the abuses that flow from them. We promote tax compliance and we oppose tax evasion, tax avoidance, and all the mechanisms that enable owners and controllers of wealth to escape their responsibilities to the societies on which they and their wealth depend. Tax havens, or secrecy jurisdictions as we prefer to call them, lie at the centre of our concerns, and we oppose them."

John Christensen, who directs TJN, has recorded and reported upon the huge amounts of money flowing into offshore tax havens, mostly with the agreement of governments who thereby lose billions in tax revenue.

Whereas tax avoidance is not regarded as an illegal practise many of the transactions noted by Christensen can be characterised as tax evasion, kickbacks, capital flight and money laundering, including for the drug trade and other illicit activities, all of which carry on under the cover of client secrecy.

Although he has made his findings available to governments they appear to have been extremely reluctant to seek agreement amongst themselves to put an end to it. I wonder why!?

Some political leaders are reliant upon multinational support at election times, while others may have covert alliances with multinational investors. In one way or another the multinationals remain firmly in control.

This adds more reason for dispensing with countries wherein nefarious activities are allowed, and sometimes encouraged to take place. It further underscores the merit of replacing the present monetary system.

Surely, if such scandalous activities are proven to be taking place, there must be internationally agreed ways of putting a stop to them?

There are many regulations attaching to the movement of money through the world's banking services, designed to prevent such things as money laundering.

But we are talking about extremely large and regular movements involving corporations that know how to control the way in which regulations are applied – or manipulated – through banking services, over which some have substantial powers and controlling interests.

They also operate in countries which honour the code of confidentiality that prevails between banks and their clients, in similar fashion as between doctors and their patients.

We must not overlook the fact that governments have been seen to either approve these activities or at least do nothing to stop them. Those who might wish to call for action to be taken against offending nations are unable to do so with real effect. There are mechanisms that prohibit countries from interfering in the internal affairs of others.

The United Nations was established, inter alia, to enable member states to determine the fundamentals of democratic governance to be adopted by them and, through the process of international debate and co-operation, to work towards desirable conditions of global economic stability and peaceful coexistence.

Two other major world bodies were established to add weight to the hope for global economic stability. They are the International Monetary Fund (IMF) and the World Bank.

They were formed towards the closing period of World War II in the little U.S.A. town of Bretton Woods, New Hampshire in July 1944.

Since the war did not end until well into 1945, we can assume the Bretton Woods gathering of financial wizards were reasonably optimistic of a victory for the allied forces. They were perhaps in control of the future and knew exactly what the result was planned to be!

The alleged prime objective of the World Bank at the time was to help rebuild Europe after the war, favouring the principal aggressor Germany and the country's much despised ally Japan. An obvious choice because they were the areas in which the greatest profits would be made.

The IMF, comprising 183 member countries, was said to have been established to promote international monetary co-operation and, inter alia, to provide temporary financial assistance to countries to help ease balance of payment adjustments.

It is interesting to note that the founding chairman of the Bretton Woods committee at the time remarked that he thought the "Bank" should be the 'Fund' and the "Fund" should be the 'Bank,' and there has been a certain amount of confusion ever since.

There is no confusion about the stated purposes of the IMF:
In Article 1, paragraphs (iii) and (iv) we find clear commitments, and obviously the necessary enabling powers, which could have prevented the eventual disastrous consequences arising from fluctuations of world currencies:

> *(iii) To promote exchange stability, to maintain orderly exchange arrangements among members, and to avoid competitive exchange depreciation.*
>
> *(iv) To assist in the establishment of a multilateral system of payments in respect of current transactions between members, and in the elimination of foreign exchange restrictions which hamper the growth of world trade.*

In the light of devastating poverty, starvation and death being experienced in so many third world countries, arising very largely from the brutal devaluation of their currencies and disposable incomes, I believe the IMF members should be held totally accountable.
They have the power to proclaim a moratorium on all currency trading activities as a prelude to determining equitable and stable international currency exchange values. Or have they been working to a deliberate agenda of conspiracy to increase the survival dependency of the poor upon the favours and profitable conditional assistance of the rich? I am inclined to believe so.

The World Bank, IMF, the World Trade Organisation and the United Nations have failed the people of the world. They have become fully committed to their own definition of globalisation designed to meet the demands for infinite economic growth as defined and pursued by the multinational corporations.

There is no evidence to support claims that globalisation will unite nations in ways that will beneficially and equitably unite the entire human race. Every proclaimed endeavour to do so has failed completely. Various cultural, trading, monetary, political, industrial and religious organisations, tasked to make globalisation a beneficial reality have similarly failed. I believe failure is inevitable because political and commercial agendas are clearly determined to ensure so.

Globalisation will ensure the rich get richer, the poor remain so, and the starving millions fade away as quietly and as far out of sight as possible.

Desirable global stability at every level of humanity will only become an attainable goal when people turn their focus away from attempts to unite countries. It is more preferable and sensible for the people of the world to unite themselves as one huge family in a single world nation. We started thus as a species a mere 2-3 million years ago, so coming together again will not be something radically new.

I have to admit there is a modicum of sense in your proposal for a single nation world, preferably of our own design rather than having one thrust upon us by world leaders or multinationals. Perhaps millions of other people may also agree. However, people tend to get stuck in their ways and feel more comfortable living their lives in ways to which they have become accustomed over many years.

A single nation world is but one important part of many in the entire process of seeking to overcome our present problems. Our mixture of culturally conditioned societies will predictably resist losing traditional countries. As you so rightly say, it's what they have become accustomed to. That was, after all, the master plan of the ruling elite centuries ago and it has been working perfectly.

Our generation must apply remedial and creative forms of thinking about the legacy we intend leaving for our future generations to inherit.

We must stop thinking inside the box about things that we have become used to, and stop imagining my proposed changes will occur in our lifetime making it necessary for us to adapt to change.

Millions of today's adults are unlikely to experience the proposed lifestyle changes. The children of today might but the changes would take place gradually during their lifetime.

We have to ask ourselves if we are content to leave the children of tomorrow with the mess we find ourselves in now, or shall we plan to create a new and exciting foundation upon which they might build a better life than we have ever known?

I firmly believe countries have passed their 'use before' date and we should all start planning a more viable, secure and efficacious alternative for our future generations.

We must stop thinking small and start thinking big – very big.

I shall be very interested to see what you are intending to do about countries.

As far as I am concerned, with all the problems we undoubtedly have all over the world, people cling to the belief that their country is one of those important and essential anchors in their lives. Despite what you say, countries bind their populations together. They are something we are able to be proud of.

There is something constant, permanent and everlasting about our countries.

If you are proposing we dispose of them, and presumably replace them with something else, I don't think you are going to be very popular, and I am sure you will have few supporters for such a radical and impossible suggestion.

I accept that as a predictable, honest and absolutely natural assessment of how important countries have become in the hearts and minds of the majority of people all over the world today, with the emphasis on the word 'today.'

As mentioned earlier, I am thinking of the 'tomorrow' of many years ahead from today. The new world order that I am proposing will be for the grandchildren of today's newly weds.

Obviously, to propose an instant and radical alternative to something that many have been so willing and anxious to believe in all their lives, would be difficult to convey convincingly.

I don't want today's people to accept radical changes to be made to their present lifestyles. I want them to come together all over the world and lay foundations for a new world order for future generations to inherit from us.

Throughout the book I highlight obstacles that have to be overcome while giving my reasons for saying so. I am not proposing we come together and remove the obstacles now. All forms of adjustment would have to be thoroughly considered before remedial planning is undertaken.

We are presently considering countries so let us begin with the realities of what constitutes a country.

The word 'country' is defined as a territory, an area of land, distinguished by its people, culture, language, geography and its political autonomy.

From this we clearly see a deliberate separation of the human species into bordered territories of confinement. The perfect recipe for creating a world full of xenophobic foreigners within a single species.

One's country of birth has traditionally held a special place in the hearts of most people, the reasons for which are often difficult to put into words concisely. It's the place where our lives and personal memories begin and grow. If we remain there forever they eventually die with us, perchance to continue as a part of the memories of our families and friends.

It's usually, but not always, regarded as being the place where our family roots were metaphorically planted and where we sentimentally believe part of them always seem to remain, even if we move beyond our country's borders to another part of the world.

My roots were planted in England in May 1934, five years before the outbreak of World War II at a time when I believe the country was far more "English" than it is today.

Needless to say my childhood memories and experiences were choreographed by the scriptwriters, producers, directors and performers of reality war productions.

Having looked back to those wartime years with a more mature and experienced mind, I have seen how war has endured as one of the oldest forms of patriotic subterfuge used to great effect by political leaders. The subterfuge is designed to encourage people to remain loyally committed to their territorial boundaries, for reasons not necessarily associated with patriotism per se.

I remember as a child at the time, the patriotic calls going out in Britain rallying the public and defence forces to "fight the good fight for King and country," usually followed by stirring words to the effect that "God is on our side, the side of right."

What was not apparent to me at the time was that similar patriotic calls were being chanted on the other side of the English Channel, where soldiers of the German Third Reich were also being assured that God was on their side and would be fighting beside them in the struggle for final and glorious victory for the Fuehrer and the Fatherland.

What absolute and horrifying nonsense sovereign territories, politics, religion and war really are.

Despite what they are told, or what they might naïvely believe at the time, people on both sides of the battle line are not in fact sent to fight in defence of their countries, nor to protect the lives of their families and loved-ones. They are sent to fight, perchance to die, by order of the rulers of their respective countries, simply because the world's political system has a long and shameful history of failing to unify the nations of the world. The system has constantly failed and continues to fail because it cannot possibly succeed. The ordinary people always become the victims of dysfunctional rulers, politicians and a failed international political system.

As Russian writer Leo Tolstoi (1828-1910) so accurately put it:

"Governments need armies to protect them against their enslaved and oppressed subjects." Very true, because as soon as the people finally realise how their governments are manipulating their lives they might very well rise up and get rid of them.

In the naïvety of my maritime youth, I swore allegiance to King (and later Queen) and country like a true and well trained mentally conditioned patriotic sailor. In retrospect I realise it was the Naval way of life, the camaraderie and commitment to duty and responsibility towards each other that most of us inwardly loved and wished to preserve. Nothing to do with patriotism.

It wasn't until I ended my Naval career and joined my family shipping business that I became aware of the real purpose of countries.

I had to train myself to take more interest in politics and the working of government. I studied the business sections and editorial comments in newspapers. The more I read and the more knowledge I acquired the easier it became to understand how the capitalist system worked, and how I had unwittingly become part of it.

Although I was a novice businessman in the City of London's "Square Mile" at the time, clawing my way up the learning curve of commerce, I realise now I was discovering how the tentacles of politics intertwined with the power cables of big business. Both worshipped at the same altar of economic growth and expansionism, the product of which controlled the lives and destinies of the world's population.

With the knowledge I acquired I saw the world's Mercator's chart as a huge board game, upon which large and powerful multinational corporations and their political allies played their customised and sophisticated game of Monopoly, using vast amounts of very real money and playing for very high stakes.

International trade, banking services and shipping played important manoeuvring roles around the board.

Countries were just places on the board where resources and money were blended to produce great wealth for the winners. The people in those countries were the tools used to gather the resources and to purchase the goods produced from them.

I also saw how my tiny involvement in the international maritime freight industry made me a very small cog in this hugely powerful conglomerate, which straddled the globe serving international trade. It was awesome and remains so.

Having recalled and analysed that wealth of historical knowledge, I can see more clearly how the global masses are used by multinationals to feed their enormous and avaricious wealth generating machines all over the world.

From books I have since read by people who were intimately involved with the mechanics and purpose of those machines, I can see they have been running smoothly for many years and have fuel for many more.

> ***I can imagine how strange the 'real world' must have appeared to you after many years in the Navy, but you appear to have developed a somewhat jaundiced opinion towards it. We are all aware that corruption occurs, and that politicians in certain countries are party to it. Surely, it would be better to rid the world of corruption rather than rid it of countries. If countries are removed, with what will they be replaced? People will still want something to belong to and to be proud of.***

That's a good point and I thought I should at least assure you that I too have experienced feelings of so-called national pride and patriotism during my life, particularly during, and shortly after, a period of global war.

Incidentally, a patriot is defined as one who vigorously supports his country and its way of life. Sadly, I can think of no country in the world having a way of life I would vigorously support. But then how does one define "a way of life."

I believe patriotism should engender a two-way exchange of mutual concern and respect between a country's people and its political leaders at all levels of service delivery. I am unaware of any country having achieved this harmonious accord, other than superficially.

Nevertheless, many people still view their country as being a separate and distinctly strong entity, reserved exclusively for them, offering protection and shelter from adversaries and requiring nought but allegiance to its name, its flag and its borders.

Well, that sounds about right and I would go along with that.

Well, those areas of land called countries provide no exclusivity, no protection and are incapable of expecting or requiring anything from anyone in return.

In my opinion, no area of land called a country has a universal or divine right of existence, because there exists no single owner of the planet's huge real estate possessing the authority to allocate sections for ownership, or on indefinite lease agreements to aspirant tenants.

History shows us that ancient community leaders took land by discovery or force, drew borders around their spoils, named them, proclaimed themselves monarchs to rule over their dominions and the empires they subsequently created, and decreed their offspring must rule in perpetuity.

That might well have been the case thousands of years ago, but man has become more civilised since those times and brought order and understanding to the world, to enable nations to recognise and respect each other's existence and to formalise the names, locations and borders of all countries.

As you have pointed out, there is no owner of the planet to whom mankind could have turned for guidance and settlement, so man had to become wise enough and sane enough to do it himself in pursuit of global harmony and conciliation.

I believe that task was accomplished to the reasonable satisfaction of the majority of people throughout the world. So now you want to change all that?

It was the rulers of countries who brought the questionable order and understanding you mention, and the people they ruled were ordered to understand their positions of subservience to the rulers and their assigns.

Over the years, countries have become increasingly devalued in terms of their old so-called patriotic status. They no longer have any guaranteed future permanence at all.

For example, consider some of the changes of international countries that have taken place since as recently as 1990.

The first and obvious example would be the amalgamation of many nations throughout continental Europe into the European Union and its single currency the Euro.

Another would be the transformation of that huge single entity which used to be known as the USSR (Union of Soviet Socialist Republics). After its dissolution, fifteen new countries were added to global maps.

The political shape shifting exercise performed on the old Yugoslavia produced seven new countries.

We saw Czechoslovakia divided into the Czech Republic at one end and Slovakia at the other.

We have seen the emergence of new countries such as Yemen, the Marshall Islands, Micronesia, Eritrea, Palau and East Timor.

I have not bothered to consider name changes, such as South West Africa to Namibia, Rhodesia to Zimbabwe, Ceylon to Sri Lanka and Burma to Myanma. They are not newly created countries in the accepted sense.

The common denominators in name changes and newly created countries are the amalgam of commercial, political and religious agendas and preferences. The so-called 'will of the people' has never been a serious consideration.

My proposal for change considers the planet as being a whole single entity inhabited by, amongst others, a population of human beings comprising a single nation species.

After all, we are all children of the Universe who have come together on a planet we have called Earth. We came together either through the more probable evolutionary process, or by divine order, or the creations of inter-stellar visitors.

Let us remain children of the Universe and return to our original roots as one huge undivided family.

The ordinary people of the world who have been compelled to accept the status quo of segregation unquestioningly, must reflect upon history and decide whether or not segregation was the right way to go.

Then we should decide whether or not we and our families, past, present and future have been, or will ever be, real beneficiaries in the segregation process. If we decide humanity has not benefited, what process would have been more equitable and beneficial?

Having been told that all men are born equal we should be asking ourselves why there is so much inequality in the world, and why some people appear to be born more equal than others.

If fair consideration is given to my proposal for the future, let it become a point of departure for planning a more equal and fair way in which future generations might live together in a world full of abundant assets and resources, which they can share more equitably than we have managed to do. I am sure the need for change on their behalf will quickly become a more compelling and attractive idea.

The "wise" and "sane" motivations to which you alluded earlier were not driven by the enabling will of the people. They were forced upon them by the territorial, political and religious leaders in command at the time, none of who had been democratically elected by the people to act in their best interests.

You also mentioned global harmony and conciliation, implying the determination of sovereign nations would ensure their longevity for all time. In reality the world has never experienced complete international harmony and conciliation, for the simple reason that a large number of nations, each with its own agenda, will never accomplish complete agreement on every other country's demands.

The long established practise of segregating nations and their people into First World, Third World, Developed, Under-developed,

Developing and various other forms of demeaning categorisation, has always favoured the rich and perpetuated poverty amongst the poor, because it was always intended to be so.

The world has become an exclusive oyster bed of infinite growth for the rich and powerful from whence they reap a steady harvest of pearls. The little people have no option but to keep providing their labour as human resources and pearl gatherers.

I want to pick up on something you said much earlier, about nobody actually owning the planet, which I suppose after discounting religious fanaticism is probably true. Who amongst the global masses – as you call us all – is going to decide where we shall all live, work, play, multiply, and eventually be laid to rest?

Surely this is going to bring us right back to a "fittest of the fit" scenario and an eventual global dictatorship.

That's an excellent point.

Rest assured there will be no openings for a new breed of dictators or rulers of the world within the Global Administration form of governance that I propose.

Our lives have been ruled by a subliminal global dictatorship for centuries which will be dissolved by the Global Administration, which could never have happened in the past because, as history shows us, the people of the world were denied the opportunity to unite as a global collective. They were corralled within their respective border fences and trained to regard all others as foreigners and potential enemies. The xenophobia seeds were planted centuries ago and have been germinating successfully for years.

The types of rule have changed over the years culminating in the mixture of imperial, political, religious and military formats in various parts of the world today.

In the majority of cases the changes have taken place without the participative input of the people.

The multinationals rule the world

The politically controlled public sector has never been able to gain firm control of the wealth generating power of the commercial and industrial private sectors. Ergo, if you can't beat them, join them, which is the state of play throughout much of the world today.

The large multinationals have quietly and expertly dictated the way the wealth generating game is played. They hold all the aces and all the trump cards. They are the world's covert dictators, running their brilliantly customised New World Order under the globalisation brand. Some carefully selected politicians are invited to conditionally share some of the benefits.

Reformation and the so-called values and social justices of democracy remain mass hypnotic illusions.

The only thing that has changed over the years is the categorisation given to people en mass, brought about largely by the industrial revolution and all that evolved commercially and technologically thereafter. We are all now referred to as 'human resources,' the essential beasts of burden required to keep the wheels of the wealth generating business turning.

We have also been given a secondary classified of being the large and loyal pool of essential consumers, purchasing the goods and services the human resources produce. Consumers have been encouraged to purchase everything their hearts desire. They have been given access to credit facilities to make it all possible and encouraged to take out loans to acquire the additional luxuries they cannot really afford. This should compel them to work harder and longer to pay off their debts.

They are told it's good for the economy, good for the country and good for growth, which means it must obviously be good for everyone in the long run, right?

Wrong, wrong, so disastrously wrong.

We have already covered the hazards associated with this practise. Suffice it to say it is not good for those who allow themselves to get into debt, which thankfully would never happen in my proposed World Governance Standard because it would be impossible for people to live beyond their means.

The vision I have for the future, in a single nation world, with every future man, woman and child sharing equitably the abundant resources of the planet, would make the need to constantly want more to have no reason or purpose.

From time to time you have been slipping in the words "World Governance Standard," alternating sometimes with "Global Administration." Talk of a World Governance Standard worries me somewhat, having read a number of hypotheses on the subject of New World Orders, some of which throw in talk of conspiracy theories and the like. Is your mention of a World Governance Standard and Global Administration the same thing or are they two different things? It would help me to understand more clearly where you are going.

I use the words 'World Governance Standard' because that is what the adoption of my proposal would bring about. It might otherwise be referred to as a New World Order.

As already mentioned, we have had what could be termed an 'Existing World Order' for many years, which has been changed into a New World Order branded as Globalisation.

My proposal encourages the people of the world to change Globalisation into a World Governance Standard, replacing the present inefficient and dysfunctional structure comprising more than 200 individual countries, each with their own interpretations of what Globalisation means, into a single nation structure that represents the entire world community.

At present each of the existing countries has its own form of sovereignty and governance. Some 190 of them are members of the United Nations which, as we have already covered, attempts unsuccessfully to engender harmony in and between all member countries according to its mission statement.

Under existing world order conditions the UN has failed to achieve its mission objectives. It will continue to fail for as long as money, politics, religion and national sovereignty remain the traditionally essential component parts of the existing world order architecture.

My proposal for a reconstituted World Governance Standard will enable those UN mission objectives to be achieved, conditional upon a radical revision of prevailing global conditions.

Included in those revisions would be the replacement of the present cumbersome, divergent and all too often corrupt multi-national government structure. The replacement would be a single world nation comprising the entire human race as its citizens. The planet would become one very large country.

The World Governance Standard would replace and remould the objectives of the United Nations. Remember, the UN does not currently include all the world's nations, nor all the world's people. As a governance co-ordinating body the UN would be replaced by the Global Administration, being a single and totally inclusive global governance body.

Replacing the UN with the Global Administration

The UN's fundamental mission statement could possibly be retained with minor changes to the wording, but with radical changes in the body's structure and policy implementation to appear thus:

1. it compiles, generates and analyses a wide range of economic, social and environmental data and information, upon which the Global Administration Assessors will draw to review common problems and to take stock of policy options;
2. it facilitates the negotiations of Regional Senators in all inter-administrative bodies on joint courses of action to address ongoing or emerging global challenges;
3. and it advises the global population through their Regional Senators on the ways and means of translating policy frameworks, developed at the Global Administration level, into action programmes at all Regional levels and through technical and resources assistance, to reinforce global regional capacities.

If this wording is compared with the UN's present version, it is almost identical. The intended core objectives certainly are.

However, my proposal provides a more direct, rapid response facility for implementation at ground zero worldwide, where speed of service delivery will be paramount, and which will become more crucial in the not too distant future when climate change kicks in fully.

The fundamental comparative changes will be:

The UN:

Point one of the current United Nations document wording only enables interface between Member States – not the entire global community – to debate common issues they share, and to consider policy options relative to those Member States only.

Comparison:

My version refers to Global Administrative Assessors who would be permanent active members of an Action Congress. Each member will be in direct contact with the individual global Regional Senators throughout the entire world, not just parts of it.

The UN:

UN's point two again refers to Member States only.

Comparison:

Mine refers to Regional Senators who would provide the conduits between the Global Administration and the people at ground zero throughout all global Regions, via the various Divisional Controllers, who would in turn report to their Section Commanders stationed at the Regional Senate offices.

The UN:

UN's third point becomes reliant upon the time consuming and protracted scheduling of interfacing with various Member State countries, converting conference and summit proposals into any number of potentially workable solutions for problems relating specifically to those countries.

From experience we know that everything would predictably move through the various traditional committee debate sessions, becoming subjected to the laboriously conventional parliamentary protocols including opposition party submissions, the assessment of possible variants with legislation, Parliamentary Acts, common law, the Constitution if applicable, and all manner of other statutory provisions that might be in conflict, or at variants with the enactment of the proposed solutions.

Comparison:

It has to be realised that a more efficacious system must be established, equipped and manned to engage proactively to ensure essential service deliveries within the shortest possible time, if we are to save or salvage the lives and possessions of people when confronted by the full and fearsome consequences of global warming and climate change.

It will become increasingly necessary to use our best endeavours to also save all wild life threatened with extinction and all food sources essential to them as well as to ourselves.

Under climate change condition, endangered regions may have only a few weeks, days or even hours to be in a state of readiness to protect people and properties. They might well be confronted by a succession of life threatening occurrences.

The mechanisms of traditional governance are already failing in conventional domestic service delivery. They will not satisfy the much higher demands for management competency and for resources needed to address the anticipated disasters associated with climate change. Let us not forget that climate change has already started, and under-resourced disaster management workers in a number of countries are having great difficulty managing emergencies of lesser magnitude than experts are advising us to anticipate in the future.

This relates directly to my third point, which enables any number of global issues to be addressed simultaneously, directly at the supreme Global Administration level of the decision making process, from whence action plans, or additional support for locally prepared plans, would be rapidly disseminated to all locations together with support resources tailored to meet the immediate needs of each location and its adjoining territories.

Hence the need for an early establishment of the environmental and disaster management bodies mentioned earlier.

The entire Global Administration architecture, including the command chain infrastructure, and the necessary equipment and disaster management resources, would have been designed and equipped with one paramount objective in mind – to deal quickly and expeditiously with every imaginable disaster likely to occur anywhere around the world, proactively where possible and reactively where unavoidable.

All other customary and less demanding social issues will obviously be attended to more easily, and no doubt more quickly, being processed through such a dedicated and permanently active fast track system, even though the issues may not be classified as disasters or life threatening.

I have deliberately recommended a Global Administration, structured to assume full and total control of global governance matters, because a dedicated central command centre is the only option to effectively address the disastrous and potentially chaotic conditions that climate change is bringing with it.

However, it must not be confused with a single seat of governance ruling over a collection of many global nations. It will be administering the domestic governance of a single global nation, supported by dedicated and active regional branch offices worldwide.

I'm nevertheless beginning to detect a "Big Brother" scenario in the making here which I am sure many others might be anticipating.
You are proposing to hand the world over to an as yet unspecified number of people, to do with as they please, who could enrich themselves beyond the wildest dreams of any aspiring world dominator. I don't think this idea is going to fly at all.
Also, what will happen if a climate change disaster befalls the Global Administration command centre wiping it out completely?

You raise some very good and understandable points.
When the foundation principles and objectives for my book were being planned and researched, long before climate change became a necessary consideration, the "Big Brother" comparison was anticipated.

The fundamentals of the Global Administration architecture are explained in more detail further on. They comprise what I regard as a point of departure discussion arrangement to stimulate debate, of global proportions, by as many people as possible.

Solutions to our problems, and to the continuation of mankind's survival on this planet, will not reside under the control of one "Big Brother" person or group alone.
Many minds, belonging to apolitical professionals nominated and elected, quite literally, by people all over the world, will be charged with planning the administrative responsibilities of other chosen professionals, having the collective competence to address every conceivable problem and need arising on a totally worldwide basis.

Far too many people, elected and monitored by their worldwide peers, will be involved in the decision making processes to permit a "Big Brother" occurrence arising.

Also of course, with conventional money and land ownership removed from our lives completely, the historical attraction for one person, or the elitist minority groups we presently have in our midst, corruptly amassing great wealth and power would no longer be possible.

As to the command centre being wiped out by a calamitous event, it is not proposed that a single location will accommodate the command centre.

As will be seen later, the world will have been divided into ten Zones:

- nine of which would have a Province encapsulating the land masses within each Zone.
- Each Province would have a dedicated command centre located within one of its Regions, being an interactively connected part of the total Global Administration network.
- All command centres would be constantly linked, presumably by satellite or submarine technology and manned by shifts of Global Administrative Assessors on a permanent 24/7 basis.

Global Administration will not be like a single conventional debating chamber, attended by a limited number of ever-changing nation leaders from time to time. It will be a permanently active decision making and action taking entity, acting upon information continuously flowing from the Assessors around the world, with such decisions taken upon a collective consensus basis by the people's elected representatives within every Provincial Region around the world.

Ideally, each Province would have a permanent audio-visual link with each of its Regions, which in turn would be networked with their sub-set locations.

The objective would be to enable a continuous and optimal audio-visual global communication interaction, in order that Global Administration Assessors will be able to arrive at rapid consensus on appropriate action to be taken to address worldwide problems seen in real time.

This location spread of the Global Administration executive would in no way dilute the functional competence of the decision making process. Indeed, it is expected to stamp an accurate and appropriate measure of priority upon each and every need arising.

An inherent advantage of fragmentation would be the closer proximity of parts of the Global Administration to all sectors of the entire global population.

That certainly sounds a little more reassuring, but I'm still not entirely convinced. So, like most other people, I'll wait and see what else you have to say.
Meanwhile, if you intend dispensing with countries, replacing them with Zones, Provinces and Regions etc., will they all have borders and restrictions of movement similar to countries?

That's a fair question, and I am sure the answer will give you cause for further reassurance.

The manner in which countries would be transformed into demarcated global Zones and Provinces without restrictive borders, is preceded on the following page by a simple organogram of the fundamental components of the proposed world governance structure.
It provides a clear indication of how the global population is intended to take control of their own destinies – from the bottom up!

In the light of so many problems presently occurring worldwide and the distressing effects they have upon so many people, the demise of country names and territorial boundaries is not expected to be as traumatic as might initially be imagined by present generations. This will become more apparent when a full understanding of a global cashless society and the many related advantages are included in the preparatory process.

It should also be remembered that the entire process of change will have a transitional period of at least 25 years before implementation.
This will provide adults at the commencement date of the transitional period time to adjust to what will become their new lifestyles. Children and others born close to and after the commencement date will grow

naturally into it. We know how children are far more receptive and adaptable to change than adults.

My proposal brings the power of total global governance under the control of the people – all of them.

It also places a lot more responsibility directly upon the people of future generations who would, throughout the transitional years, be shown and advised how to handle or assign this responsibility competently.

I have every confidence that people of tomorrow's generation will learn how to apply and refine the nuances of total global governance much easier and more responsibly than their elders.

World Governance organogram

NOTES ON FUNDAMENTAL HEADLINE FUNCTIONS

Supreme Council
Nine Councillors and nine deputies comprising elected members from the Provincial Administration.

❶ The Supreme Council will, inter alia, be guardians of the Global Constitution and ensure adherence of its provisions. It will formalise all duly approved Laws of the World and be the supreme adjudicators of all appeals. It will function as the Commander in Chief of the global defence forces.

Global Administration
Located throughout each of the ten Zones. The size and composition of the GA will only be determined and established after an expert assessment has been undertaken by the many disciplines involved.

❷ The Global Administration will be mandated by the Supreme Council to direct and control all activities necessary to protect and preserve the Constitutional rights and privileges of all life forms, protect the environment and ensure optimal deployment of all global resources without fear or favour.

Provincial Executive
An appropriate number of eminently competent Executives and deputies appointed by the Regional Council.

❸ The Provincial Executive will control the legislative processes in all social service matters, including global policing and defence force deployments. They will be responsible for Constitution revisions, writing Laws of the World, administration of the justice system, and for ensuring a transparent, ethical and participative governance standard obtains globally throughout all Provinces in accordance with the provisions of the Constitution.

Provincial Administration
240 Administrators and deputies elected from the Regional Council.

❹ Provincial Administrators will liaise directly with the Global Administration ensuring optimal co-ordination of activities throughout Regions in each Province. They will have responsibilities for global communication, infrastructure, statistical and Status Card data capture and processing.

Regional Council
Comprising 240 Regional Councillors and deputies throughout nine Provinces, nominated and elected by the global community through the People's Congress.

❺ Regional Councils will be the conduit link between the People's Congress and all world governance authorities, and will manage all practical aspects of service delivery and management of all prime public services within their Regional communities.

People's Congress
Comprising elected representatives of the people in Regional Sectors, Districts, Areas and Locations in each of the nine Provinces.
This will be the point from which appointed Regional Councillors, Provincial Administrators and Executives, Supreme Council members and Global Administrators will originate, representing a "Bottom-up" line of governance and ascendancy.

❻ There will be nine Congressional chambers worldwide, each of which will be administered by eminently qualified people nominated and elected by residents within each Province. All matters affecting every aspect of global living conditions are expected to emanate from, and be motivated by, the entire global community through their respective People's Congress chambers. The process of collective and participative secular governance of the people, by the people and for the people will be the foundation of the People's Congress.

Conversion of countries

The final appearance of a World Governance Standard Mercator's chart will be determined by those best able to do the job professionally and expertly.

As a conceptual point of departure these are the fundamentals that I have considered:

Territorics:

Northern Territory – all above the equator;

Southern Territory – all below the equator.

Zones:

In the Northern Territory:

Zone 1: 180° W from the present Greenwich Meridian to 75° W

Zone 2: 75° W to 15° E

Zone 3: 15° E to 105° E

Zone 4: 105° E to 180° E

Longitudes 180° W and 180° E are obviously the same line and would replace the present International Date Line, leaving the location of a possible alternative or more appropriate Planet Date Line to be decided upon. The line might run directly between both poles without the present variations.

In the Southern Territory:

(also from the Greenwich Meridian)

Zone 5: 180° W to 120° W

Zone 6: 120° W to 60° W

Zone 7: 60° W to 15° E

Zone 8: 15° E to 75° E

Zone 9: 75° E to 180° E

Zone 10: 60° S to 0° (South Pole) through the global 360° circumference.

Provinces:

Provinces numbered 1-9 would be within the same boundaries as Zones 1-9, relating only to the land masses within those Zones (historical, present and future), whether or not inhabited.

Regions:

Regions are the portions within Provinces bounded by their 15° lines of longitude and latitude.

The number of Regions within Provinces is expected to be:

- Province 1: 42;
- Province 2: 36;
- Province 3: 36;
- Province 4: 30;
- Province 5: 16;
- Province 6: 16;
- Province 7: 20;
- Province 8: 16;
- Province 9: 28.

Zone 10 would initially have no Provincial or Regional contents. It is recommend, if practical, that it have a Global Administration centre and be in audio visual contact with all other centres.

There would be 240 Regions representing the total planetary land portions within the remaining nine Zone Provinces. This corresponds closely to the number of conventional countries worldwide today.

Sectors, Districts, Areas and Locations within Regions.

These places of decreasing sizes, by whatever alternative names might be decided upon, would be determined through agreement between the Regional Administrators and various community groupings such as existing Residents' Associations and other recognised community organisations.

Influencing factors would be:

- the preferences of existing communities prior to the time of changeover;
- the possible environmental developments planned for the Regions and their sub-sets;
- the proposed movement of environmental work forces into or from the Regions and

- any other reasons to be addressed and agreed upon in public forums.

The location of every community settlement would be coded as its appropriate Provincial place of residence, possibly incorporating the sub-set location, and recorded into every community resident's Status Card, in much the same way as postal codes are presently compiled for parts of the world.

This will enable a constant and continuous census, location and logistics monitoring process, every time a Status Card is used for purchasing goods and services.

Such a process will be essential for ensuring equitable and sustained allocation and distribution of resources exactly where they are required.

Facilities will be available for tourism and for temporary and permanent relocation between Provinces, enabling Status Card holders to retain the full and undisturbed use and purchasing power of their cards anywhere in the world.

Failure to use the enabling facility prior to visiting or moving to a different Province would render the Status Card provisionally unusable in that Province until such time as corrective measures are taken.

Border Posts and Customs and Immigration control points and the use of passports would not be required for any form of global travel movements, all of which would be regarded as domestic.

Provided there was no intention of using one's Status Card for purchasing goods and services in a neighbouring Province, it would be possible to move freely back and forth on a regular basis. Indeed, one could live in one Province and travel back and forth visiting friends in neighbouring Provinces without any inconvenience whatsoever.

It could become extremely embarrassing to run out of fuel in the neighbouring Province, only to find that your Status Card could not be used to top up the tank.

Exactly, but embarrassing is not the word I would use!

Yes. Stupid might be more appropriate. Anyway, thank you for that explanation. I now have a much clearer idea of what you are proposing, and I must say the change from countries to Zones and Provinces is not as drastic as I had been imagining.

In fact, in sporting terms, one could still have one's local Sector and Regional teams to support, and instead of a National team, there would be a Provincial team. Yes, I think I could live with that.

Well, there you go. You appear to be getting the feel for it already.

The single world nation and Status Card monitoring process dispenses with traditional country border posts and movement control formalities.

It enables people to have greater freedom of movement to all parts of the planet, with the unique and value-added benefits of doing away completely with conventional currency exchange control.

Status Cards will automatically provide the essential and constant statistical information to manage the provision of supplies, utility services, energy and other resources on a planned and equitable basis.

In the event of climatic variables creating conditions unsuitable for long-term habitation in certain locations, it would be possible to plan and execute the orderly relocation of large numbers of identifiable people with comparative logistical and administrative ease.

Incorporated in a comprehensive resettlement information process, people would be shown how future coastal areas and inland river town locations are expected to become affected by rising water levels. People would be shown which of the existing coastal countries and islands are expected to become uninhabitable due to climate change and tidal conditions.

The categorisation of 'uninhabitable' as community settlement areas, would also take into consideration those regions expected to lose all essential transportation connectivity facilities.

The millions of people in those global areas would be shown where suitable resettlement sites are available for relocation purposes.

As important as human resettlement areas will obviously become, they will only be part of a total global strategy.

Plans for reshaping our present multinational world into a single nation entity will have to factor in dedicated space reserved for all forms of wild life, as well as global spreads of land for agriculture, live stock, habitation and the hugely complex range of life support features essential for survival.

Parallel with this would be a huge and specialised resettlement plan, dedicated to the extraordinary needs of perhaps a quarter of the world's present population, including those who presently have no formal and permanent residential status whatsoever.

They and the many thousands of dedicated professional helpers and carers will require, and receive, very special and deliberate settlement consideration.

Survival of the species on a massive scale would never otherwise be possible if conventional money, traditional political governance and territorial boundaries remain firmly entrenched features of our world order.

As I keep saying unapologetically, the beneficial aspects of global resources must be made available to the entire human race on an equitably shared basis, which is impossible today.

I recommend reading a report by International Alert[22] titled: "*A Climate of Conflict - the links between climate change, peace and war*" by Dan Smith and Janani Vivekananda.

Chapter 3 captioned "The Unified Solution," contains some very interesting and pertinent observations which underscore my proposals for a single world nation:

> "The community is the vital level for action to adapt to and meet climate change but international cooperation is also essential. Climate change and its physical consequences do not respect national borders so policy and action to address the problem must be developed internationally. This truth has formed the cornerstone of efforts to mitigate climate change for two decades already.
>
> The knock-on socio-economic consequences do not respect national borders either. Large-scale migration, loss of economic output, loss of livelihood security, increased political instability and greater risk of violent conflict will all have consequences that cross national borders. The logic that promotes international cooperation for mitigation works in the same direction when it comes to adaptation.

Furthermore, in many countries that face the double-headed problem, the government is going to be either unwilling or unable – or both – to take on the task of adaptation and peace building. In many of the countries most at risk, the government – and more than that, the system of governance – is part of the problem. The task of helping communities adapt to climate change cannot be left to such governments. There is no alternative except international cooperation to support local action."

These calls by International Alert for international cooperation, and the reasons for so doing, correspond very closely with my own observations. International cooperation cannot be relied upon today to play a role in survival.

International Alert and I are both aware of the need for action to be taken on an expansive global basis.

The principal difference between International Alert's call for action and my own, is that theirs will need many national heads of state to be in agreement to act, many of whom have already been identified as being unwilling to do so.

Charles Darwin knew something about survival when he said:

"It is not the strongest of the species that survive, nor the most intelligent, but the one most responsive to change."

I say, let us be aware and fully informed of the inevitability of change and be proactively responsive to it.

I confess you have put forward a number of pretty compelling reasons for uniting the global population into a single nation environment.

Although the reasons are well founded and certainly well intentioned, they are unprecedented and enormously challenging and perhaps practically impossible to implement.

I think most people will consider the risks far too great to embark upon such a venture having no precedence and no guarantee of success.

Also of course, like me they will probably be wondering who would get the ball rolling. Where are the people with the skills, the abilities, the time and the energy to come together and start the process?

You might be right, but as far as the challenges and guarantees of success are concerned, how do you expect these might be achieved by world leaders if they were to embark upon a "save the world" campaign of their own making?

How much less challenging might a politically inspired campaign be? What precedents exist to guide politicians in planning such a venture? Finally, which campaign do you believe is more likely to succeed:

- one that is totally reliant upon the uncertainties of sustained international leadership cooperation, and totally dependent upon gaining unlimited access to every available dollar in the world or;
- one that requires no conventional political intervention whatsoever, and needs no traditional money to get the job started and established as a dependable and sustainable way of life?

The efficacy of a politically driven solution will, in all probability, be choreographed by the terms and conditions prescribed by multinationals intent upon protecting their considerable investments, demanding the retention of the traditional wealth generating currency system and their country workstations.

Multinationals will be well aware of the threat to their survival under a new World Governance Standard. They can be expected to do everything within their considerable power to prevent this happening.

As to the elements of competence and expertise necessary to address the future problems, a politically motivated campaign would have to draw upon precisely the same private sector skills that the people would hope to energise. Such skills are conspicuous by their absence in the corridors of political power.

Those people who possess the necessary skills and competence would be encouraged to make themselves known, and to become available for nomination as leaders and drivers in the proposed World Governance Standard's Global Administration, uninhibited by political, commercial and financial constraints.

They would have the enviable opportunity to write, produce and direct the most exciting chapter in mankind's continuing journey of evolution.

They would also have the ability to decide which option will be more beneficial for themselves:

(i) the one that keeps them subordinate to political and multinational dictates or

(ii) the one that enables them to be the rightful masters in their own particular disciplines.

Governance of the planet should be by a large body of apolitical specialists, nominated from within the demarcated Regions of the world, and elected by the people within those Regions to become their contracted representatives and creators of the founding executive bodies within the Global Administrative authority.

The people of the world will be contracted with that authority, which will itself be contractually obligated to the people, in terms of the provisions that will bind both parties to the adherence of the formalised terms and conditions of the contract.

This will set the mould of a unique global participative governance of the people, for the people and by the people, which has never been attempted before.

Chapter 8

Solving the Problems

Preface
Starting at the micro level

When a man and woman affirm their love for one another in marriage, they embark upon a voyage of life that will present them with responsibilities and commitments in a partnership, the like of which they might never have experienced before.

Sadly, statistical data relating to divorce and broken marriages worldwide, certainly in South Africa, suggests a large percentage of newlyweds are completely unprepared and unskilled for the responsibilities of marriage in today's world.

Any number of human frailties may contribute to an eventual and sad parting of the ways. Predominant among these are inabilities to accept commitment and a lack of tolerance of the opinions of the other.

One common failing is an inability to abandon selfish lifestyle preferences as a commitment towards achieving shared interests, based upon mutual love and respect for each other. A marriage built upon a foundation of commitment, tolerance and sharing is more assured of success than one that is not.

Children born into such a parental environment are more likely to develop into responsible, respected and valued members of the community in which they live and the greater society in general.

A successful marriage represents participative governance at the microeconomic level which, if repeated on a global basis will contribute so much towards the success of tolerant and participative governance at the macroeconomic level.

If the successful and happy marriages of men and women can become reasonably assured through the adoption of these principles, we can expect the marriage of many countries into a single nation world can be assured with equal success and harmony.

But how is the enabling climate created in preparation for this enormous 'wedding of nations' to take place and to be joyously celebrated? How can it be encouraged to remain committed, tolerant, sharing and enduring?

Such a union is only possible by the will of the people. People who demand an end to the brutality of wars, of terrorism, of crime, of corruption, of illiteracy, of poverty and starvation.

People who demand an end to all that stands between them, their children and all future generations and a world in which contentment, happiness, tolerance, opportunity and peaceful coexistence become customary rather than a forlorn dream.

OK. Your point is well taken. So how do you propose stimulating the will of the people?

Hopefully, all that has been covered so far, together with things that people already know they would like to change themselves, should be sufficient to have already stimulated their desire to be part of the process of making a difference in our world, as quickly and as peacefully as possible.

Added to this will be a growing awareness of the global warming and climate change phenomenon and how its devastating consequences are gradually being revealed and experienced worldwide.

Another devastating revelation is the inevitable, unavoidable and rapid devaluation and collapse of the world's monetary system.

Humanity must prepare itself to become confronted with worsening and unrelenting disasters that will impact upon the widespread societal problems mankind has created and endured over many years.

If conditions are going to be as bad as many scientists warn u to expects, and as you obviously believe, won't people tend to become more concerned about their own personal survival rather than survival of the whole global population?

I'm sure many will indeed think more about themselves and their loved one's rather than about others. Self survival is a strong instinct. We must hope they will have time to give urgent consideration to the need for all mankind to change its lifestyle, in order to deal with the future in a more united and co-operative way.

No man is an island but the human race can unite to become a single nation world.

There is a growing majority of people the world over who demand change in many of the worrying issues I have covered. Lifestyle conditions for such a large percentage of people have deteriorated to such an alarming degree, that the majority no longer need to be stimulated to wish for change. They want it and they want it as quickly as possible. The problem is, of course, few know exactly what sort of change they actually want nor how to make it happen.

Whether or not they have the will, the inclination and the motivation to unite and to make the world a better place in which to live, needs to be seen and to be tested.

There has always been a tendency for so many people to expect and demand that others, who they believe are paid to do so, take the responsible action to look after their interests and security for them.

"Why should I bark when I own a dog?"

Unfortunately, our species has permitted wide divisions of socially segregated communities to develop, having such wide disparities between the haves and the have nots.

Throughout the world today some 854 million people suffer from hunger. In South Africa alone 14.3 million are virtually starving, which is about 32.5 percent of the total population.

One child dies somewhere around the world every five seconds.

In South Africa the lack of clean potable water is the cause of more deaths of children yearly than HIV Aids and malaria combined.

My proposals for change are for the entire human race, the haves, the have nots and everyone in between. I wonder how fertile and imaginative are the hearts and minds of those who will read them?

Who amongst them will take up the challenge and have the will, the determination, the courage and the ability to transform a proposal for change into a reality of renewed opportunity?

I really don't think you need worry yourself too much about that right now. I can't comment upon the value of your proposal because I still don't yet know exactly what it is. I've expressed a few reservations of my own, so get it out there and see what happens. If it can withstand the harsh and vigorous dissection and examination to which it is bound to become

> ***subjected, somebody out there on your wavelength might just pick it up and run with you. I imagine that most people will expect you to start the ball rolling though.***

Yes, I rather think they might and if I were younger with a lot more energy I would certainly do so.

Fortunately, there are many competent and socially concerned people throughout the world, with high levels of energy and determination, who are able to get the ball rolling a lot faster than me.

They are the people who think outside of the box when looking for solutions to problems, particularly the big ones. They are the type of people I hope will study my proposals and become inspired to motivate others to become pioneers in a global renaissance.

❖

Summary

Having shown why I believe our existing world order of Globalisation must be changed, I believe a summary of the four causes of conflict and instability that I have identified will be in order.

Money:

The introduction of money automatically created conditions of inequality in our lives. It brought opulence to a few, poverty to many and an assortment of volatile variables in between. It also gave purpose for crime, corruption, exploitation and conflict, which have grown stronger over the years.

Money has become the source of power for the wealthy elitist minority, and misery for so many others. It draws the line in the sand that separates the haves and the have nots.

Politics:

Politics has become the perfection of subliminal subterfuge, having been expertly designed to convince us we are masters of our own destinies, and that our political leaders will ensure a "better life for all." The growth of information technology has revealed that honesty and integrity are rare commodities in the corridors of political power and that political leaders can no longer be trusted to protect our interests.

Religion:

Religion has become a highly successful and powerful business over the years.

Through its various and often intransigent doctrines, it has skilfully employed elements of mystery and spiritual fantasy in the exercise of control over the hearts and souls of followers for centuries.

It promises afterlife heavenly rewards for the faithful and horrors of eternal suffering and damnation in hell for the disbelievers.

Countries:

Countries rich in resources have become the pastures for wealth generation by elitist minorities using communities of human resources conditioned to do so for them.

Countries were created by conquerors and imperialist rulers to keep the people they ruled behind borders they had marked around their dominions. They transformed the people of the world from a single human species into a world of xenophobic foreigners.

The time has come for the people of the world to wake up and unite to remove dominions, borders and countries and to become once again a single species living together in a single world nation.

Together we can ensure an equitable distribution of our planet's resources to the benefit of all and to all others with whom we share space on Earth.

Let us move on to see how that can be achieved to the ultimate satisfaction and benefit of all.

Chapter 9

The Plan for Change

A New World Governance Standard

Foreword:

The English novelist Samuel Butler said:

"All animals, except man, know that the ultimate of life is to enjoy it."

Considering mankind's reckless pollution of Earth's delicately balanced environment, many animals might have thought, as their species joined the growing list of extinction statistics, life would have been far more enjoyable and assured if man lived on another planet.

Because man has a penchant for shooting himself in the foot while continuing to produce the means to do so, he would have probably polluted that one too.

Hopefully this chapter will encourage man to think more deeply, more laterally and on a much bigger scale than ever before. He will certainly need to think differently, because my plan for change flies defiantly in the face of the long established traditions, conventions and customs which mankind has become deliberately conditioned to accept and abide by.

The plan invites mankind to scuttle the slave ships of multinational and political imperialism, and create a World Governance Standard that benefits every life form on the planet without fear or favour.

Let us be guided by Gautama Siddharta (563-483 BC), Hindu Prince and founder of Buddhism:

"There are only two mistakes one can make along the road to truth; not going all the way, and not starting."

Let us boldly employ our own initiatives and determination to lay strong foundations upon which to build our own New World Order and take bold steps to get started.

What should we strive for in our new customised world order?

A glimpse into the future

If we are to understand the objectives and consequences of the proposed changes, we should try to see the effects they are intended to have upon future lifestyles and the benefits that should accrue to future generations.

Because this is not possible in real time I decided to transform the concept into a picture of words in order that you might share my vision of a future life on Earth.

I have put together an anecdotal biography featuring 54 year old Cindy and her 61 year old husband Frank, living anywhere in the world, five years into the new World Governance Standard era.

They were approaching their mid-twenties when married, one year after the commencement of the twenty five year preparatory transitional period which preceded the new era.

Like all others of their age they remember the old world order days and make regular comparisons between lifestyle conditions 30 years ago and those of the present time.

The preparatory period had been a little inconvenient at first as old lifestyle customs were gradually replaced by those that would become normal in future.

The story begins:

This morning Cindy boarded the free community "Hopper" 'bus which passes close to her home. She was going to town to do a little shopping at the Mall and to keep an appointment with her dentist.

As it glided to a stop close to the newly renovated community centre, about 50 metres from the Mall entrance, she remembered what a hassle the trip used to be by car and the problems she always seemed to have finding a parking space followed later by the nerve wracking drive home in heavy traffic.

Very few cars were parked there this morning. As she strolled towards the Mall entrance she was nevertheless glad she and Frank had decided to scale down to a small electrically operated car.

The decision had actually been made much easier when she resigned her position at the bank six years ago, just a year before the whole global banking business finally closed down.

Once the new Credit system was formally activated banking services throughout the world were no longer required.

She entered the Mall and headed towards the huge double storied MallMart store which gave new meaning to 'one-stop shopping.'

Cindy found shopping very much easier than in the 'old days'.

There were far fewer brand names for products now but still a comprehensive selection of types within each product range from which to choose.

All products had their own identities incorporated in the bar code. The product names were automatically printed on the sales slip at one of the many check out points.

Details of each item were electronically relayed by the check out till to each vendor's control system for reconciliation and inventory purposes.

Cindy was well aware of the process and it was of little more than academic interest to her now.

She was only picking up a few items today so she tossed the collapsible shopping trolley she had brought with her into one of the store's trolleys and made her way in.

From experience she knew exactly where to find what she wanted but, for those shopping at the MallMart for the first time, there were well displayed and elevated product section signs mounted in strategic places, and isle signs with more descriptive product listings.

As she drew level with one of the canned goods aisles she noticed her friend Julia fumbling with something that appeared to be giving her a problem.

She wheeled over to her and after the usual exchange of greetings asked Julia what was giving her a problem.

Julia explained it was the first time she had used one of the store's hand-held bulk buy scanners and she was having a problem getting a screen print of what she had scanned in so far.

The scanners were very popular with people doing a big shop, which they didn't want to trundle round the store and then spend time at the check out, unloading and then reloading it to wheel out to the car.

One simply scanned the bar code of every item being purchased then proceeded to one of the specially marked check out points where the scanner would be plugged into the system. Shoppers would then be asked if they intended picking the items up from the store's delivery bay themselves or have them delivered to their home address. If the latter a small delivery fee would be added to the account.

The shopper would then place her Stat Chip (Status Card) on the till reader, have a thumb or retina scan for Card reconciliation purposes, and her account would be debited accordingly. This automatically triggers two hard copies of the payment receipt to be printed. Apart from the date and time stamp all receipts are allocated a bulk buy transaction number for each day of trading.

If shoppers intended collecting their goods personally they would leave the store, go to the car and drive to the delivery/collection bay area.

A highly visible display screen on the wall showed the next transaction number and the covered drive-through collection lane number.

When the waiting shopper sees her number displayed she would drive to the appropriate lane number to pick up her goods.

They would be loaded into her car and checked off against the check out receipt. A signed copy would be handed to the delivery marshal.

If a shopper had arranged to have them delivered she would drive home and await delivery, signing off in similar fashion upon completion.

Reverting to Julia's little problem Cindy showed her how to operate the "basket check" function on the scanner, which enables each recorded item to be screen printed by pressing the appropriate scanner pad key and deleted if required.

Cindy bade Julia farewell and finished her shopping. She checked out, loaded the items into her collapsible trolley and departed the MallMart.

Her dentist was also in the Mall, not too far from the store entrance, and she made her way there.

She was a little early for her appointment but the surgery had been fairly quiet so she was shown directly into the 'torture chamber.'

The customary pleasantries were exchanged and Cindy handed her Stat Chip to Norman the dentist.

He ambled over to his computer, placed the Chip on the reader pad, pressed the appropriate buttons and her full recorded history of dental treatment over the past twelve years became available for viewing on the screen.

Norman was only interested in the last treatment he had performed which had been a small filling of an upper first molar. The 'before' and 'after' x-ray shots were there on the screen together with a summary of work done.

While admiring his artistry his assistant had been settling Cindy into what she called the 'astronaut's armchair.'

He came over, peered into her obediently opened mouth, studied his work in real time and confirmed it to be in order. He inspected the rest of her ivories for tell-tale signs of decay or anything else requiring his professional attention.

He informed her everything was fine as he made his way to his computer to record the inspection on the system and onto her Chip.

She received a 'no charge' clean bill of oral health together with her updated Stat Chip. With the customary farewells she collected her trolley and set course for the coffee shop she always frequented when visiting the Mall.

Under the circumstances perhaps a close encounter with two Danish pastries would be perfectly acceptable she thought to herself as she quickened her pace.

The Mall site was about 300m above sea level and approximately 10k from what was now colloquially referred to as the 'new' coastline.

She located a window seat which overlooked the surrounding lawny gardens, beyond which was a backdrop of land recently cleared for a large new housing project, abutting what had once been agricultural land that was no longer arable, stretching towards the distant and misty new coastline. It was called new because it was originally 3k further away before tidal levels increased.

As she attacked her second Danish, with no guilty feelings whatsoever, she was remembering the small coastal town that used to be more or less where she was now looking about 3k out to sea.

She recalled it being a quaint little place with wide expanses of glorious beach, a small amount of light industry and commerce and a population which she always thought comprised more retired people than actively employed folk, which was probably true at the time.

Its economy seemed to have been dependent very largely upon seasonal tourists, deep sea fishing, surfing and other water activities.

It quickly became a popular place for up-country business people to build large and expensive holiday homes, the vast majority of which were built as close to the beach as possible.

Inevitably, the town sprouted real estate agents like toad stools and property prices rose faster than the mercury on a scorching day.

She remembered a newly wed young couple, both of whom had grown up in the community, becoming unable to afford to set up home because property prices for even the smallest hovel, needing lots of TLC, shot up to ridiculous heights.

This calamitous course of events occurred in small villages and towns all around the country's extensive coast line.

Frank used to say it had become an era of money making misery for those who didn't have enough.

Then climate change moved up a gear and started to pick up speed.

Within the space of twenty three years the little town's beaches and protective sand dunes were battered and sucked out to sea by raging waves and back tides caused by rising sea levels and stronger currents.

The town became completely submerged by the encroaching sea and the executive houses had since become underwater dwellings for sand, kelp and all manner of marine life.

When the tide comes in now its waves are breaking upon what was once farm land some three kilometres inland from the original coastline.

Most of the town's original community is now living in the enlarged town in which the Mall resides. New housing estates are being erected to accommodate people moving away from up and down the receding coastline.

This sort of thing is happening all around the world. In some areas complete countries have almost been wiped off the map.

She sighed softly, beckoned the young waitress for her tab and busied herself to leave for home.

She had been momentarily saddened by memories of the buried town but the Danish pastries more than compensated.

She settled her bill in the customary way with her Stat Chip and collected her trolley from the coffee shop's little parking bay.

Tipping was no longer possible because, like all workers, table staff received a full salary through the Credit allocation system. Also, in a cashless society there would be no means by which tips could be paid to the staff.

She waited for a few minutes for the Hopper and was soon on her way home.

Frank arrived home at about the usual time 18:20 looking a little more chipper than usual.

As he took the coffee Cindy handed him he asked if she would like to get away for a few days "out of season."

That was an expression that only people of their age really remembered and understood.

For the past thirty-odd years climate change had thrown spring, summer, autumn and winter into a mixing bowl, tossed in a liberal helping of adverse weather conditions and spread the concoction all over the planet's crusty surface like chunky marmalade on a slice of toast.

It was all quite normal for the world's youngsters who automatically adapted to conditions with relative ease on a daily basis, while their elders were taking an eternity to come to terms with the disappearance of the old traditional seasonal periods.

Responding to Cindy's remark about being too busy to have some time off, Frank said that orders for two of the product lines his factory produced had dropped off and new orders were not expected for about two-to-three weeks.

Management had rescheduled work programs enabling the work force to take three days off on a roster basis.

Temporary lay-offs of this type had become regular occurrences throughout the world, normally arising because of disruptions caused by severe weather conditions and seismic activities.

Although road and rail transport routes linking raw material sources and processing plants were the earliest and most long suffering victims of these occurrences, on-carrying routes from processing plants to the many other users and refiners of products were becoming similarly affected.

A number of cluster industries had been built around or closer to raw material sourcing and energy locations. They had proved to be reasonably successful for certain end product purposes. But of course there are so many products requiring an extensive inventory of materials to produce the finished goods they manufactured.

There had also been a few disasters where entire industrial clusters were razed to the ground by earthquake activity.

Fortunately, Global Admin.'s multi-million strong Damage Reaction and Recovery Force, strategically equipped and located around the world, could be mobilised very quickly with all the necessary resources to be on site where needed.

It was also extremely fortunate that global industry and commerce was no longer in private ownership hands nor under the whole or partial control of the old state enterprise structures.

In fact none of those long established and customarily accepted activities were owned and operated by anyone now.

Cindy recalled her time at the bank. She saw how consumer debt increased, savings accounts evaporated, foreclosures increased, client numbers decreased, retailers experienced declining trade, all of which had more than a ripple effect deep into the markets. Unemployment increased as did the ranks of the poor. It was a very distressing time.

None of the planet's resources were owned or traded by anyone now and the words 'economic growth' had been relegated to history.

Under sensibly controlled conditions mankind now carefully harvested and processed resources to the shared benefit of everyone while protecting the needs and welfare of the environment and of all other life forms.

The harvesting, processing, manufacturing, assembly and distribution tools were now regarded as essential instruments for the achievement of this goal managed and staffed by people skilled to do so.

Maintenance, repair, replacements and all new structures were provided on order from the Regional Infrastructural Controller's office, which constantly monitored service delivery within its mandated area of responsibility.

Factory management and staff, like all other employed people, were allocated equitably proportioned amounts of Credits for their services.

Funding was provided to accommodate daily operational needs.

When Cindy had been discussing with her colleagues at the bank the imminent cessation of global banking services, and wondering what they would do in the future, one of her friends in accounting said she thought there might be an exciting and interesting future in global product pricing.

She actually went that route and had found the work to be challenging, fascinating and very rewarding.

It took Cindy, and no doubt millions of others around the world, quite a while to get her mind around the imminent new cashless Credits system, and to work out how far her allotted disposable income of these new units would stretch. She thought at the time that home budgeting was going to be a problem.

As Credit allocation schedules and projected product prices began rolling out she was initially apprehensive. Then she began factoring in the old traditional expenses that would no longer apply.

No taxation, no inflation, no bank overdrafts and interest, no mortgage repayments, no mortgage insurance, free or low-cost community transport services, no need for life insurance or retirement annuity contributions, no Municipal/Council rates, only utilities consumed (water, electricity and gas), free health care and hospitalisation, free education – which would please her adult children who had families of their own, but no longer affected Frank and herself - no import duty and taxes on goods from other parts of the world and a number of other features that previously impacted upon prices and the final purchasing power of disposable income.

Gradually the future began to look far less daunting than she had been anticipating.

Indeed, their combined incomes would put them on par with their net financial position after fixed costs immediately prior to the changeover.

As time progressed it became increasingly obvious they were becoming considerably better off than before and would certainly be so in their retirement.

Five years into the World Governance Standard, she and Frank agreed they were definitely better off than before and social conditions generally were greatly improved.

If only global warming would cool off and weather conditions could get back to normal – as they still remembered them!

On the social front crime had taken a very noticeable dive, particularly in housebreaking and common larceny.

With the departure of cash from society all the many traditional money-related crimes no longer occurred, and gang battles between youths became a thing of the past.

Drug trafficking had at last been completely wiped out and registered drug addicts were able to get their fixes free of charge from clinics, as the required condition towards curative treatment with the aim of becoming rehabilitated.

It was still early days to know how successful this was but the clinics and courses were certainly well attended, which was very reassuring for everyone including the addicts. After all, now that drugs were no longer available on the streets it made sense to register for free treatment.

Alcohol consumption had also declined quite sharply, mainly because so many of the raw materials had been decimated by changes in climatic conditions or destroyed by a variety of storms, floods, mud slides, heavy frosts and fires in traditional crop growing regions around the world.

It was generally assumed that recovery of the alcoholic beverage industry was receiving a zero priority grading by Global Administration when measured against the more essential and pressing needs for food and particularly for water security.

Not surprisingly, many long forgotten home brewing recipes were revisited by the older generation and home brew clubs reported amazing increases in their respective memberships.

Cindy chuckled inwardly remembering Frank's attempts at making some plum wine.

She had insisted he did it all in the garage keeping the smell of his fermenting plonk away from the house, as well as that irritating plop-plop noise from the air-locks.

It took seven months to produce his first batch which, in all fairness was not too bad, but not as dry as they would have both preferred.

It didn't go to waste and there are still three bottles maturing in the wine rack.

An important ingredient in home wine making is patience and Frank did not have sufficient to keep the hobby going long enough to try his hand at making another batch.

Cindy was still thinking about the plum wine when Frank asked her again about having a few days off.

She smiled apologetically and confessed her mind had been wandering back to the past – which she found herself doing quite often.

I must stop doing that, she thought to herself.

Still smiling, she reminded Frank about their weather damaged garden and that they had promised each other to do some recovery work over the weekend.

She also reminded him about the residents' meeting scheduled for Saturday evening relating to proposals for building the new hospital and perhaps extending two of the schools.

As she collected the coffee cups and departed for the kitchen she added, with a mischievous smile on her face, that he might also care to use the time to give wine making another go!

The Saturday evening resident's meeting at the Community Centre was very well attended with 1 817 registrations recorded by the Stat Chip process.

Registration was a common requirement at such meetings because the official Agenda and Minutes had to be filed with the District Controller's (DC) office after all meetings together with a verifiable record of attendance. This was necessary to ensure that voting on matters raised at meetings – which would have been recorded in the Minutes – could be measured by the DC's assessors. This would enable them to determine the level of support or opposition by community members of matters raised at meetings.

It was an essential ingredient for the participative governance process and had become well supported by residents and DCs alike.

In the 'old days' attendees at such meetings, which were held in formally ordered communities around the world, would have been required to provide their ID numbers, names, addresses and probably communication details on attendance registration lists provided before being allowed access to meetings.

Depending upon attendance numbers, it could take an hour or more to complete the ritual, generally by hand, before a meeting actually got under way.

With 1 817 people passing through usually six Chip registration points, the process could be completed within about twenty five minutes.

All Stat Chip scanners supplied to authorised users would only be enabled to access encoded data specific to the transaction relationship between the user and the Chip owner.

For example, scanners at the resident's meeting venue would only be enabled to access data relating to the owner's name, ID number and residential address details.

When placed on any scanner pad the Chip interrogates the scanner's access authorisation and triggers the result onto the scanner's small screen. In this case it would have been "LIM-ID" meaning limited access – personal ID only.

When Cindy settled her bill at the Mall the check out scanner would have shown "TIL-AC" meaning it was an authorised vendor's till scanner enabled to access the owner's ID number, to relay the transaction amount to the Chip, which would confirm funds available, deduct the amount from its present stored balance and authorise transmission of the purchase price, together with all purchased product bar codes to Regional Accounting.

The whole process usually took about 5-10 seconds depending upon the volume of purchases.

At the dentist it would have been "HC-DEN" enabling access only to Health Care–Dental information.

All Chip owners could have their own scanners as an encoded plug in accessory to a computer which enabled them to have full "read only" access to all data on the Chip.

The read only access prohibited editing or deleting of any encoded information on the Chip, other than changes to residential address and communication numbers. Such changes would only be formalised with online authorisation sent to the Chip from District Control.

Having become computer literate during her time at the bank, Cindy had no problem coming to terms with the Stat Chip and its many useful features and advantages.

Frank, on the other hand, pleaded insanity and insisted Cindy did all the reconciliation formalities for him in case he discovered a way of deleting everything without even trying.

Very sensibly she refused point blank.

She reminded him of the words he had used some time ago when she told him she had experienced problems with her washing machine. "When all else fails, read the instructions," he had told her.

He got the message and within an hour had mastered it perfectly.

After the first week he proclaimed the Stat. Chip to be "the best thing since sliced bread."

Meanwhile, back to the meeting, where a customary review of the previous meeting's Minutes was conducted and recorded as having been read.

With the influx of displaced families from adjoining weather affected Areas within the District, there was a growing need to review infrastructural upgrading to enable newcomers to pick up their lives as quickly as possible.

New prefab housing estates were progressing on schedule and utilities had been routed for eventual connections.

Two of the schools to which incoming children were becoming enrolled were expected to start exceeding the 20-per class levels very soon.

Plans were already in motion to construct a new wing at Burlington School, while the extension of the south wing at Tromsworth was already in progress.

The Residents' Association secretary informed the meeting he had discussed matters with all parties and it was proposed that Tromsworth should remain on course without changes or delays.

The new wing at Burlington can be enlarged and a second floor has been provided for.

After allowing for the increased number of children coming from the neighbouring Areas, class levels would be approximately eighteen leaving two vacant rooms each for the primary and secondary sections.

In response to questions he said that further reduction in class levels, rather than having empty class rooms, had been considered but the availability of teachers was presently a worldwide problem.

It would of course be resolved eventually but not within the immediate future.

As a sideline to underscore the present teaching staff problems globally, he reminded the meeting of the huge education dilemma confronting the world 15 short years ago, about ten years before the change over.

An estimated one billion people throughout different parts of the world were reportedly illiterate or functionally so, and it became an imperative to bring them to a level of reasonable literacy, sufficient for them to comprehend the fundamentals of how the World Governance Standard would operate, how they were intended to benefit from it, and what they would be required to do to acquire those benefits.

The biggest problem at the time focused upon those throughout Africa, the Middle East, South East Asia, China, the Far East generally and South America, and particularly in those countries where millions had been impoverished, brutalised, exploited and were starving and disease infected.

Housing, feeding, clothing and medical attention had to be prioritised before any form of deliberate fundamental education could be considered.

Because they were the very people who were intended to be the principal beneficiaries of the social and humanitarian benefits of the new Standard, nothing would prevent it from coming to pass, not even worsening weather conditions.

Real and functional illiteracy in other developed parts of the world would be easier to overcome by comparison.

In the United States of America for example, where some 49 percent of the total population was thus categorised, and in the United Kingdom and the rest of Europe having levels of about 30 percent, these were regions where existing facilities and social conditions were more available and conducive to addressing the problems.

During that ten year period before the change over, approximately 600 000 volunteers from around the world and from various disciplines including education, had registered to become part of the solution. Almost 250 000 educators registered every year since to contribute their skills to this huge task.

Fortunately, increasing numbers of university students were turning towards a career in education but it takes a while before they are sufficiently skilled for deployment.

The Residents' Association secretary got his point across very well and his audience became assured that matters would be improving in the fullness of time.

The last item on the Agenda was the new hospital.

All social services were working under pressure and constantly coming up with new and innovative ways of addressing problems of service delivery disruptions.

The only sustained feature of service delivery in these times was the determination and dedication of those who worked so hard to make it happen.

Ever changing climatic conditions had put an end to long term plans for sustainability in many of mankind's endeavours.

Rapid adaptation and mobility were the foundations upon which planners based their strategies for addressing all manner of occurrences affecting a range of essential services.

A workable Plan 'B' was no longer an option. There had to be a series of options ranging as far into the alphabet as possible.

The private medical facilities, which used to be linked to medical aid schemes, had become part of the entire catalogue of medical services brought together under a single universal and free Health Care Service (HCS).

The building of hospitals, which was the Agenda item under consideration at the meeting, was dependent upon a number of criteria. These included the Area's population size and anticipated growth rate, its existing facilities, access to infrastructure and utilities and the incidence of needs. All of this would be measured by the HCS Controllers against the immediate and future availability of staffing and equipment.

Hospitals were no longer built as enduring monuments to the expertise of architects in grateful memory of the financial benefactors who made them possible.

The working life of a hospital, like all other constructions, could no longer be guaranteed or accurately predicted.

Hospitals were now built to a common prefabricated modular plan, with double storey capabilities, to any predetermined size, and every piece of equipment from the humble bed pan to the most highly sophisticated scanner was completely mobile.

The prefab hospital units also included very adequate staff accommodation and common dining and relaxation areas.

Arising from practical operating experience under variable conditions and in different terrains, quick response and rapid emplacement field hospitals had undergone a number of design improvements and refinements which made them extremely efficient.

To a large extent they were self-sufficient in terms of medical personnel, hygiene attendants and a facility assembly and maintenance crew, all of who moved as a complete unit from site to site as soon as permanent staffing arrangements had been finalised.

The meeting was informed that a Class 3 field hospital unit with a 75-bed accommodation had been allocated to the Area as a temporary measure.

The site was nearing completion in preparation for its arrival and the unit was expected to become operational in six or seven days.

Another suitable site had been reserved for a much needed and more suitable prefab hospital which was expected to be erected and operational in about three months time.

The secretary informed the meeting the elapsed time from making application to HCS for increased medical services, to when the prefab hospital will become operationally ready, would be three days short of five months.

Having the temporary field hospital up and ready so quickly was going to relieve the immediate pressure on the Bennington Hospital and bring much needed relief to the community at large.

A vote of thanks came from the floor accompanied by an appreciative round of applause and the meeting came to a satisfactory conclusion.

Returning home aboard the Hopper, Cindy and Frank were recalling how similar meetings were held in the old days remembering how long it took before anything ever materialised, if at all.

Political considerations always took precedence over the needs of the community and political processes always seemed to grind agonisingly slowly.

It might have taken 2-3 years before getting an agreement to provide a new state hospital and then another couple of years to get it finally built, equipped and operational.

A private hospital might have received approval and been built in half the time.

As Frank pointed out, everything in those days depended upon the availability of land, money, political will and competency, which was not the case today.

Nobody owned land any more and the old political structures had thankfully been wound down and scrapped.

Land was allocated to a community within a designated Regional Area and the community elected its own Area Management Council (AMC), from those making themselves available for nomination and election, which then became officially recorded with the Regional Controller.

The community then elected its Residents' Association which acted as a conduit between the people and the AMC. A close collaboration enabled participative decision making processes in the manner by which the Area developed and grew.

Residents' Association management could be re-elected or replaced at the Biennial General Meeting, and through the Association the community could take steps to call for disciplinary actions to be instituted against inefficiencies occurring within the AMC.

Through the mechanisms of professionally managed bodies, who were accountable to the people who put them in office, the people were empowered to develop, run and maintain their communities in a spirit of majority consensus to the benefit of all.

When new roads and buildings were needed and approval had been secured from the Regional Infrastructural Controller, which was never unreasonably delayed or declined, all that remained to fulfil the need were the material and human resources to get the job done.

Money was no longer part of the equation, which had always been a delaying factor in the old world order days.

The new World Governance system made progress so much easier and quicker to accomplish. As Frank often said, "best thing since sliced bread."

They arrived home with time to spare before watching a movie they particularly wanted to see.

A global newscast was drawing to a close as they comforted themselves in front of the screen.

Their minds were still lingering in the past as they waited for the movie to start. Cindy was thinking how much more pleasant viewing had become now that violence, bad language and pornography no longer featured on any of the TV channels.

Frank had commented similarly several times in the past but was presently thinking how the absence of advertising made viewing more pleasurable.
With the end of commercialism advertising died overnight. He was overjoyed to see a closure to the seemingly endless inventory of feminine cosmetics and wrinkle removing creams invading his space.

He was also pleased to see the end of what he called "retailer's contempt of consumers' intelligence."
They had been doing it for years and seemed to relish in depicting the mentality of consumers as being slightly below chimpanzee levels.
"Only 999,99 – You save a whopping 200,00." Did they really believe consumers were so absolutely stupid they would believe that 999,99 was a whole lot cheaper than 1 000,00?
Also, why could he never recall seeing the product previously advertised at the higher price?
Damned insulting, he was thinking to himself as the movie credits came on screen.
As he settled back to watch he switched off the past and with a smile reminded himself he was now living in "better than sliced bread" times.

The end.

What did we learn from this imaginary glimpse into the future?

We were made aware that climate change was affecting people's lives worldwide to varying extents. We also learned what 'good' days might be like perhaps 40-50 years from now.

We saw how people had empowered themselves to control their lifestyles, their community development, structures and growth.
They had greater control over their children's education facilities and over health care.

The old bureaucratic, and so often corrupt, political system had been completely dispensed with. So too had conventional money, which throughout history had been at the root of so much crime, corruption, debt misery and a cause of drug abuse, alcoholism and domestic violence.

Domestic budgeting and household shopping had become much easier to handle, and free or low-cost public transport had encouraged the downgrading or demise of family car ownership.

Given this impression of predicted changes in lifestyle conditions in the future, one should be able to extrapolate the probabilities of changes closer to one's own present life style.

Yes, but on the question of Credits replacing conventional money, you didn't explain how prices will be calculated, nor how they will compare to present day costs. I'm sure that most people will have a particular interest in that aspect of life in the future.

Yes, I am sure you are right so let us look at how the new monetary system is intended to work and how the process will affect the shaping of new lifestyles.

It is important to first underscore some of the fundamental differences between man and all other life forms on the planet, in terms of essential life sustaining needs. Those which are common to all are clean air, clean water and clean ground in which edible food can grow, all of which are freely available from our planet's abundant natural resources.

Man's evolution has advanced to the point where his non-essential lifestyle needs are rapidly exceeding his very essential life sustaining needs, which is placing increasing pressure upon his ability to sustain access to, and harvesting of, resources necessary to fulfil both needs. The reason for this calamitous state of affairs is because he created an unnatural resource which attracts a far greater demand for possession by mankind than all other resources and needs. Possession of this unnatural resource has become absolutely essential. To be without it renders one unable to survive at all.

The unnatural resource is called money.

Mankind has been confronted with many problems throughout history, some worse than others, the most persistent and unfriendly of which has been money..

We examined money earlier so nothing will be gained by covering that particular ground again. It is nevertheless very important that we understand exactly how money controls our lives and everything we do from the minute of our birth until the moment we die. It then controls what happens to our body after death.

Notwithstanding the abundance of water, air and arable soil that might be available to mankind, a very high percentage of people will, under the prevailing lifestyle conditions, perish without access to money.

So how will the pricing of goods and services be processed and how will the new electronic money, the Credit, replace conventional money?

To be honest, I do not know exactly how, but people with the appropriate knowledge, vision and skills will know exactly how and will provide the answers. Meanwhile, let me mention some of the things that I am sure will be taken into consideration to arrive at the answers.

Global resources of every type will have been catalogued and inventoried. Much of this information is already available from existing statistical records and existing records will also provide data relating to the annual consumption rates of various resources.

Although incomplete, records relating to world population numbers will also be available, which will be more accurately refined during the preparatory Status Card allocation work.

These three criteria relating to available resources, rates of consumption and global population will provide an appropriate point of departure for determining the next four paramount considerations:

1. The life expectancy of essential non-renewable resources over a determinable period of time;
2. The corresponding consumption rate of each resource per capita of population;
3. A preliminary scale of values for each of the resources;
4. The minimum amount of disposable income (Basic Income Grant) necessary to ensure a sustainable survival.

The job of the valuation professionals will be made easier knowing that most of the historical input costs for producing goods and services will no longer apply in the future. For example:

i) Exploration, harvesting and processing of resources will be conducted as social services to the entire global population, under the auspices of the Global Administration;
ii) There will be no private ownership of resources, nor of any commercial activities traditionally associated with their harvesting, processing and distribution;
iii) Scaled incomes of all human resources associated with all levels of production will be paid by Global Administration, as will plant, machinery and maintenance.

The minimal input costs recoverable from consumers, related directly and indirectly to the consumption of other resources such as power, water, fuel and lubricants throughout the entire production and delivery process, will be recovered from retail prices.

This is a very simplified overview of pricing fundamentals to which all manner of variables will undoubtedly be factored in for consideration by the valuation team. Two traditional factors that will never arise for consideration will be inflation and the present need for continuous economic growth.

The new monetary system and uniform pricing structures will necessitate changes in present global income variables. Because of differing cost of living indices in countries around the world today, the customary incomes for identical job descriptions vary considerably between countries.

The intention to establish a universal global pricing structure and a common cost of living index worldwide, will entail establishing a uniformity of disposable incomes worldwide. Butchers, bakers and candlestick makers will receive identical disposable incomes regardless of where they reside in the world. This philosophy is better understood by remembering the entire world will be a single nation rather than the multi-nation planet we have today.

As mentioned previously, the Credit will be no more than a unit of acquittal against the inventory stock of resources purchased by consumers.

Credits will have no traditional investment or savings capabilities because there will be nothing in which to invest and no interest bearing saving accounts.

Because Global Administration will assume liability for the major basket of 'costs' relating to the maintenance, servicing and distribution of goods and services worldwide, an appropriate allocation percentage of Credits will be reserved for the purpose of allocating disposable incomes to those who perform those functions. Further adjustments will be made to enable Global Administration to accommodate its own material and resource needs in the performance of its contractual services, which will include, inter alia, those relating to environmental management and damage control.

The remaining balance will become an important point of departure for determining equitable Credit allocations to the global community.

Obviously a great deal of fine tuning will ensue, but the essential ingredients for a stable global economy will be known and in place and available for accurate accounting purposes.

OK, hold it there. I think I'm slowly beginning to understand your proposed system but I need to be absolutely sure before hearing any more about it, otherwise I'll be lost and won't be able to see the bigger picture.

As I understand it, you are telling us the world belongs to no-one and in your World Governance Standard, no member of the human race will ever be able to own any part of it – not even the piece of ground his house is built upon. In fact, he may never actually own the house either.

On that basis, traditional farmers, fruit growers and mining conglomerates etc., will not own the land they work, but they will still be able to work the land and the mines.

They will no longer own the buildings, equipment, plant and machinery. Your Global Administration will assume responsibility for running costs, repairs, maintenance and

replacements as required and will pay those who make it all possible.

This principle will presumably apply for every form of approved business operation around the world.

I assume the previous business owners would be able to continue doing whatever they had always been doing, and employing the same people they employed before. But now they do not have to pay the people for the work they do. Together with the people they employ, they would receive payment in Credits from the global system, equal to the Credits shareholding allocated to them, which would depend upon the work they do and their position up the promotion and responsibility ladder.

So as I see it, all the planet's resources would be valued and everyone would be allocated shares, or Credits, depending upon the work they do regardless of what part of the world they live in.

I can't quite decide whether you are talking nationalisation on a total global scale, with one governing body controlling everything, or whether it is a form of global socialism.

Also, if people decide to do absolutely nothing all their lives, I get the impression they would receive a Basic Income Grant for life which would allow them to survive at the bottom rung of the ladder in reasonable comfort. If everyone decided to do just that, to lay back and do no work at all, the system would collapse, right?

You appear to have got the broad principle of the proposal mapped out reasonably in your mind. The bigger picture will hopefully become clearer as we move forward.

By reference to your mention of farmers, fruit growers and miners who would no longer own the land or mines they worked. This issue becomes clearer when we use the analogy of deep sea fishermen. They have never owned the seas and oceans, only the right to do what they do – catch quotas of fish.

Similarly, the farmers, fruit growers and miners would no longer own – or need to own – the land they work. Indeed, there are many today who do not own the land or mines they work. They own the right to work them.

In the future, they would simply continue doing what they do best, without having to concern themselves with input costs or making a profit for themselves or for shareholders.

Shareholdings and profits would no longer be features of society. Since there would be nothing in which to invest there would be no need to generate profits in the traditional sense.

The world will always need what people today traditionally produce, and their contractual mission in life would be to continue meeting those needs and to be rewarded appropriately by their Status Card disposable income rating.

They would, of course, have commitments to meet, subject always to climatic conditions and other forces affecting their output abilities.

The purchasing value of a Credit will remain stable globally. In times of a surplus of certain products the values of such products may be reduced to encourage extra sales thereby minimising wastage.

If products are in short supply, the prices may remain unchanged but rationing might be introduced to enable equitable distribution.

Your comparisons with nationalisation and socialism are interesting and understandable.

Because both today are largely dependent upon money, derived through the conventional function of capitalism and of trading with other capitalist nations, they cannot be properly compared to the system I am proposing, because conventional capitalism, money and trading would no longer feature in our lives.

If you are searching for words to describe the system I have in mind, perhaps "shared resource management" might be appropriate.

One of the fundamentals of present day political governance is that taxpayers have to fund expenditure on social services, and on everything else at which government chooses to throw our hard earned money. If there is a change of ruling party after a general election, we are confronted by a different body of politicians who invariably create another – or additional - set of targets at which to throw more of our money.

My system would be completely apolitical, run along sound conventional business management lines without the need to generate profits, dividends and taxes.

As to your concern about the system collapsing if everyone chose to survive on a BIG and do no work at all, the short answer is 'yes,' it would collapse, and the human race will have committed mass suicide – much to the enormous relief and joy of the remaining life form species on the planet!

The BIG only has value, purpose and meaning for as long as there are others who provide the goods and services enabling the BIG beneficiaries, and everyone else, to benefit and to survive.

The granting of BIG allowances will be very carefully controlled and monitored to prevent abuse and exploitation.

I have little doubt there will be millions of people who will be focused beyond the BIG level, anxious to do everything possible to reap the biggest rewards their skills and abilities permit.

Having spoken about Credits quite a lot, this is an opportune moment to explain in greater detail the purpose and function of the Status Card, as well as its intended benefits for the holder in particular and for the global community at large.

The Status Card

This would become one of the most important, if not the most important material possession of every member of the global community. It will be virtually indestructible, trackable if misplaced and of no value whatsoever to anyone other than its legitimate and recorded owner.

It would contain every scrap of pertinent recorded history of the owner from cradle to grave, and its size and appearance might be similar to a conventional USB data storage stick.

Input of record data will only be permitted from authorised and enabled input sources. It will be impossible for existing recorded data to be accessed, viewed, deleted or changed in any way other than by authorised persons using specialised official equipment.

Storage capacity will be measured in gigabytes, as decided by those charged with administration of the Status Card design project.

Fundamental records will include things such as the holder's full name, ID No:, photograph (periodically renewable), finger/hand print, retina scan, DNA, blood type, allergies and birth certificate.

Subject to availability from authoritative sources prior to the time of introduction, it should be possible to scan in additional historical records, including existing certifications of marriage(s), divorce(s), education, qualifications, awards, health, criminal convictions, permanent residential location(s), employment records and whatever might be considered essential or desirable at the time.

From all information captured the Administration will then allocate a Status Credit Rating, which will guarantee and safeguard the unambiguous identity of the Status Cardholder, as well as all rights, privileges and entitlements accruing thereto.

It will also become a convenient and trackable alternative to previous identity documents, passports and visas which will no longer be necessary in a single nation world.

The Status Credit Rating will determine the number of Credits (yearly disposable income) allocated to the Cardholder applicable to his/her employment status and employment position at the time.

People having no knowledge or understanding of Credit Cards, who might have handled only small amounts of money – or possibly none at all – will undoubtedly take longer than most to become competently informed users of Status Cards.

Amongst those will be the world's totally illiterate and impoverished masses, as well as orphan and abandoned children and those who have been previously deprived of any form of social identity or formal existence.

Bringing them into the World Governance system to enjoy the benefits to which they will be entitled will be enormously difficult, and will probably take many of the transitional years to accomplish.

Exceptions to the fundamental system set-up might be tribal communities presently living in very remote regions of the world. Those who have little or no knowledge of the larger global community at all, and certainly no understanding whatsoever of conventional money. People who will have maintained simple lifestyles suited to their culture, their remote environmental setting and evolutionary status.

The uniquely special interests and welfare of this particular grouping will be protected, in keeping with the determination of global ecological protection and preservation. They are, after all, the epitome of primitive living ecology and raw humanity and must be protected, respected and preserved.

It might even be decided that protective measures would include leaving them completely outside the prime global renaissance process, guaranteeing them protection from incursions by access and possible contamination by the rest of humanity.

Leaving them to their own ancient traditional devices until such time as integration into the greater global community becomes inevitable and beneficial to them, might become a preferred decision.

Educating the other disadvantaged sectors will be an enormous international human relations task, for which adequate provisions in terms of human and material resources will be allocated under strict humanitarian control.

It will become extremely important that the Status Card's purpose becomes clearly and unambiguously understood before introducing it into all levels of society.

The Status Card will endure for life, concluding with death certification data of its long time owner and its eventual surrender to the appropriate administration archive depository.

Recorded Status Card transactions refer to data, of whatever nature, actually stored in the Card's memory.

Not every transaction will necessarily be recorded on the Card.

Day-to-day purchases, which generate a hard copy printed receipt at the check-out, will not be recorded in full on the Card, only the total purchase value, date and location reference. The complete transaction will, however, be recorded at the networked Regional and Provincial data collection centres for resources stock control and for Card and ownership reconciliation purposes.

This form of data collection will enable reconcilable assessment of resource types and volumes consumed at all Status Card income levels. This will accurately monitor and ensure equitable distribution, particularly at the BIG level.

Basic Income Grant

Let us now consider the BIG principle to see how a present day human tragedy might be transformed into a worldwide beneficial experience.

For many years some nation leaders, the World Bank, the I.M.F. and poverty relief organisations have attempted to overcome or relieve the tragedies of homelessness, poverty, starvation and the horrors befalling innocent men, women and children who get caught up in national defence force and rebel guerrilla battle exchanges in certain countries.

Billions of dollars have been thrown at the problems, much of which has been converted into arms and ammunition by the political recipients, rather than being used to bring the intended relief to the people in need.

In truth of course, conventional and unsustainable financial aid loans and grants will never solve this desperate human tragedy.

The need to determine the BIG level, together with additional benefits attaching thereto, will be treated with priority for reasons that have been repeatedly focussed upon earlier.

Members of our homeless and destitute global community, who are most in need of the BIG, will be settled and housed initially in what will become their own provisional social settings throughout selected parts of the world.

Although the accommodation and settings will be very modest by general standards, many of the settlers will regard them as the closest encounter with luxury ever.

These settlement sites might also be situated close to areas where high numbers of trained manual workers will be needed for agricultural, rudimentary environmental recovery, restoration, renewal and maintenance work.

Facilities will have been established at those sites to enable full education opportunities for children, and fundamental tutoring for adults, moving onto skills training for the environmental work in which they will be enabled to engage.

As soon as they are sufficiently skilled and able to join other working groups in the field, thereby becoming formally employed, their BIG status will end. Their status will have moved a notch or two up the Credit Rating scale and their income will have increased accordingly.

Others will be similarly accommodated and trained to add their numbers to what will become a huge Damage Reaction and Recovery Force, stationed at strategic locations around the world. They will be similarly rewarded for their valuable contribution to this essential work.

Counted amongst some of the biggest rewards received by these previously disadvantaged people will be the attainment of their self respect and dignity, which the majority will have never experienced in their previous lives.

Some may be relocated away from the places where political and military persecution had characterised such long and torturous periods of their previous existence. They will become part of what appears to be at least two billion people scattered around the world who will have instantly qualified for BIG facilities. From their numbers perhaps 650 million would become available for training and employment where required.

You are talking huge numbers here. More than twice the population of the United States. Surely you are not suggesting they would all be instantly housed, fed, educated, trained and employed in environmental and damage control work?

No, not at all.

Their circumstances will certainly qualify them for BIG facilities, and arrangements will be made throughout the widely spread regions where they presently are, to relocate, organise and provide them with suitable temporary shelter and to put them under the administrative care of people competently skilled to look after them.

They will need to be recorded into the global system, which I imagine will be thwart with identity verification problems, to enable them to be provided with their Status Cards when they are eventually accommodated in their specific community settings, and enabled to use them after a process of education and training.

It will be an enormous task, taking many years to accomplish, employing many people to do it. There are already armies of people qualified and able to address such issues, and the task will be considerably easier to accomplish when the present day political and financial restrictions and conflict situations have been removed.

As to there being perhaps 650 million available for training and deployment, this is a reasonable assumption but it is not suggested for a moment they would all be instantly trained and employed.

They will simply represent a huge pool of currently disadvantaged and unemployed people to draw upon, rather than having to divert huge numbers of skilled people from other forms of employment into environmental and damage control fields of work.

Also, 650 million people is not an excessive number to be employed worldwide on emergency and environmental services.

We have become accustomed to addressing and overcoming many adversities when they arise. In the future we can expect to have no option but to be fully prepared to deploy large numbers of specifically dedicated and trained human resources and equipment on a huge scale, in attempts to prevent such adversities arising in the first place, particularly in regions allocated for livestock, forestry and agricultural activities and other essential life support purposes.

My philosophy is, big problems need big ideas to find big solutions, and we have to think big to find them.

As said before, climate change is with us. Its effects are just beginning to be felt. The time for preventing it from occurring has long passed. We have to adapt to prepare ourselves for a whole new lifestyle to address the consequences of unprecedented climatic conditions and to forget about trying to prevent the unpreventable.

Please allow me a moment to recap here, just to make sure I am slowly getting the bigger picture coming into view now.

We would have a moneyless global society and a full inventory of all resources which have been variously valued in Credits.

Taking an estimated average global population over a period of 500 to 1 000 years, we work out how many Credits there will be for each person. We then manipulate the mean value to allow for a beneficial BIG which is increased proportionally to a top-of-the-pile upper level, with a series of scaled levels in between.

Everyone receives his/her allowance, credited electronically to their Status Cards to use like conventional credit cards to purchase goods and services.

Recipients of Credits include workers and management in business who will no longer be paid by the business. In fact, no-one will own businesses any more, because they will have all been converted to resource processing centres for the benefit of the world's entire population.

With money out of the picture, there will be no banks, no business profits, no stocks and shares, no taxes or duties, no insurances or private financially funded services. In fact, none of the traditional money related activities will exist at all – thankfully including crime.

Now, as good as that might sound, from personal experience I have a concern related to insurance, particularly personal insurance. What provisions will you have in place to cover the destruction or failure of one's Status Card, for damage or loss of one's home and possessions, for personal injuries, the death of a breadwinner, retirement annuities and insurance for children's higher education and the many other risks we insure against?

Yes, you certainly do appear to be getting the bigger picture coming through very well.

A destroyed or lost Status Card will be replaceable after due process. All recorded data will be installed from Provincial database archives.

Your concerns about personal insurance are all very natural, and I can certainly put your mind at rest on those subjects.

In effect all the traditional risk benefits will remain in place but no premiums will be necessary.

The World Governance Standard incorporates what might be described as a master insurance policy for the entire human race, with side benefits of survival automatically accruing to all other creatures and plant life of the world.

If you turn to the front of this book you will see the following words:

> *"Defeating crime, corruption, poverty and starvation in a single nation world, administered through an entrenched policy of collective and participative secular governance of the people, by the people and for the people."*

Money will no longer be permitted to rule our lives, nor will it remain available to enable minorities to accrue enormous wealth for the purpose of ruling the lives of others.

By enactment of the entrenched policy stated above, the well-being of the one shall be underwritten and guaranteed by the will and determination of the collective.

Lost homes and possessions will be replaced, they are only material things. Personal injuries will be freely treated professionally and expertly. Survivors of a dead breadwinner will never become materially or financially disadvantaged. The elderly shall never be wanting in their years of retirement. Children will be encouraged to advance in free education to the fullest extent of their capabilities, including tertiary levels of further education. A healthy and literate global population will be a non-negotiable prerogative.

Once you fully understand the very real humanitarian advantages of allocating equitable disposable income to every member of the human race, directly related to the value of available global resources, the vision of a much better and more sustainable lifestyle becomes increasingly attractive. It will no longer be necessary for those who are gainfully employed to allocate various amounts from their income to make provision for health care, for children's education, for home and content insurance, for retirement and the many other eventualities with which we are confronted in our present day lives.

From the questions you raise, I think you are actually starting to understand the bigger picture but can't quite bring yourself to believe it is actually possible to achieve.

When other questions come to mind, try first to answer them yourself based upon your understanding of the moneyless society and the paramount objectives of the World Governance Standard. You will find yourself coming up with some remarkable answers of your own.

Well, I do have one other question, relating to the total management and maintenance of property, plant, machinery and equipment used at the resources processing sites.

If the inventory of resources has already been allocated to everyone as Credits over an extremely long period of time, I imagine drawing upon resources for plant maintenance purposes under worsening climate change conditions is going to upset the global community's Credits allocation provisions. How will this be overcome?

Excellent question.

Earlier on I explained that a full inventory of available and previously consumed resources would be established for equitable worldwide distribution assessment purposes.

Included amongst those consumed resources would be those used for normal business operating purposes and for maintenance and replacements. There are so many falling into this very simply stated category that it is impossible to be more specific right now.

As examples, engineering replacements, heavy vehicle tyres and tracks, mine shaft lift cables, building and construction parts. They will have all been factored in during the inventory processing work, together with many more extraneous provisions not previously recorded.

Expenses of this nature have been declared and recorded by business operatives for many years. The data are presently available for future analytical and budgetary provision purposes. Upward adjustments will be factored in as best as possible to allow for additional losses anticipated from climate change conditions.

Remember, when talking about features of rebuilding, maintenance and replacement it would no longer be necessary to consider the material and manufactured costs of parts relating thereto. Global

Administration would simply be paying applicable Credit salaries to the people who produce all elements of the material parts.

Provisions for temporary and formal housing for homeless people, together with peripheral materials needed to feed and clothe them and to provide medical care, child education and adult training will also be factored in.

Other provisions would have to be made relating to fully equipping the damage control forces and those engaged in environmental recovery and restoration and for other contingencies. All these and others would fall under the 'fine tuning' mentioned earlier.

A paramount condition for ensuring mankind's survival will be the controlled access to the benefits derived from global resources. For as long as conventional money remains with us, such access will never be available to every member of the human race.

As climate change conditions worsen, the traditional harvesting and processing of resources will become increasingly expensive to sustain, if at all, due to the decreasing value of conventional money. Eventually, and very predictably, conventional money would lose its value completely and, as pointed out earlier, the consequences will be catastrophic. Money will simply lose its life support benefits completely.

Meanwhile, planet Earth's abundant resources would still be there, unharvested, unprocessed and completely wasted because people will not work to be paid with worthless money. The reduced value of disposable income will have forced the prices of available goods up beyond the reach of a growing majority of consumers.

By removing conventional money from the equation of life and replacing it with equitably distributed Credits, secured by the value of the planet's abundant global resources, we shall be able to continue the harvesting, production and consumption processes indefinitely.

Chapter 10

Handling the need for change

How will people deal with it?

Although the precise effects of the global warming and climate change phenomenon remain unknown to us, historical records and scientific predictions alert us to the probability of catastrophic consequences. The need for changes in our lifestyles becomes increasingly apparent with every passing day.

That which we already know plus that which we can reasonably expect, provides sufficient reason for us to prepare a programme for survival as quickly as possible.

We have yet to see such a programme from world leaders or any group of eminent people. We hear much about reducing carbon emissions, looking for alternative energy sources and the need to pay more attention to our potable water supplies. These important matters can only be effective as part of a deliberate and comprehensive survival plan.

If the people of the world decide to wait for a politically created survival plan, I am bound to inquire when will it be presented for public scrutiny and participative input? Indeed, will wide participative input be invited?

For the first time in recorded history our species is confronted with the horrendous possibility of extinction, or at best a huge decimation of its numbers.

As alarmist as that might sound, no official and qualified political statement has been formally released, proclaiming that total or partial extinction will not become a consequence of global warming and climate change.

Throughout my book I have told you what I believe are the four global infestations that have weighed upon our lives for millennia and the damage they have inflicted upon us.

I have shown how they have kept the masses subliminally shackled to their allotted stations in life, in subservience to powerful elitist minorities. I have added climate change to the list of manmade problems confronting us all, and stressed the need to acknowledge the possible threat of extinction that accompanies it.

The following concluding chapter outlines my proposals for solutions to prepare for a soft landing in the turbulent times ahead. It also highlights the first step towards achieving a long awaited and much needed global renaissance.

My proposals contain two very valuable bonuses:

- They will enable us to create a legacy of hope and opportunity for future generations, greater than we have ever experienced in our own lifetimes.
- If the anticipated horrors of climate change miraculously dissolve and the world's weather patterns bring a most welcome return of assured seasons, many of our own generation will be able to experience some of the benefits of the legacy we shall have created.

I hope my proposals will energise the minds of others into determining the awesome magnitude of the tasks ahead, which must be accomplished over the very short twenty to thirty years preparatory period I expect it to take.

With time being the enemy of us all, quantum leaps in technology might accelerate our pace toward salvation.

No single person can solve all the many problems with which we are confronted. It will require many minds and the supportive will and self survival instinct of the world's entire human population to unite and adapt to survive.

I hope my thoughts and words will provide the spark to set the world alight with a united will and determination to make that possible.

Remember, think big!

Chapter 11

The Solution Proposals

The long held assumption that existence on planet Earth is the guaranteed right of every life form species in the world, has never been more uncertain than right now. All life on Earth has become subject to the will of one animal species – Homo sapiens, a.k.a. us.

We are the youngest intelligent life species on the planet and, since our arrival, we have been putting all others at risk of extinction. We have now reached the point of putting our own lives at risk.

I have put forward a survival plan intended to prevent this from happening. A plan that is intended to benefit our future generations and all other life on Earth.

It will require the engagement of many skilled, articulate and altruistic minds, capable of assessing the plan to determine how its conceptualisation can be transformed into a sustainable reality.

After considering once again those words of Albert Einstein:

"There are problems in today's world that cannot be solved by the level of thinking that created them"....

I have reason to believe there are many informed and perceptive people throughout the world who fully concur. People who possess the level of thinking that is needed to address and to solve our worrying problems. I believe we are actually closer to seeing those people coming forward to take on the challenge than many might otherwise believe.

For example, it is encouraging to hear people all over the world calling loudly for global unity in these times of adversity. Politicians tell us we live in a "global village," implying we are all neighbours living in a single community. This is precisely what my proposal advocates in reality rather than as political rhetoric.

Declarations of 'togetherness' have been vocalised and demonstrated during times of unrest for years, particularly in times of war.

What can we learn from this latent instinctive desire to bond together in times of distress? Is bonding an inbred feature of mankind's natural psyche? Is there an instinctive DNA knowledge within us that makes us a common and indivisible life form species?

We are undeniably all members of the same race, the human race, so a bonding instinct should be perfectly normal.

If so we have to ask ourselves:

- Who has divided us and made us foreigners to each other?
- Who has sown the seed of xenophobia in our psyche?
- Who has restricted our natural will to freely wander the planet?
- Who has transformed the essential life support resources of the masses into wealth generating possessions for elitist minorities?
- Who has branded us 'human resources' and made us addicted to money as a reward for our labour?

If you have carefully read the earlier chapters you will know the answer. We are the culprits. We have all become our own worst enemies.

To our eternal shame we continue perpetuating the suppression of our natural spirit of togetherness and interdependence as a species.

Through a deliberate process of oppression and fear we have permitted the seeds of suppression to be sown and fertilized in our hearts and minds, by those with the power and the self-serving interests to do so.

We are shamefully allowing our children and all future generations to be conditioned to accept the same suppression and subservience.

The approaching phenomenon of global warming and climate change, together with the impending expectation of prolonged global recession, presents us with a unique, once in a lifetime opportunity to change our lifestyles and fortunes and to create a universal culture of survival. We must grasp it firmly and unite to create a uniquely different new world order for ourselves and, more importantly, for our children and all future generations. A world order founded upon participative governance that releases Earth's abundant resource assets from the grip of elitist minorities, allowing them to flow on a responsibly managed and equitably shared basis to all.

Man has progressed to a point where he now has the intellectual, scientific and technological abilities and skills to manage and maintain these assets in the best interests of all life forms, not just human.

I am sure millions of religious believers probably accept that to be a plausible interpretation of the instruction contained in Genesis 1:27-30.

Can I come in here?

I have a much better idea of what you are wishing to do, and about the benefits you are sure will be generated for everyone. However, notwithstanding your reference to Genesis, as I mentioned earlier, I'm still detecting a preamble to a journey towards communism, or socialism on a grand scale, both of which we know are failed philosophies.

Since it is your wish to change the present world order into something that has never been tried before, I think you need to give us a clear picture of how it will be defined. For example, if we become citizens of a single nation world will it be ruled as a socialist state, a republic, a dictatorship, a democracy or something entirely different?

Well, as you quite rightly point out, we would be changing our present form of governance into something that has never been attempted before and for which there are no precedents. We would actually be setting them.

For those reasons alone I can assure you once again it will bear no resemblance whatsoever to the classic forms of communism or socialism or any other 'ism' with which we might be familiar. As I have said before, they are reliant upon the capitalist wealth generating instruments of conventional money and trade, which would be non-existent in my proposed world order.

As I have said earlier, money has become a weapon of mass destruction. Vladimir Lenin (1870-1924), first leader of the Soviet Union is on record as saying: "The surest way to destroy a nation is to debauch its currency."

The western world has been debauching global currencies for years and a number of nations are now threatened by economic collapse.

I can assure you the proposed new order will not be a new form of rule in the historically accepted sense either. There will be no traditional or conventional form of territorial rule.

There will of course be a rule of law and a policing service upholding and enforcing a common law of the world to safeguard the interests of us all.

Although I have used the word 'governance' quite often, there would be no conventional political government in the traditional sense. Indeed, there would be no political parties.

We will have a Global Administration, which can be likened unto a board of directors, elected to positions of responsibility by the shareholders – the global population - and referred to as Administrators. There will be no opening for a dictatorship.

Presently, a constitutional Republic produces a form of governance that normally has a president at the top, having conditional supreme powers for both national and international purposes. That would not be the case in my proposed new arrangement.

The single nation Global Administration will comprise the democratically elected representatives from around the world, making it a true global Democracy without the traditional and conventional political structures.

The term Democracy, having an elected Supreme Council at the top, has always been uppermost in my mind. That body, as shown in the World Governance Organogram, comprising members nominated and elected from within the global constituency, would formalise the terms and conditions and responsibilities of the Global Administration, and act as arbiters in matters that might become deadlocked at the Administration decision-making level.

After all, in colloquial terms the 'buck' has to stop somewhere. Where better than at the top?

So if you are looking for a suitable and appropriate description for the form of governance by which our new world order would be conducted, perhaps a People's Democratic Administration might be appropriate. It could not be confused with a "one party state."

The more appropriate way perhaps to view the manner in which our affairs would be managed, is to regard the entire human race as conditional shareholders, as implied earlier, in a corporation called Planet Earth.

The conditions would relate to the number of shares (Credits) each of us would be entitled to receive, dependent upon our terms of employment and our contribution to society.

As shareholders, we would be enabled to nominate and elect a board of directors (Administrators) to manage the corporation's world affairs with diligence and efficacy.

The working capital would be the planet's entire stock of resources, and the board of directors would be charged to manage and maintain the stock and to ensure the shareholders (that's us) receive redeemable dividend vouchers for life. They would be of sufficient value expressed in Credits, to ensure we are all able to enjoy long and comfortable lives.

The corporation would provide us with essential social services, including full and free medical care, full and free education facilities and would underwrite our complete life insurance requirements.

The corporation would redeem the dividend vouchers (Credits) from us every time we exchanged them for goods and services for our individual needs. It would be our responsibility entirely to manage our dividend voucher accounts, and the corporation would put in place monitoring mechanisms that will prevent us from exceeding our allowances.

That is a very brief overview of the basic fundamentals of lifestyle conditions I envisage under the proposed new world order conditions, and a new culture of survival.

Well I must say that gives me a much clearer vision of the future you have in mind, and I have to say it's looking much better than I was anticipating.

Thank you, I'm delighted to hear that.

There are many problems to be overcome and the equitable replacement of existing money is one of the most important solutions to get right. As I have said before, and I think most will agree, money has become one of the most unstable and hazardous survival instruments in our lives.

I have great expectations that our youth will study the proposed changes very carefully, looking for benefits and advantages to which they can relate in much more positive ways than their elders might.

After all, this book is also for the youth of today as well as those of tomorrow. They are the age group from which future leaders will emerge.

For all of you, young and old, who believe in the message to mankind contained in Genesis 1:27-30, I think you will detect a similar message throughout my book, particularly in the Solution Proposal which follows.

We all now have an opportunity to change course for a better future. The moment is perfect. Our world leaders are drowning in confusion, they distrust each other and have lost all sense of direction. Let us show them how a real global village must be created.

Solution Proposal - Preamble

If there is common agreement that 'survival of the species' means the survival of all life forms including ourselves, achievement of that desirable objective will necessitate many deliberate and carefully planned considerations.

A cardinal consideration will be that since mankind cannot engage in collective debate on a survival strategy with all other life forms, and being cognizant of their inalienable right of presence on the planet with us, mankind must now accept the enormously responsible 'Executor' responsibilities on their behalf, as directed in Genesis.

There is a rather distasteful interdependence for survival throughout the entire life form collective, which necessitates many being essential to the food chain requirements of others. Many have traditionally been, and will probably remain, victims of man's own carnivorous tendencies. If we are to survive, then clearly all others must survive, and we must ensure they do.

Other considerations will focus upon the way land and resources must be deliberately and responsibly shared rather than selectively and exclusively plundered, and how the entire process of change must prioritise the cleansing, repair, restoration and a deliberately sustained maintenance of our planet's environment and ecology.

A New Monetary System - The Credit

In review, I believe it has become necessary to give priority to this aspect of change for a number of reasons, not least of which are:

- Our present world monetary system is heading inevitably and predictably towards a total collapse;
- There are far too many different currencies in the world, the majority of which are now traded as volatile commodities on the open market;
- Currency trading has had destabilising effects upon global economies and more importantly upon the purchasing power of disposable incomes;
- This practice is having devastating effects upon the innocent citizens of every nation;
- Currencies are no longer measured in value against a stable element of collateral security but, as already mentioned, rather against what is becoming an unstable so-called 'reserve currency' such as the US dollar, which is also traded;
- This tendency has already given rise to the printing and circulation of unsecured fiat money in the world's money market, leading inevitably to negative equity and insolvency on a massive scale.

There are many other reasons why money as we understand it today, has long outlived its purpose of providing citizens with a dependable, stable and secure form of disposable income, and a unit of exchange for broad trading and survival purposes.

With the approach of global warming and climate change, world leaders are confronted with many very serious problems that will require huge financial resources to solve. These problems cannot, and will not, be solved by the use of unstable conventional money.

As a prelude to underscoring the Credit's intended benefit in our lives, let us first review and categorise just a few of the existing monetary transactions that will cease to exist at the change over to the Credit.

1. **Investments**. None of the planet's resource assets, including land and sea, will be owned by mankind.
   All business functions will be operated, ideally by their conventional and experienced management and staff, under contract terms with the Global Administration. There will be no need, purpose or opportunity for commercial, industrial or private shareholder financial investments. The global community will effectively become the sole collective preferential shareholders.

♋

2. **Financial security.** All income, from the Basic Income Grant level upwards, will be guaranteed by the Global Administration. Payments will be made directly to the recipient's Status Card account without deductions. Only the recipient will have secured access to amounts credited to his or her account. The Status Card system will enable owners to have use of their Status Cards on a worldwide basis. The system will monitor transactions and disable owners from attempting to exceed their subsistence allowance.

♋

3. **Cash sales**. People would no longer be able to buy or sell personal items privately between each other, because they would not have the Status Card transaction facilities to do so. Facilities will be made available, similar to those presently in place, where second hand items could be accepted for resale. The store would be licensed to check the authenticity of ownership of exchanged goods, and to credit the depositor's Status Card and debit the buyer's.

♋

4. **Insurance**. As mentioned earlier, there would be no facilities available for any form of traditional insurance cover whatsoever, particularly the present worrying need for medical insurance. All risks would be underwritten by Global Administration.

It is anticipated a high, and perhaps increasing percentage of claims, will become related to conditions arising from global warming and climate change which, under traditional insurance provisions might become "Act of God" exemptions. Such claims will be processed through the Global Administration's social responsibility mechanisms. Household and personal effects will be subject to verifiable ownership certification. All historical data relating to claims will have been analysed to ensure fair and optimal cover, avoiding fraud and exploitation.

♋

5. **Taxation, Municipal/Council Rates, Excise Duty etc.** None of these features of present day revenue generating instrumentation would apply under Global Administration conditions, prevailing in a single nation world functioning in a moneyless domestic environment.

♋

The aggregated yearly availability of resources over a provisional budgetary period of one millennium, expressed as a value in Credits, will be allocated to provide sustained global maintenance at two levels:

1. Graduated tiers of disposable income for the entire human race;
2. Planet administration, ecological and environmental management and maintenance, production and distribution.

The division of Credits is provisionally expected to be one third for human disposable income, and two thirds for all other matters related to Global Administration's responsibilities.

The human factor:

Humanity must expect, and prepare, to experience high levels of unavoidable decimation due to predicted climatic change activity and a probable increase in levels of disease and food scarcity.

We are warned that fatalities might be as high as one billion worldwide.

Prior to the changeover to a Global Administration, conventional disposable income will have become virtually worthless due to recession and climate change factors.

Inevitably, people will be confronted by the urgent need to decide upon a population size for the sustained survival of future generations.

Although six billion was an earlier estimation, greater accuracy will undoubtedly be more determinable at a future time, when prevailing conditions and future forecasting will enable a more informed decision to be made.

Graduated disposable income

In today's world, we are reasonably assured of the availability of most things necessary for our needs. Unfortunately, we do not always have sufficient money to buy them, particularly those people who are on low or fixed incomes.

In contrast to today's volatile money, the Credit will have very long periods of assured value stability.

The consumption of budgeted resource stocks will be continually monitored through Status Card transaction analysis, for stock control and Regional replenishment purposes.

Processing data over a predetermined period of time will enable analysts to constantly assess the equitableness of Credit allocations at all levels of graduated disposable income.

Upper and lower percentages of monthly and annual usage will have been determined for benchmark monitoring purposes. This will ensure that all disposable income ratings are accommodating the anticipated demands at each level, particularly the BIG.

An ideal aggregated consumption at all levels should not exceed 98.5 percent, and be not less than 97 percent, exhibiting a desirable inclination towards responsible budgeting and a conservation ethic.

Tendencies above or below these two levels will automatically trigger a thorough analysis of actual resources consumed at each level. Analysed results will enable appropriate remedial adjustments to be introduced, either immediately or over a determinable period of time.

The need to maintain a firm and non-suppressive control over a global budgetary provision will be necessary and obvious, particularly throughout the early years of Credit usage.

At points of sale, Credits will be expressed to the nearest decimal point of the one hundred un-named units comprising the whole.

Every product and service will be bar coded at the place of origination, incorporating the codes and percentages of various resources contained therein and recorded for sales reconciliation.

The Status Card will be the source to activate the conduit through which bar code data will flow for stock acquittal.

The Card may embody mechanisms to enable consumers to apply self regulation in the maintenance of budgetary control.

Consumers will never be able to get into debt because traditional credit facilities will no longer be available. There will, however, be facilities enabling people to apply for special grants or for adjustments to their level of Credit allocation but, the reasons would have be very compelling and soundly based.

Planetary maintenance:

This heading cannot begin to convey the enormity or multiplicity of tasks it encompasses, nor the size of the work force to be employed, or the calibre of essential administrative and managerial skills and competence required to drive its many component parts.

Three umbrella portfolios are expected to be created: Oceanic, Terrestrial and Aerial, each of which will presumably form their own dedicated task force units, specialising in the various families of sciences relative to each portfolio.

Oceanic

Within this portfolio, for example, there might be task force units specialising in search and destroy patrols against any piracy and illegal fishing, with others maintaining protection and servicing for legitimate merchant marine operators, as well as for equally legitimate fishing operators and for various other task force units at sea.

Other units will focus upon such things as pollution control, marine life monitoring, maintenance, protection and farming for restocking if necessary. A well stocked and sustainable sea harvesting activity will become an increasingly important life support feature.

Others will monitor meteorological conditions at sea, enabling early warning alerts of activities expected to affect terrestrial locations.

Terrestrial:

Terrestrial protection, recovery, maintenance and management issues will be greater in number than Oceanic, the categories of which will also be far more numerous.

It is from the terrestrial regions that the majority of resources are harvested and there will be particularly heavy set-up and operational demands made upon them for equipping and for logistical maintenance purposes.

Specialised divisional task force units will be established, directed to ensure sustained and optimally controlled harvesting and beneficiation of all essential resources.

All existing global commercial activities of every description will come under the control of their allotted centralised and specialised portfolio units, ideally retaining the existing management and personnel structures worldwide.

Existing administrative and managerial members from each classified industry will be invited to become part of centralised control bodies.

The intention will be to consolidate fragmented industry types into a number of single synergetic units. For example, all existing forms of mining might become consolidated under the single Mining Resources portfolio. The various types of mined products, or mining processes, might then become portfolio Divisions of Mining Resources worldwide.

The operational, maintenance and servicing costs for the entire global industrial portfolio would be funded from the Planetary Maintenance reserves (the provisionally assumed 66.6 percent Credits allocation mentioned earlier.)

Graduated tiers of disposable income for the entire human race component not employed within the Planetary Maintenance structures would be funded from the equally assumed 33.4 percent reserve balance.

One of the prime objectives of the proposed business consolidation process, would be to focus upon quality and durability. It would also ensure the non-negotiable insistence upon conservancy of resources, of energy consumption, and of ecological and environmental friendliness. There will be an adoption of single branding for all product lines and minimal choices within those lines.

Exclusivity, custom design and the excesses of minority elitist opulence would be unavailable.

While the recycling of waste would receive a high and deliberate priority, a sharp worldwide decline in the levels of waste is expected to occur due to the adoption of the high quality and durability process.

Aerial:

Aerial protection predominantly embodies the sciences relating to the life sustaining elements of unpolluted air and the rain that falls to the ground. If the air we breath and the water we drink and that which falls upon the crops we grow for food become toxic and life threatening, all other life preservation endeavours will be severely compromised.

Clean air and water security are absolutely essential to mankind's fight for survival under ever worsening climate change conditions.

Summarising Planetary Maintenance

Conservation will become one of mankind's paramount survival objectives. Lifestyles will be geared to provide future generations greater peace and order in their lives than was ever achieved by mankind throughout its relatively short time on Earth.

Lifestyles will be geared to instil ethics for work, play and life in the psyche of all generations.

So many of our past and present generations sacrificed these ethics at the altar of greed, corruption and violence. They were sacrifices that made them totally dependent upon money and material possessions for their very existence. Future generations must not inherit those dreadful inherent vices.

Predictably, poverty and starvation have become some of the most brutally inhumane consequences of those sacrifices, as well as the dawning of global warming and climate change. We are reaping what we have sown.

Future generations must not be made to suffer the consequences of the contaminated fruit we have cultivated.

Clearly, avoidance of that calamitous possibility is the responsibility of our present generation. It is a responsibility we shirk at our own peril, because to do so might very well mark the extinction of our species. We must all start thinking big and learn to adapt to survive. The choice is ours and ours alone.

Annexure

(Links may have changed since preparation of this Annexure.)

1. Al Gore's "An Inconvenient Truth"

web site at : http://www.climatecrisis.net/

2. The Ticking Time Bomb

http://www.americanantigravity.com/blogs/40/Ticking Time-Bomb.html.

3. Tyranny of Good Intentions

http://www.liberty-tree.org/ltn/tyranny-of-good-intentions.html

4. The Creature from Jekyll Island by G. Edward Griffin

http://www.amazon.com/Creature-Jekyll-Island-Federal-Reserve/dp/0912986212

5. Dag Hammarskjöld Foundation's "*What Next*" publication "Carbon Trading"

http://www.dhf.uu.se/press_release_carbon.html

6. The Arms Deal : read "*After the Party*" by Andrew Feinstein

Website of an extensive record of events:
http://www.armsdeal-vpo.co.za/
and an article published in the South African *Mail & Guardian* newspaper, 23 February 2007 07:20 by investigative reporters Stefaans Brümmer and Sam Sole.

7. Piero Scaruffi Report:

http://www.scaruffi.com/politics/dictat.html

8. Beverly K. Eakman

(Home web page: http://www.beverlye.com/).

9. Zwelinzima Vavi, general secretary COSATU.

Unemployed were better off under apartheid: *Mail & Guardian/SAPA* Johannesburg, 27 October 2007 03:34

10. The Gautrain project – Project web site is at:

http://www.gautrain.co.za/index.php?fp=1

11. The Intergovernmental Panel on Climate Change, draft copy 16 November, 2007.

http://www.ipcc.ch/

12. Religion of India:

http://www.thetruehistoryandthereligionofindia.org/th_endorsements.htm

13. Islam

Muhammad by Drs. Zahoor and Haq.
http://www.scribd.com/doc/17643/Muhammad-by-Dr-A-Zahoor-and-Dr-Z-Haq

14. Digital Islamic Library:

http://www.al-islam.org/index.php and
http://www.al-islam.org/restatement/
The True Call:
http://www.thetruecall.com/home/modules.php?name=News&file=article&sid=269

15. William Muir:

http://en.wikipedia.org/wiki/William_Muir

16. Bible Probe:

http://bibleprobe.com/muhammad.htm.

17. Angel Gabriel and Muhammad

http://www.thespiritofislam.com/books/imk/index.html#chap0203
Under Chapter 2 : Was the Spirit Really the Angel Gabriel?

18. Flavius Josephus:

http://bible.crosswalk.com/History/BC/FlaviusJosephus/

19. Noah's Ark

web addresses: http://www.arksearch.com/
http://images.google.co.za/imgres?imgurl
http://www.raindrop.org/rugrat/fun/cark.gif&imgrefurl
http://www.mssscrafts.com/oldtestament/noah.htm
http://en.wikipedia.org/wiki/Noah's_Ark
http://www.noahsarksearch.com/
http://skepdic.com/noahsark.html

20. Professor Israel Shahak – "Jewish History, Jewish Religion."

http://www.biblebelievers.org.au/jewhis.htm

21. Tax Justice

http://www.taxjustice.net/cms/front_content.php?idcat=2

22. International Alert: Climate of Conflict

http://www.international-alert.org/climate_change/index.php
For PDF file:
http://www.international-alert.org/pdf/A_Climate_Of_Conflict.pdf

23. King Asoka

King Asoka, the third monarch of the Indian Mauryan dynasty.
Died in 232 B.C. in the thirty-eighth year of his reign.
http://www.cs.colostate.edu/~malaiya/ashoka.html

About the author

Bob Robertson

Born 1934, Hertford, England.
Government school education at eight different schools during the troubled and unsettling World War II period (1939-1945).

Joined the Royal Navy in 1949 at the age of $15^1/_2$ as a boy radio telegraphist.

Eight years general service duties during which he was at the Montebello Islands off Western Australia for the explosion of Britain's first atomic bomb October 1952.

Two years (1953-1955) land-based duties in South Africa at (what was then) Cape Town Radio Station at Slangkop, Kommetjie.

Back to the UK for a one year posting aboard the corvette H.M.S. "Truelove" on fishery protection duties in the North Sea and Arctic Circle, aboard which a mutiny occurred. (No-one was hanged at the yardarm!)

Stationed at Combined Military Head Quarters in Nicosia, Cyprus (1955-1956), during the Greek/Turkish conflict.

Got his 'wings' for aircrew duties in the Royal Naval Fleet Air Arm in 1956, and spent a further three years naval service on land and aircraft carrier (H.M.S. "Bulwark") flying duties.

Married 1957, and was privileged to spend almost fifty wonderful years with his wife Yvonne who sadly died in 2006.

His five children born in Malta, England and South Africa now live in various parts of the world.

Left the Navy in 1960 and joined his London-based family shipping business.
Emigrated to South Africa in June 1969, and is still there.
A number of interesting shipping related jobs during the early years in his new country, including the Moçambique Cahora Bassa Dam project organising equipment logistics; the design and development of aligned shipping documentation; export development services and early preparation for containerisation.

Joined the executive management team of South African Foreign Trade Organisation (SAFTO) in 1971, assisting existing and prospective exporters to establish international markets.

Went solo in February 1972 and formed South Africa's first container shipping line, Enterprise Container Lines (ECL) four years ahead of the country's planned introduction of containerisation.
ECL provided connecting carrier services to Europe, Scandinavia, the United Kingdom, Mediterranean, the USA, Canada, South America and Japan via Rotterdam.

One of ECL's ships m.v. Nortrans Karen

Delivered a number of corporate sponsored addresses to members of the shipping and related industries over a five year period.

ECL was sold to the national flag carrier South African Marine Corp. (Safmarine) in 1977.
Remaining on the peripherals of shipping he formed his own specialised publishing company for the shipping industry in 1980, and produced two alternate weekly newspapers.
The titles were eventually purchased by Lloyd's of London Press, by which time he had moved into the new and rapidly growing electronic media industry.

Became a founding member of the United Democratic Movement (UDM), an opposition party to the ANC in South African politics, and was chairman of the Gauteng Finance Committee for a while.

Sold his business in 1999, resigned from the UDM and slipped into retirement in 2000 at which time he began researching material for his book.

With many years of world travel behind him (34 countries) and experiences gained while in the international shipping industry, talking with people from all walks of life in various parts of the world, his long-felt belief that mankind desperately needs to actively and boldly campaign for a complete overhaul of the present world order became compelling.
In simple terms, he saw the world on an upward spiral of turmoil, and the rapidly approaching catastrophes related to climate change were going to make life desperately unbearable for millions of people worldwide, particularly the greatly disadvantaged poor and starving masses.

The book was originally intended for a South African readership, but climate change moved the goal posts to make it a book appropriate for global readership.